Women in Sport Leadership

Although women and girls participate in sport in greater numbers than ever before, research shows there has been no significant increase in women leading sport organizations. This book takes an international, evidence-based perspective in examining women in sport leadership and offers future directions for improving gender equity. With contributions from leading international sport scholars and practitioners, it explores the opportunities and challenges women face while exercising leadership in sport organizations and evaluates leadership development practices.

While positional leadership is crucial, this book argues that some women may choose to exercise leadership in non-positional ways, challenging readers to consider their personal values and passions. The chapters not only discuss key topics such as gender bias, intersectionality, quotas, networking, mentoring and sponsoring, but also present a variety of strategies to develop and support the next generation of women leaders in sport. A new model of how to achieve gender equity in sport leadership is also introduced.

Women in Sport Leadership: Research and Practice for Change is important reading for all students, scholars, leaders, administrators, and coaches with an interest in sport business, policy and management, as well as women's sport and gender studies.

Laura J. Burton is an Associate Professor in Sport Management in the Department of Educational Leadership in the Neag School of Education at the University of Connecticut, USA. Prior to completing her PhD, Laura worked as an athletic trainer from 1995 to 1998. Her research focus is on gender issues in sport leadership, including examining how stereotypes impact women in leadership. She currently serves as the Editor of the *Journal of Intercollegiate Sport*.

Sarah Leberman is a Professor of Leadership and is the Dean Academic for Massey University, New Zealand. Her research focus is on women in leadership within sport and academia. She was a Fulbright Senior Scholar in 2007, which she tenured at the University of Minnesota, USA. She was a member of the New Zealand Olympic Committee, Women in Sport Group and the Manager of the Women's Junior Black Sticks and Black Sticks teams.

Routledge Research in Sport Business and Management
Available in this series:

Women in Sport Leadership

Research and Practice for Change

Edited by Laura J. Burton
and Sarah Leberman

Routledge
Taylor & Francis Group

LONDON AND NEW YORK

First published 2017 by Routledge

2 Park Square, Milton Park, Abingdon, Oxfordshire OX14 4RN

52 Vanderbilt Avenue, New York, NY 10017

Routledge is an imprint of the Taylor & Francis Group, an informa business

First issued in paperback 2019

British Library Cataloguing-in-Publication Data
A catalogue record for this book is available from the British Library

Library of Congress Cataloging-in-Publication Data
Names: Leberman, Sarah, author.
Title: Women in sport leadership : research and practice
    for change / edited by Laura J. Burton and Sarah Leberman.
Description: Abingdon, Oxon New York, NY : Routledge, 2017.
Series: Routledge Research in Sport Business and Management ; 9 |
    Includes bibliographical references and index.
Identifiers: LCCN 2016055580 | ISBN 9781138686168 (hardback) |
    ISBN 9781315542775 (ebook)
Subjects: LCSH: Sports for women. | Leadership in women. |
    Sex discrimination in sports. | Sports administration—Social aspects.
Classification: LCC GV709 W5747 2017 | DDC 796.082—dc23
LC record available at https://lccn.loc.gov/2016055580

ISBN: 978-1-138-68616-8 (hbk)
ISBN: 978-0-367-23325-9 (pbk)

Typeset in Sabon
by Apex CoVantage, LLC

This book is dedicated to all women and girls worldwide who exercise leadership in sport in a myriad of ways on a daily basis.

'The success of every woman should be the inspiration to another.

We should raise each other up.'
(Serena Williams)

'Kei a tātou tēnei ao; kei a tātau hoki ēnei iti kahurangi.

This is our world; these are the challenges we must strive to overcome.'
(Māori proverb)

Contents

Figures

Tables

Acknowledgments

Thank you, Sarah for joining me on this project. This book is a reflection of the integrity and thoughtfulness you bring to all aspects of your work. I am so thankful for our friendship and for the opportunity to continue collaborating on work to make the world better for girls and women in sport.

Thank you to my wife Kathryn for your love and support of me while working on this book. And thank you for the leadership and strength you provide to our family. You inspire me everyday. Also, thank you to my parents Joan and Richard, for their continued love and support.

—Laura J. Burton

Thank you, Laura for inviting me to co-edit this book. I have very much enjoyed our journey together. This has truly been a sharing of minds and hearts. I look forward to our ongoing friendship over the years to come.

Thank you to my daughter Phoebe and husband Brett for your support throughout the process of writing this book, including time away at the University of Connecticut and many weekends. I could not do all the things I do without you.

—Sarah Leberman

Thank you to all our colleagues who have contributed to this book in numerous different ways.

—Laura and Sarah

Contributors

Johanna A. Adriaanse is an Associate of the Business School at the University of Technology Sydney, Australia. Her research expertise is in the area of gender and sport. She has been a visiting scholar in the USA (Smith College, Massachusetts), the Netherlands (Utrecht University), and Norway (Norwegian University of Sport Sciences). She has been the Co-chair of the International Working Group on Women and Sport (IWG) from 2006 to 2014 and has served on the Board of Women Sport International since 2005.

Michael J. Bryant is currently an Assistant Professor of Sport Management at the University of Minnesota-Morris, USA. In addition to supporting his students' academic progress and professional preparation, he is most interested in research that bridges theory to practice with emphasis upon leadership, diversity, and inclusion in athletics. A native of Edmonds, Washington, he spent several years coaching and in athletics administration at the college level before transitioning to the classroom.

Lindsey Darvin is currently a PhD student and graduate research assistant in the department of Tourism, Recreation, and Sport Management at the University of Florida, USA. Her research areas and interests include women in sport leadership, gender equity in sport, and athlete development.

Heidi Grappendorf is an Associate Professor in Sport Administration at the University of Cincinnati, USA. Her research interests include how gender role conflict impacts women's careers in the management and leadership of sport organizations, women's career progression, and the overall under-representation of women and diversity in sport. She has over 50 national and international presentations, and over 30 publications including predominantly peer-reviewed journal articles, in addition to six book chapters. She was named the 2015 NASSM Diversity Award winner.

Meg G. Hancock is the Chair of the Health & Sport Sciences Department and an Assistant Professor of Sport Administration in the College of Education and Human Development at the University of Louisville (UofL), USA. Her research interests include career development and gender diversity in the sport industry. Prior to Louisville, she worked with coaches, student athletes, and college administrators at Dartmouth College, USA.

E. **Nicole Melton** is an Assistant Professor in the Mark H. McCormack Department of Sport Management at the University of Massachusetts, Amherst, USA. Her research focuses on diversity and inclusion in sport organizations. She examines the antecedents of workplace or team inclusion and the subsequent performance benefits of creating such environments. In addition, she explores ways to empower sport employees and athletes to become effective change agents for social justice within sport. Prior to academia, she played collegiate and professional golf and then worked as a consumer test analyst for NIKEGOLF.

Claire Schaeperkoetter is a doctoral research fellow and graduate teaching assistant in the Department of Health, Sport, and Exercise Sciences at the University of Kansas, USA. Her research interests include examining how the intersection of organizational structures, financial goals, and environmental pressures contribute to organizational programming and decision-making.

Vicki D. Schull is an Assistant Professor in the Human Performance Department at Minnesota State University, Mankato, USA. Her research interests include leadership in sport, gender relations in sport, issues in intercollegiate athletics, and organizational change in sport organizations.

Nefertiti A. Walker is an Assistant Professor in the Mark H. McCormack Department of Sport Management in the Isenberg School of Management at University of Massachusetts, Amherst, USA. She completed both her BA and MBA from Stetson University, USA and her PhD from the University of Florida, USA. Her research interests are gender, diversity and inclusion, and organizational behavior in sport.

Janelle E. Wells is a Visiting Assistant Professor in the Sport and Entertainment Management Program at the Muma College of Business at the University of South Florida, USA. She always had a livelihood in sports, which earned her a collegiate athletic scholarship, progressed into the coaching ranks, and then translated into the private sector and classroom. She is an advocate for advancing professional competencies, developing progressive inclusive organizational strategies, and connecting sport scholars and practitioners.

Chapter 1

Why this book? Framing the conversation about women in sport leadership

Sarah Leberman and Laura J. Burton

Introduction

As we began work on this book, we considered why it is so important to provide a detailed discussion of the state of research on women in sport leadership. One of our primary motivating factors for embarking on this work is the ubiquitous nature of sport—sport is everywhere—in the media, in parks, and in educational institutions, and in many parts of the world, girls and women are participating in sport in record numbers. However, decisions about what happens in sport, including girls' and women's access to sport, are still predominantly made by white, heterosexual men. This affects what we see in the media, such as how often women athletes are portrayed in active non-sexualized ways (Fink, 2016), the amount of coverage afforded female athletes in all forms of media (Bruce, 2016; Cooky, Messner, & Hextrum, 2013), and the amount of prize money and level of salary female athletes receive in sport (Women on Boards, 2016). Further, we need to know who is on the board of national and international sport federations, holding leadership positions in interscholastic and intercollegiate athletic administration, and who is provided the opportunity to coach our children. It is critically important to know who leads our sports organizations and why only a privileged few continue to hold power. It is our goal to provide insights into these critical questions in the chapters that follow, and in the final chapter to suggest ways forward to increase both access to and equity in sport leadership.

Framing the conversation

Sport participation by women and girls has increased over the past 40 years, due to both legislative interventions, such as Title IX in the USA, and programs at national, regional, and local levels worldwide, which encourage girls and women to be physically active. The 2012 Summer Olympics in London were touted as the Women's Olympics with a record number of female participants, and the requirement since 2014 that all Olympic Sports be available for men and women, with women's ski jumping being added to the competition. However, this increase in participation has not been matched by a significant increase in the proportion of women in leadership positions within sport at any level, but in particular at the national and international level. The International Olympic Committee (IOC) set a target of 20% representation on national sport governing bodies and National Olympic Committees by 2005 for its member countries. However, by 2016 this figure had only been achieved in some countries by some sports (27 out of 135 National Olympic Committees who responded to the survey) (International Olympic Committee, 2016; Women on Boards, 2016). Women remain underrepresented in leadership positions throughout sport; women hold less than 20% of board director positions, only 10% as board chairs and only 16% of chief executive positions (Adriaanse, 2015). In most cases sport is still a male-dominated environment, where women, despite an increase in opportunities to prepare themselves through education and training, are still largely underrepresented in leadership roles the world over.

The 2016 Rio Olympics served to reinforce this pattern. For the first time there were seven countries with a majority of women delegation in terms of athletes –Puerto Rico (66%), China (61%), Canada (60%), United States (53%), Bahrain (53%), Australia (51%), and New Zealand (51%). Overall women athletes made up 45% of the competitors. However, the 2016 International Sports Report Card on Women in Leadership Roles (Lapchick, 2016) paints a very different picture in terms of off-field participation by women. Men run 33 of the 35 international federations affiliated with the Olympics. Currently, only two women lead international sport federations: Marisol Casado the International Triathlon Union (ITU) a summer sport federation and Kate Caithness a winter sport federation—World Curling. The report provides some disappointing figures with respect to women in sport leadership roles. Only 5.7% of International Federations presidents were women, 12.2% were vice-presidents, and 13.1% were executive committee members, and only 24.4% of the IOC members were women. More concerning perhaps is the fact that a number of international federations have no women on their executive committees despite having high levels of participation by women—International Association of Athletics Federation, Federation of International Basketball Association, International Golf Federation, International Handball Federation, and the International Swimming Federation. At a national level the figures are not much better. Only 9% (389/4303) of national presidents across the world were women.

Some sports organizations are taking positive steps to address these challenges. For example, the Commonwealth Games Federation (CGF) launched its Gender Equality Taskforce in July 2016. The focus is to achieve equality in both opportunities and participation for athletes, coaches, team and technical officials, and in governance in all events and organizations linked to the CGF by 2022 in Durban. The CGF elected its first woman president,

Louise Martin, in 2015 and constitutionally is committed to gender equity having both women and men represented in vice-presidential elections (Commonwealth Games Federation, 2016).

Other issues affecting women in sport during 2016 included, for example, the US Women's National Team Soccer pay equity claim (March 31, 2016), where five members of the US national women's soccer team filed a complaint with the Equal Employment Opportunity Commission charging US Soccer with wage discrimination. The women were paid nearly four times less than the men despite being more prominent, better known and successful and exceeding projected revenues by $16,000,000 (Powell, 2016). Similarly, Australia's leading women surfers are seeking pay equity. The difference in prize money for the same surf event can be as much as AUS$40,000 (Atkins & Burns, 2016). The gender pay gap in sport is only being reduced very slowly. Some sports, however, have taken strategic decisions which are positively impacting women in their sport. For example, women cricketers in both Australia and the United Kingdom are being paid more equitably as a result of increased game attendance, TV coverage, and sponsorship opportunities (Women on Boards, 2016).

Business case for diversity

Most Organization for Economic Cooperation and Development (OECD) countries have a strong pipeline of female talent with more women graduating with tertiary qualifications than men. However, this is not yet translating into equity within senior management and governance, or in terms of pay. Research demonstrates the benefits to business of both gender and ethnic diversity—it improves financial performance, widens the talent pool, supports enhanced innovation and group performance, encourages adaptability, and improves employee retention. It is therefore important for policymakers and sport organizations alike to identify strategies which capitalize on the many and diverse strengths women and people of different racial and ethnic backgrounds bring to the workforce and to the development of successful sport organizations as we move through the 21st century (Badal & Harter, 2014; Catalyst, 2013; Equal Employment Opportunities Trust, 2010; Pellegrino, D'Amato, & Weisberg, 2011). Within sport, intercollegiate athletic departments in the United States that adopt an inclusive culture and were racially diverse had better performance outcomes (Cunningham, 2009). Further, athletic departments supporting an inclusive culture that had a higher number of LGBT employees performed better (more team success) than other less inclusive athletic departments (Cunningham, 2011). This research suggests that diversity benefits organizations for a wide variety of reasons. Despite the evidence, the practice in sport worldwide is quite different.

Sport is also seen as an important vehicle for achieving gender equality more broadly, as evidenced in the United Nations 'Advancing Gender Equality through Sports: 2030 Agenda' (United Nations Women, 2016). The terms 'gender equality' and 'gender equity' are often used interchangeably:

> Gender equality is the result of the absence of discrimination on the basis of a person's sex in opportunities and the allocation of resources or benefits or in access to services. Gender equity entails the provision of fairness and justice in the distribution of benefits and responsibilities between women and men. The concept recognizes that women and men have different needs and power and that these differences should be identified and addressed in a manner that rectifies the imbalances between the sexes.
>
> (European Commission, 2014, p. 47)

We favor the term 'gender equity,' as 'gender equality' tends to perpetuate the existing structures that privilege men particularly with respect to career paths, for example (Bailyn, 2003; Schein, 2007). Gender equity, in contrast, seeks to ensure that everyone is treated fairly, but not necessarily in the same way and therefore better accommodates difference.

Why are women still underrepresented? Why then after over 40 years of initiatives and interventions and research to evidence that diversity is positive for outcomes across a number of measures is the representation of women in leadership positions within sport organizations and on governance boards, nationally and internationally, still not equitable? Women's representation in leadership positions in sport organizations has declined in some areas (intercollegiate sport in the United States) and is virtually non-existent in other areas (international professional sport), with overall progress being glacial (Fink, 2016; Knoppers, 2015; Shaw, 2006; Shaw, 2013; Shaw & Hoeber, 2003; Women on Boards, 2016). Scholars have studied this area extensively over the past 30 plus years and their research reveals there are numerous forces at societal, organizational, and individual levels that impede women's opportunities for leadership positions in sport. Chapter 2 provides a detailed discussion on these factors. Some countries, such as Norway, have introduced quotas at a national level to ensure gender equity on boards (see Chapter 6 for a discussion in the context of sport).

At the end of this introduction, we provide a conceptual framework (Figure 1.1) to examine this issue taking into account the available scholarship to date. In our framework we focus on three main areas that must be addressed to advance women in sport leadership—institutional practices that reinforce the dominant male hegemony within sport (e.g., Cunningham, 2010; Shaw & Frisby, 2006) (see Chapter 3), inherent biases, often unconscious, toward women in sport and sport leadership (e.g. Burton, 2015; Burton, Grappendorf, & Henderson, 2011) (see Chapter 4), and the lack of understanding and recognition of intersectionality. Intersectionality means that not all women are the same, and as such hold multiple identities, some of which are more immediately apparent including race, ethnicity, and disability, and others which are not, such as sexuality, class, and religion (e.g., Palmer & Masters, 2010; Walker & Melton, 2015) (see Chapter 5).

To counter this situation, Shaw (2013) argued that gender needs to be at the center of sport policy development, with the analysis being scrutinized through a gender lens. Her key message, drawing on radical feminist theory, is the need to ask questions in different ways, which places the onus on the organizations and structures which drive the sport sector, rather than on what women can do to help themselves. The example she provided related to the Black Ferns, the very successful New Zealand women's rugby team:

> rather than asking how the Black Ferns can fit within the male domi-nated landscape of high performance sport, questions should be framed by 'how do our assumptions about gender limit funding and the potential for meaningful development for the Black Ferns and women's rugby?'
>
> (Shaw, 2013, pp. 312–313)

Working to address the three core areas highlighted above and placing gender at the forefront of structural decision making will go some way to redressing the ongoing gender equity issues present in sport leadership.

Starting young

If we wait for these structural changes (institutional structures, removal of bias, understanding of intersectionality) to take place in sport organiza-tions, we will continue with the very slow progress toward gender equity. Because if we have few women in strategic decision-making positions, the status quo is likely to prevail. Therefore leadership development programs for women in sport still need to be available, as do networking, mentor-ing, and sponsoring opportunities (see Chapter 8). Looking to the future, rather than waiting until women have entered the workforce for leader-ship development opportunities, we believe providing these opportunities when girls are aged between 10 and 12 will assist in equipping them with an understanding of who they are, what their values and strengths are, and how to navigate in the world of sport in order to exercise leadership, beyond being sport participants. Learning about leadership and exercising leader-ship are very different. Therefore providing multiple avenues for practicing leadership (Raelin, 2016) will enable girls once they are women to have had exposure to the complexities of leadership within sport before they enter the sport industry per se. Similar to the thinking that elite athletes or expert musicians require 10,000 hours of practice to attain that level (Ericsson, Krampe, & Tesch-Römer, 1993), we would argue that a similar amount of time is required to exercise leadership in the strongest possible way for each woman (see Chapters 7 and 8).

Working together with men to lead change

At the same time we need to provide agency to girls and women enabling them to become part of the structures which set the strategic direction of organizations and develop policies, such as becoming CEOs or being members of a board, so that in conjunction with similarly thinking men they can work together for change from the structural perspective. A number of groups now exist advocating for men to be part of the solution—for example, HeforShe (www.heforshe.org/en), Male Champions for Change (Australian Human Rights Commission, 2013) and NBA Lean in Together (2015). The role of men is critical in supporting structural change. The Canadian Association for the Advancement of Women and Sport and Physical Activity (CAAWS) provides 10 key ways in which men can support girls and women (CAAWS, n.d.).

1   Speak up.
2   Celebrate women athletes.
3   Train and certify women coaches and officials.
4   Recruit women leaders.
5   Pay-it-forward and mentor.
6   Invite women.
7   Nominate women leaders.
8   Communicate opportunities.
9   Educate yourself and others.
10   Promote women and sport leadership networks.

Importance of values and a 'sense of place'

The importance of values in shaping leadership behavior and of authentic leadership within the context of sport are very pertinent to the discussion in this book, highlighted by the fact that women may choose to exercise leadership in many different ways which may be positional (e.g., CEO, board member) and/or non-positional. Similarly, we are very mindful that readers of this book will come from many diverse socio-cultural contexts. This is important to know, as where we come from and the experiences we have had fundamentally shape how we choose to be in the world. The values, passion, and strengths we have inform many of the decisions we make and it is therefore important to start with an understanding of who we are and how we understand our place in the world. Māori, the indigenous people of Aotaeroa/New Zealand, call this knowing your *turangawaewae*, often associated with their tribal affiliation(s). It is about knowing where you feel centered and what makes you who you are. Once you are clear about this, it is much easier to stand strong in the face of different perspectives and be respectful of these, rather than being threatened by them. Amanda Sinclair's

(2010) work focusing on knowing your 'sense of place' makes a similar point. She focuses on the importance of knowing your sense of place when learning and reflecting on leadership. Her key argument is that identities (e.g., gender, ethnicity, sexuality, belief system) and places (e.g., country, socio-economic context) have been largely absent from the leadership literature and yet form such an important part of thinking about both leadership and what it means to be a leader. She suggests that we have multiple identities and often these are contradictory, requiring constant negotiation depending on the situation we are in.

Sinclair advocates for the importance of 'placing ourselves,' by thinking about the places we have come from and are in, and the multiple identities that we have, when we are thinking, studying, and practicing leadership. She encourages us to ask, 'Where do I come from?' and 'How do I situate myself within this?'. Importantly, this also means that we cannot and do not speak for all women, as depending on where we come from informs our perspectives and we have very different lived experiences. So it is about giving voice to women individually and collectively to affect change.

Exercising leadership

Individual leaders, in sport or any industry, cannot be 'successful' on their own. Leaders need the support of followers and the systems that underpin their organization. If we think of a successful sports team, success is based on performance of the group, rather than only attributable to the captain or coach, because without the team there would be no success. The team also includes the off field/off court team members, who provide the infrastructure within which these successful teams operate. In her book *Leadership for the Disillusioned* (2007), Sinclair argues that we need to think "about leadership as a way of being that is reflective and thoughtful about self; that values relationships and the present; that is connected to others and embodied; that is not narrowly striving or ego-driven; and that is liberating in its effects' (p. xv). She encourages us to reflect upon our own experiences of leadership and how these experiences inform the way we are both leaders and followers. Similarly, she highlights how the leaders we should aspire to be are often business leaders, and questions how the voices and knowledge of certain groups of society are privileged while others (i.e., those not leading businesses or sport organizations) are marginalised. These observations are at the core of what is required to challenge the dominant structures supporting leadership within the sport industry. Leadership is more than a position or a title, it about being a person of influence, which can be exercised in many different ways.

Donna Ladkin (2010) also questions the traditional approaches used for studying leadership, adopting a phenomenological approach to exploring the notions of leadership and leaders, taking account of time and context, which are particularly pertinent in the global and multicultural environment within which sport operates. Ladkin argues that leadership is a 'moment' of social relation, as it cannot exist independently—it requires people, a context, a purpose, and a point in time, and therefore moves beyond the focus on one aspect, namely that of the leader. The way we interpret this leadership moment is very much dependent on our own perspective and experience and how we are positioned in relation to that moment. What experiences do we bring to the situation? Are we the parent, coach, umpire, or CEO?

Reinforcing this perspective, recent work by Raelin (2011, 2016) shifts the focus from leadership as an individual act to leadership as the process of people working together to accomplish a particular outcome. The emphasis is therefore on understanding "where, how and why leadership work is organised and accomplished" (2011, p. 196), rather than on who the individual is. Process and context are therefore vitally important, instead of the outcome per se. Raelin argues that leaderful practice, as distinct from leadership-as-practice, requires collectiveness, concurrency, collaboration, and compassion. Leaderful practice focuses on the democratic approach involving all stakeholders in working toward outcomes. "Leadership is thus a meta-capability that encourages movement from day-to-day actions by individuals to core processes and capabilities that subsequently shape individual behaviour" (2016, p. 141). What this means for scholars examining sport leadership is that it is time to move away from the more individualistic approaches to leadership which have provided the majority of leadership research in sport management toward research that takes more account of context and the multiple realities of leadership. Raelin (2016) advocates for leadership as collective agency, where "we need meaning makers, who can actively participate in the affairs of the community and can be called upon to offer meaning to the community, especially when it may face contested terrain or periods of uncertainty or insecurity" (p. 146). If we substitute the sport sector for community, the pertinence of this becomes obvious, particularly with respect to women in sport leadership.

Power

The word 'power' is often associated with negative connotations. Consider in contrast the notion of 'power-with,' rather than 'power-over' others, from the Native American perspective (Starhawk, 1987). This provides a different frame for how power can be interpreted. In the context of women and leadership, Barbara Kellerman (2012) in her book *The End of Leadership* provides a very useful discussion on the words 'power,' 'authority,' 'influence,' and 'voice.' In short, power and authority are usually associated with positional leadership and bring with it certain accountabilities and responsibilities. Whereas, influence and voice can be exercised without position, although this may be more difficult.

In order to affect structural change in the sport sector, we need women to be in positions of leadership, as this is where strategies and policies are developed. We acknowledge the importance of having women in positions of leadership in sport so that women are shaping the strategic direction of sport organizations. These positions include, for example, CEO of sports organizations, athletic director, or member of sport governing bodies. However, positional leadership in sport has its own inherent biases—women who are prototypical leaders, by exhibiting more masculine rather than feminine behaviors (Burton, Barr, Fink, & Bruening, 2009)—which does not fit all women in sport who wish to contribute to leadership. At the same time we need women to exercise leadership through their influence and voice in a myriad of different ways within the sport sector, irrespective of whether they hold a formal leadership position. Women exercise leadership daily within sport organizations in ways that are not positional and therefore difficult to count and make visible. In order to effect wholesale change in sport, it is important not only to understand how more women can be provided with opportunities to be in leadership positions, but also to respect that some women may choose to exercise leadership in non-positional ways. If we consider leadership as practice and a collective endeavour as suggested by Raelin (2016), then this is even more important in our quest to redress the gender equity issues prevalent across the sport sector.

Women helping women: Queen Bee phenomenon

Unfortunately, once women are in leadership positions they do not always bring other women through and often once successful hold numerous leadership/governance positions, rather than, for example, tapping other women on the shoulder and advocating for them to be on boards. So women need to advocate for women. The assumption is that once women reach leadership positions they will mentor and advocate for younger women and serve as role models (Duigud, 2011; Mavin, 2008). However, research by Derks, Van Laar, and Ellemers (2016) suggests this is not necessarily the case, and that women in male-dominated organizations assimilate to the prevailing culture. This response is often termed the 'Queen Bee syndrome.' Derks and colleagues argue that this behavior is "in response to the gender discrimination and identity threat that women leaders experience in some work settings" (p. 457). Interestingly, they cite the example of the Dutch company KPN scraping quotas as they were not attracting the gender diversity they were seeking. Hurst, Leberman, and Edwards (2016) examine the Queen Bee phenomenon from a relational perspective (Fletcher, 1999) by seeking to understand what the expectations of women's hierarchical workplace relationships are and how they are experienced, as these expectations are situated within societal gender-based expectations (Litwin, 2011). Understanding these relationships as situated within the wider organizational context and their impact on career decisions can assist organizations in developing strategies to maximize the hierarchical relationships between women in the workplace, that is, how to facilitate policies and practices that enable women to support women. However, Krawcheck (2016) argues that the Queen Bee syndrome is at an end for four reasons—the business case for diversity is hard to ignore; women are building their own tables not just asking for seats; one woman's success clears the way for others; and more women are recognizing their power to change things.

Importance of context

Given the importance of context in relation to leadership, we are very mindful that countries across the world have different sport systems and therefore not all research is necessarily transferable beyond the specific locale within which it has been undertaken. The reality is that most of the research on women in sport leadership is situated within North America and primarily the US intercollegiate sport system. The intercollegiate system is unique in the world as it situates elite sport within a higher education framework. Despite this situation many of the broader findings are likely to apply in most OECD countries to a greater or lesser extent. Sport in most European countries, as well as Australia and New Zealand, is based on a regional/state and national/federal sport organization structure, which operates within a range of government policies. Sport structures are different again in many African and Asian countries, where opportunities for women are often compounded by cultural and religious norms.

Conceptual framework

The following conceptual model (Figure 1.1) has been developed to frame our thinking for the book. We acknowledge that there is an ongoing debate about whether our focus should be on structure or agency in endeavoring to increase women in sport leadership. Critical feminist theorists advocate for a focus on structure, whereas more liberal feminists argue that agency is of primary importance.

We suggest that at this point in time we cannot afford to only focus on one, but instead we need to be active in both areas to reduce the gap between them as depicted by the space between structure and agency and the blue arrows in our model—showing an increase in agency and a decrease in structural issues. Institutional practices, gender bias, and lack of understanding about intersectionality are the three main areas we believe have not been fully addressed. These require further examination in order to close the gap between structure and agency, which once closed would ideally obviate the need to have the numerous leadership and empowerment programs for girls and women that exist today.

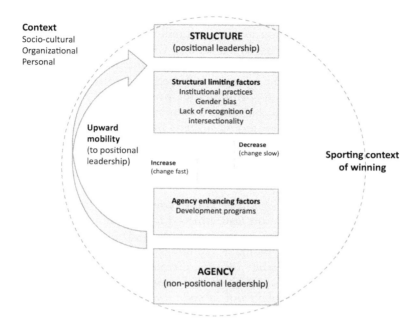

Figure 1.1 Structure-Agency conceptual model for why women remain underrepresented in sport leadership © Sarah Leberman and Laura J. Burton

Structural change takes time and is often slow, whereas programs to increase agency can be comparatively fast and effective. The size of the boxes for structure and agency suggest that the progress in changing structures has been smaller than for agency. We also recognize that the comparative sizes will be variable both within and between countries. For example, in a country such as Norway that has quotas, the size of the structure box would be similar to that of agency. In the end, individuals create the structures we are part of symbolized by the curving arrow on the left of the model. We need more women to be part of those structures to affect change. Facilitating this through programs that develop women's and girls' self-confidence, self-awareness, resilience, and networks as well as social capital are not about 'fixing the women,' but about enabling them to seek those positions of power and authority within the sport sector.

We therefore start with an overview of the structural issues affecting women's sport leadership, which has been the main focus of the extant research with respect to women in sport leadership. Chapter 2 reviews the scholarship to date and explores new areas of research that enhance our understanding of the opportunities and challenges for women in all areas of sport leadership globally. Chapters 3–5 discuss the three key areas we believe are influencing our ability to make genuine progress—institutionalized practices, the impact of bias on women when exercising leadership in sport, and the lack of appreciation and understanding that intersectionality has on women's progress in sports organizations. Chapter 6 focuses on whether the use of quotas is the way to improve gender equity in sport leadership as experienced in many Nordic countries. Chapters 7 through 9 highlight the role of agency in creating opportunities for women to be prepared for the world of sport. Chapter 10 challenges the dominant 'win at all costs' paradigm within sport organizations and suggests that fundamental changes are required in the structures of sport organizations, informed by the concept of the quadruple top—and bottom-line, in order to achieve gender equity in sport leadership. The Appendix outlines a research agenda highlighted in the process of writing this book.

We hope this book will challenge you to consider your personal values, strengths, and passion for sport leadership—why you are interested in sport leadership, what difference you wish to make and in which context—as this will guide the choices you make and how you lead. Leadership is about influence. Positional leadership adds the dimensions of authority and perceived power. The interplay of these three concepts is crucial for understanding how leadership plays out in sport on a daily basis. Our overall objective is to provide an evidenced-based discussion, together with a suggested way forward and recommendations for future research on women in sport leadership so that gender equity in sport leadership may be reached within our lifetimes.

References

Adriaanse, J. (2015). Gender diversity in the governance of sport associations: The Sydney Scoreboard Global Index of Participation. *Journal of Business Ethics*, *137*(1), 149–160. http://doi.org/10.1007/s10551-015-2550-3

Atkins, M., & Burns, A. (2016) Female pro surfers want industry to get on board regarding sexism concerns. Retrieved from www.abc.net.au/news/2016–04–15/female-surfers-call-for-end-to-sexist-culture-in-sport/7329932

Australian Human Rights Commission. (2013). Male champions of change. Retrieved from www.humanrights.gov.au/our-work/sex-discrimination/projects/male-champions-change

Badal, S. & Harter, J.K. (2014), Gender diversity, business-unit engagement, and performance. *Journal of Leadership & Organizational Studies, 21*(4), 354–365.

Bailyn, L. (2003). Academic careers and gender equity: Lessons learned from MIT. *Gender, Work & Organization, 10*(2), 137–153.

Bruce, T. (2016). New rules for new times: Sportswomen and media representation in the Third Wave. *Sex Roles, 74*(7–8), 361–376.

Burton, L.J. (2015). Underrepresentation of women in sport leadership: A review of research. *Sport Management Review, 18*, 155–165.

Burton. L.J., Barr, C.A., Fink, J.S., & Bruening, J.E. (2009). "Think athletic director, think masculine?" Examination of the gender typing of managerial subroles within athletic administration positions. *Sex Roles, 5–6*, 416–426.

Burton, L.J., Grappendorf, H., & Henderson, A. (2011). Perceptions of gender in athletic administration: Utilizing role congruity to examine (potential) prejudice against women. *Journal of Sport Management, 25*, 36–45.

Canadian Association for the Advancement of Women and Sport and Physical Activity. (n.d.). Retrieved from www.caaws.ca/gender-equity-101/what-men-can-do/

Catalyst. (2013). Why diversity matters. Retrieved from www.catalyst.org/knowledge/why-diversity-matters

Commonwealth Games Federation. (2016). Gender equality taskforce. Retrieved from http://us2.campaign-archive2.com/?u=f10a798540c235ff87d5c474b&id=cd58f441cd

Cooky, C., Messner, M.A., & Hextrum, R.H. (2013). Women play sport, but not on TV: A longitudinal study of televised news media. *Communication & Sport, 1*, 203–230.

Cunningham, G.B. (2009). The moderating effect of diversity strategy on the relationship between racial diversity and organizational performance. *Journal of Applied Social Psychology, 39*, 1445–1460.

Cunningham, G.B. (2010). Understanding the under-representation of African American coaches: A multilevel perspective. *Sport Management Review, 13*(4), 395–406.

Cunningham, G.B. (2011). The LGBT advantage: Examining the relationship among sexual orientation diversity, diversity strategy, and performance. *Sport Management Review, 14*(4), 453–461.

Derks, B., Van Laar, C., & Ellemers, N. (2016). The queen bee phenomenon: Why women leaders distance themselves from junior women. *The Leadership Quarterly, 27*(3), 456–469.

Duigud, M. (2011). Female tokens in high-prestige work groups: Catalysts or inhibitors of group diversification? *Organizational Behavior and Human Decision Processes, 116*, 104–115.

Equal Employment Opportunities Trust. (2010). *The Business Case for Diversity*. Auckland, New Zealand: Author. Retrieved from www.eeotrust.org.nz/toolkits/index.cfm

Ericsson, K.A., Krampe, R.T., & Tesch-Römer, C. (1993). The role of deliberate practice in the acquisition of expert performance. *Psychological Review, 100*(3), 363–406.

European Commission. (2014). *Gender Equality in Sport: Proposal for Strategic Actions 2014–2020*. http://bookshop.europa.eu/en/gender-equality-in-sport-pbNC0114573/

Fletcher, J.K. (1999). *Disappearing Acts: Gender, Power and Relational Practice at Work*. Cambridge, MA: MIT Press.

Fink, J.S. (2016). Hiding in plain sight: The embedded nature of sexism in sport. *Journal of Sport Management, 30*(1), 1–7.

HeforShe. (n.d.). Homepage. I want my voice to make a difference. Retrieved from www.heforshe.org/en

Hurst, J., Leberman, S.I., & Edwards, M. (2016) Women managing women: Intersections between hierarchical relationships, career development and gender equity. *Gender in Management: An International Journal, 31*(1), 1–14. http://dx.doi.org/10.1108/GM-03-2015-0018

International Olympic Committee. (2016). Fact sheet. Retrieved from https://stillmed.olympic.org/media/Document%20Library/OlympicOrg/Documents/Reference-Documents-Factsheets/Women-in-Olympic-Movement.pdf

Kellerman, B. (2012). *The End of Leadership*. New York: HarperCollins.

Knoppers, A. (2015). Assessing the sociology of sport: On critical sport sociology and sport management. *International Review for the Sociology of Sport, 50,* 496–501.

Krawcheck, S. (2016). Four reasons why gender equality in the workplace is closer than you think. Retrieved from www.fastcompany.com/3063877/strong-female-lead/four-reasons-why-gender-equality-in-the-workplace-is-closer-than-you-think

Ladkin, D. M. (2010). *Rethinking Leadership: A New Look at Old Leadership Questions*. Cheltenham: Edward Elgar.

Lapchick, R. (2016). Gender report Card: 2016 International Sports Report Card on Women in Leadership Roles. *The Institute for Diversity and Ethics in Sport*. www.tidesport.org/women-s-leadership-in-international-sports.html

Litwin, A. H. (2011). Women working together: Understanding women's relationships at work. *CGO Insights, 33,* 1–7.

Mavin, S. (2008). Queen bees, wannabees and afraid to bees: No more "best enemies" for women in management? *British Journal of Management, 19,* S75–S84.

NBA Lean in Together. (2015). Pass it on with #LeanIn together. Retrieved from http://leanin.org/together/men

Palmer, F. R. & Masters, T. M. (2010). Maori feminism and sport leadership: Exploring Maori women's experiences. *Sport Management Review, 13,* 331–344.

Pellegrino, G., D'Amato, S., & Weisberg, A. (2011). *The Gender Dividend: Making the Business Case for Investing in Women*. Retrieved from www2.deloitte.com/content/dam/Deloitte/global/Documents/Public-Sector/dttl-ps-thegenderdividend-08082013.pdf

Powell, M. (2016). *Men of Soccer Don't Get It, as Ususal*. Retrieved from www.nytimes.com/2016/04/02/sports/soccer/womens-soccer-pay-powell

Raelin, J. (2011). From leadership-as-practice to leaderful practice. *Leadership, 7*(2), 195–211.

Raelin, J. (2016). Imagine there are no leaders: Reframing leadership as collaborative agency. *Leadership, 12*(2), 131–158.

Schein, V. E. (2007). Women in management: Reflections and projections. *Women in Management Review, 22*(1), 6.

Shaw, S. (2006). "Scratching the back of Mr X". Analyzing gendered social processes in sport organizations. *Journal of Sport Management, 20*(4), 510–534.

Shaw, S. (2013). Feminist analysis of sport policy. In I. Henry & L-M. Ko (eds.) *Routledge Handbook of Sport Policy* (pp. 305–313). London: Routledge.

Shaw, S., & Frisby, W. (2006). Can gender equity be more equitable?: Promoting an alternative frame for sport management research, education, and practice. *Journal of Sport Management, 20,* 483–509.

Shaw, S., & Hoeber, L. (2003). "A strong man is direct and a direct woman is a bitch": Analyzing discourses of masculinity and femininity and their impact on employment roles in sport organisations. *Journal of Sport Management, 17*(4), 347–376.

Sinclair, A. (2007). *Leadership for the Disillusioned: Moving beyond Myths and Heroes to Leading that Liberates*. Crows Nest, NSW, Australia: Allen & Unwin.

Sinclair, A. (2010). Placing self: How might we place ourselves in leadership studies differently? *Leadership, 6*(4), 447–460.

Starhawk. (1987). *Truth or Dare: Encounters with Power, Authority and Mystery.* San Francisco: Harper.

United Nations Women. (2016). Advancing gender equality through sports. Retrieved from www.unwomen.org/en/news/stories/2016/3/sport-an-important-vehicle-to-achieve-gender-equality

Walker, N. A., & Melton, E. N. (2015). The tipping point: The intersection of race, gender and sexual orentation in intercollegiate sports. *Journal of Sport Management, 29*, 257–271.

Women on Boards. (2016). Gender balance in global sport report. Retrieved from www.womenonboards.net/Impact-Media/News/Sportswomen-win-gold,-but-still-paid-in-bronze

An evaluation of current scholarship in sport leadership: multilevel perspective

Laura J. Burton and Sarah Leberman

Introduction

As we have noted in the introduction of this book, there has been glacially slow progress toward the advancement of women into sport leadership. We have identified three main factors that we believe hinder women's progress toward greater access to sport leadership positions, institutional practices (see Chapter 3), bias (see Chapter 4) and the lack of recognition of inter-sectionality (see Chapter 5). However, we would be remiss if we did not provide a full account of the depth and breadth of scholarship that has been conducted to date seeking to better understand why, given the increasing number of girls and women playing and watching sport (e.g., in the United States, see Acosta & Carpenter, 2014), there are still so few women leading in the sport sector at all levels, within both the amateur and the professional realm.

A multilevel approach

Fink (2008) noted that research examining gender issues in sport are "situated in multi-level, sometimes subtle, and usually taken-for-granted structures, policies, and behaviors embedded in sport organizations" (p. 147). A multilevel perspective can help to better understand the underrepresentation of women in sport leadership, as "sport organizations are multilevel entities that both shape and are shaped by myriad factors" (Cunningham, 2010, p. 396). We therefore adopt a multilevel perspective to examine the lack of women in sport leadership positions (Burton, 2015; Burton & LaVoi, 2016; Cunningham, 2008; Cunningham, 2010; Dixon & Cunningham, 2006; LaVoi & Dutove, 2012).

From a societal (macro-level) perspective, we will first review research that has examined institutionalized practices of gender in sport, including social expectations and stakeholder expectations of leadership and the gendered nature of leadership expectations within the domain of sport. At the organizational (meso) level, we examine the stereotyping of leaders, how organizational culture is constructed around gender, issues of discrimination, including those unsupportive of the work–family interface, and how gendered practices influence hiring and retention of women in leadership positions. Finally, from an individual (micro) level we turn toward women's expectations of and in leadership positions, turnover within leadership positions, and how internalized gendered stereotypes impact individual career selection and advancement. In order to capture the most current research advances in this area, the majority of work presented in this chapter has been published in the last 15 years.

Sport leadership as masculine

Prior to beginning this review, we first establish that sport is a gendered space, meaning that sport is used to "actively construct boys and men to exhibit, value and reproduce traditional notions of masculinity" (Anderson, 2009, p. 4). Further, competitive sport serves as a social institution that defines certain forms of masculinity as acceptable (i.e., exclusively heterosexual and physically dominant), while denigrating others. Sport also supports heterosexual and physically dominant masculinity by suppressing all other forms of masculinity and subordinating women (Connell, 1995). Unfortunately, women are often situated as 'other' in the social institution of sport, and the presence of women in sport, as athlete, coach, manager, or leader, is under constant scrutiny (Fink, 2016; Kane, 1995), as most recently evidenced during the Rio 2016 Olympic Games (e.g., Guest, 2016).

Any discussion of women in sport leadership must include an understanding of gender as fundamental to both organizational and social processes in the sport sector. Connell (2009) describes gender as a social process and advocates for an examination of gender from a relational perspective. Gender can have an influence on organizational practices, such that images, cultures, interactions, and gender-appropriate behaviors are linked to socially constructed masculine or feminine ideals within organizational operations (Acker, 1990,1992; Britton & Logan, 2008). This understanding of gender as a social process helps us examine how and why gender is such a powerful factor in the social and organizational processes that define sport organizations (Kihl, Shaw, & Schull, 2013).

Influence of power

Gender not only shapes identities, but also operates as an axis of power. Therefore power must be addressed within the context of sport leadership as it highlights the influence of gender in interactions, structures, and processes of sport organizations (Shaw & Frisby, 2006). Power is "the influence over a group or individual and provides the ability to change another person's behavior, actions, or attitude" (Kane, 2015, p. 5). Leaders typically wield six sources of power within sport organizations. Reward power is the ability to provide rewards to subordinates, while another source, coercive power, carries aspects of punishment if subordinates do not meet expectations. Legitimate power is derived based on leaders formal positions or titles, while leaders holding referent power command "such a presence of personality that group members are compelled to follow" (Kane, 2015, p. 6). Leaders can also hold expert power by holding particular skills, knowledge or expertise, and informational power is a situation-specific form of power that provides leaders with knowledge to support subordinates in meeting specific tasks (Kane, 2015).

A newly developed conceptual model that examines how power is manifest in the promotion and selection of women to top-level positions in organizations is equally applicable when considering how women are selected and promoted to senior leadership positions in sport organizations (Auster & Prasad, 2016). An antecedent component to the model is the dominant ideology created by those in positions of power that perpetuate role incumbent schema used to assess candidates for leadership positions (Auster & Prasad, 2016). Further, power as held by similar 'in-group' members (predominantly white, heterosexual men) results in individuals from out-groups facing increased bias when seeking promotion to higher level positions when compared to experiences of in-group members, because "in-group favoritism is a critical aspect of the social dominance that occurs as committees make promotion decisions" (Auster & Prasad, 2016, p. 186).

Power held by those on hiring committees negatively impact those who do not reflect 'in-group' membership, as committee practices including the committee selection, evaluation of candidates, decision making protocols, and meetings are impacted by social dominance processes and such processes influence promotion bias and promotion outcomes (Auster & Prasad, 2016). As an example, stakeholders within the sport sector were found to use power to reinforce the gendered norms of an intercollegiate athletic department in the United States. Work by Schull, Shaw, and Kihl (2013) noted that stakeholders interested in maintaining power in a women's athletic program actively supported the hiring of a male athletic director for a newly merged athletic department that would control both the men's and women's programs. The stakeholders' support for a male athletic director was based on the perception that if a female athletic director was to be selected, she would be "eaten up alive" (p. 71) by members affiliated with the men's athletic programs. Stakeholders associated with the women's athletic program actively campaigned for a specific type of male candidate, instead of campaigning for a female candidate. As a result of the power and political influence enjoyed by stakeholders aligned with the men's athletic department, they had access to key decision makers and financial support of the university, as well as access to critical constituents in the media. Finally, the criterion outlined to support the hiring of the new athletic director, though appearing to be gender neutral, "privileged a certain type of masculinity in the sport context—a man who values gender equity" (p. 76).

Another indicator of the link between power and gender within the structure of sport organizations is evidenced through the positioning of women (legitimate power) within the major governing bodies of sport (e.g., IOC, FIFA, NCAA). Scholars have noted that women were underrepresented in positions of power or influence within the major governing body of intercollegiate sport in the United States, the NCAA. Women were poorly represented on executive leadership committees (less than 25%), and even fewer women hold positions at the director level (less than 18%). In addition, women were not represented on committees governing men's intercollegiate sports, yet men held over half of the positions on the Committee on Women's Athletics (Yiamouyiannis & Osborne, 2012). Further, when considering international sport federations, women held only 13% of positions on boards of directors and only 8% of board chair (president) positions (Adriaanse, 2015).

Power also has an influence on gendered relations in sport organizations. Power is linked to gender within organizations in at least three different ways. First, power connects to gender in the structure of organizations, as men who are overrepresented in higher status jobs have higher pay and more status within organizations. Second, power is demonstrated through social practices that perceive men as powerful and women as compliant, and therefore positions and tasks are constructed to favor men. Finally, power can be used in the process of gender identity formation within the organization such that external forces of power "endorse particular meanings of gender, and internal pressures dictate the degree of one's compliance" (Ely & Padavic, 2007, p. 1131). Work by Claringbould and Knoppers (2008) revealed that male leaders of national sport associations in the Netherlands used their power to maintain boundaries that allowed for male leadership to dominate, and women's participation was limited to those women who fit the model of leader as defined by the male leaders in those organizations.

Socio-cultural (macro) perspective on women in sport leadership

Sport does not operate in a vacuum. It is a reflection of wider societal norms and practices operating within both individual nations and globally. A socio-cultural (macro) level approach to examining why there are so few women in sport leadership requires situating sport as a gendered institution, where all processes in sport operate within a shared understanding of sport as masculine. Most individuals working in the sport sector share an assumption that work and organizational practices are gender neutral, which serves to reinforce male dominance in sport leadership (Burton, 2015). Sport organizations have institutionalized masculinity as a way of operating, where male activity is privileged, and masculinity and masculine behavior are regarded as leadership qualities necessary in sport (Cunningham, 2010; Fink, 2016; Shaw & Frisby, 2006). For those who do not embody this type of masculine behavior, perceptions of their skills as leaders and the individual's recognition of leadership ability is called into question.

The demographic information of an organization, meaning what types of people (based on race/ethnicity, religion, gender, sexual identity) hold certain positions, influences perceptions regarding who is appropriate for particular positions, and therefore appropriate to perform particular work, within an organization (Ely & Padavic, 2007). Men dominate leadership positions in sport organization in the United States and internationally (Acosta & Carpenter, 2014; Lapchick, 2015, 2016; International Working Group on Women and Sport, 2014; Smith & Wrynn, 2013). Women hold fewer than 25% of senior leadership positions across all US professional sports leagues (Lapchick, 2015). The one exception is the Women's National Basketball Association; however, women only hold 33% of general manager positions within that league.

Internationally, women hold fewer leadership positions in sport organizations when compared to men, including in volunteer and professional-level organizations (Claringbould & Knoppers, 2008; International Working Group on Women and Sport, 2014). Within the Olympic movement, the International Olympic Committee has for the first time met its self-imposed threshold of at least 20% of the board composed of women member, as of 2016 22% of IOC members were women (IOC, 2016, Smith & Wrynn, 2013; Women on Boards, 2016). However, within national Olympic governing bodies (NGBs), 85.3% of those governing bodies are composed of all-male leadership teams, while 14.1% have male/female leadership teams, and only one (.5%), Zambia, has an all-female leadership team (Smith & Wrynn, 2013). Overall, women held only 13% of positions on boards of directors and only 8% of board chair (president) positions on international sport federations (Adriaanse, 2015). Based on these data, the demography of leadership positions in sport organizations is highly skewed to male leaders. This skewed gender ratio serves to reinforce the notion of masculinity and masculine leadership as the norm in sport.

As a result of the assumption that a certain type of masculinity (heterosexual and physically dominant) is required to lead sport organizations, men maintain control of athletic director positions at the highest level of intercollegiate sport (i.e., Division I Football Bowl Subdivision), holding 93% of those positions (Lapchick, 2015), and have higher rates of organizational success (e.g., rates of career advancement) (Whisenant, Pedersen, & Obenour, 2002). In addition, women continue to be underrepresented as athletic directors in merged intercollegiate athletic departments (those that historically had both a male and a female athletic department that was then joined) (Grappendorf & Lough, 2006). Women's access to athletic director positions at the interscholastic level has been constrained by this assumption of masculinity, as women held less than 15% of those leadership positions (Whisenant, 2008).

Organizational (meso-)level perspectives on women in sport leadership

In order to understand how processes contribute to gender inequity and disparity within organizations, it is important to understand the practice of gender within organizations (Martin, 2003). Organizational-level factors include structure, governance, policies, and various other organizational operations.

Operational and functional practices

The operations and functional practices within sport organizations also serve to disadvantage women in leadership. For instance, within sport organizations in the United Kingdom, social processes including humor, informal networking, and use of dress codes were adopted that sustained masculine work practices (Shaw, 2006). The structure of a volunteer grassroots sport organization board of directors demonstrated that men and women held positions considered appropriate based on gendered assumptions. Women on the board were responsible for clerical work and home/kitchen duties, while men on the board handled facility management and maintenance (Sibson, 2010). Within intercollegiate athletic administration in the United States, women athletic administrator duties followed a more stereotypical feminine approach toward work focused on caring for student-athletes (Inglis, Danylchuk, & Pastore, 2000). Similarly, on a majority male board of directors for a national sport organization in Australia, men controlled all of the significant positions (external relations, strategic decisions, finances) and the sole female on the board held the position of marketing director (Adriaanse & Schofield, 2013). In a US-based women's professional sport organization, men marginalized the women in the organization by minimizing women's strategic influence in marketing strategies and undermining women's authority by requiring the women to conduct menial tasks below their level of authority (e.g., vacuum the office, take out the mail) (Allison, 2016).

Organizational policies and procedures

Organizational policies and procedures can influence access for women to leadership positions in the sport sector. International conferences in support of women in sport that have convened over the past 20 years end with a legacy, that is, calls for action, declarations or other initiatives to improve gender inequality in sport and sport leadership. Examination of the legacies of five of these conferences (Brighton Declaration, Windhoek Call for

Action, the Montreal Toolkit, the Kumamoto Commitment to Collaboration and the Sydney Scoreboard) revealed that legacies supported increasing the number of women in leadership roles, providing greater access to power and influence by increasing the number of women in decision-making positions, and creating a culture that values women's input and participation in sport organizations (Adriaanse & Claringbould, 2016).

When examining recruitment and selection and how perceptions of fit influenced the hiring of women onto boards of directors for national sport organizations in the Netherlands, incumbent male board members were able to maintain control of and therefore power over the board by both "affirming and negating affirmative action policies and policing 'fit' during recruitment and selection processes" (Claringbould & Knoppers, 2007, p. 503). In addition, women applying for those positions did not question the criteria used for selection even as they struggled to comply with the demands made by the male board members.

Work–family and family–work interface scholars have also examined how the organizational practices of sport organizations can be gendered. This work has most often focused on the experiences of women in coaching (in the United States) and examined organizational structures, policies, and procedures supported by organizations (Bruening & Dixon, 2007; Dixon & Bruening, 2007; Dixon & Sagas, 2007). Using an integrated theory of work–family conflict in sports, Dixon and Bruening (2005) highlight organizational-level constraints women face including job pressures and job stress, work and hours of scheduled work, and the work–family culture of an organization. At an organizational level, the demands of coaching and the expectations of spending many hours in the office contributed to significant work–family conflict for female head coaches (Dixon & Bruening, 2007). Similarly, women noted staying in current head coaching positions longer when they received organizational support (i.e., supportive athletic directors) to help manage work and family obligations (Bruening & Dixon, 2008). Leberman and Palmer (2009) report similar findings, based on their research with mothers who were sport leaders in New Zealand. Their findings suggested that women actively sought work environments which enabled flexibility so they could meet the demands of work and family. Most of the women, however, did not actively challenge organizational structures and instead developed strong support networks which enabled them to fulfill their roles. Organizational practices that failed to support the balance of work and family obligations placed greater burdens on women than men within those organizations.

Organizational culture

Organizational culture defined as "the set of shared, taken-for-granted implicit assumptions that a group holds and that determines how it perceives, thinks about, and reacts to its various environments" (Schein, 1996, p. 236). The organizational culture of the majority of sport organizations internationally support and perpetuate norms, values, and behaviors that reinforce hegemonic masculinity. Organizational culture impacts women's experiences in sport organizations, as "cultures of similarity that marginalize women are institutionalized within sport organizations" (Cunningham, 2008, p. 137). Even with research to support that an organizational culture "that values diversity and capitalizes on the benefits such differences can bring to the workplace" contributes to success (Cunningham, 2008, p. 137), there are few sport organizations that adopt or demonstrate these characteristics (Cunningham & Fink, 2006).

Sport organizations that foster an organizational culture with top management support that valued gender equity had more positive organizational outcomes for women, and men. These positive outcomes included stronger organizational commitment and intentions to stay in the organization (Spoor & Hoye, 2013). Importantly, organizational practices that supported women had a similar impact on the men working in that organization, including higher commitment and greater intention to stay, indicating that providing support for women can have a more significant impact on the entire organization (Spoor & Hoye, 2013) and is therefore beneficial to the organization as a whole.

When considering diversity in US intercollegiate athletic departments, scholars noted that a majority of intercollegiate athletic departments operate in cultures that value similarity, and the majority of people in athletic departments support the norms, values, and beliefs of white, Christian, able body, heterosexual men (Fink, Pastore, & Riemer, 2001). As a result, women and other minority groups exist as 'other' within intercollegiate athletic department cultures. In addition, intercollegiate athletic departments in the United States foster and support organizational cultures that valorize heavy workloads and time in the office (Dixon & Bruening, 2007). This type of culture places significant time demands on individuals in the organization and can have different impacts on the ability of men and women to attend to the demands of work and family. Further, many intercollegiate athletic administrators noted only modest support for work–life supportive cultures in their athletic departments (Dixon, Tiell, Lough, Sweeney, Osborne, & Bruening, 2008). The difficulty of being able to successfully integrate work and family needs has led many women to leave their careers in sport organizations (Dixon & Bruening, 2005; Inglis et al., 2000; Leberman & Shaw, 2015).

Social processes

Social processes, as a component to organizational culture, can also be analyzed to understand the informal, everyday practices taking place within an organization (Acker, 1992). Informal networks within sport organizations were important social processes within these organizations, with both an old boys' network and old girls' network having influence (Shaw, 2006). Dress codes, another way culture is expressed in an organization, were also gendered within sport organizations, as men, perhaps to demonstrate a more formal businesslike attitude, may wear neckties and jackets, while women may adopt more casual tracksuits (Shaw, 2006). Use of humor is another aspect of organizational culture and when considered in the context of gender equity can serve to undermine organizational sanctioned gender equity programs in sport organizations (Shaw, 2006).

Stereotypes

Stereotypes regarding appropriate leaders are created external to sport organizations, yet stereotypes influence women's experiences of leadership within sport organizations (for a more detailed discussion of stereotypes see Chapter 3). A prototypical leader of a sport organization is expected to demonstrate more masculine managerial behavior than feminine managerial behavior (Burton, Barr, Fink, & Bruening, 2009). Therefore, women are less likely to be considered for positions of leadership in sport, as these positions are perceived to require stereotypical masculine attributes and behaviors. In addition, when women are in leadership positions, they are unfavorably evaluated because they demonstrate attributes and behaviors perceived as incongruent with their prescribed gender roles (Eagly & Karau, 2002). Work in this area has shown that leadership stereotypes within the context of intercollegiate sport have negative impacts on women, as they were perceived as capable of success in leadership positions, yet considered unlikely to be hired for such positions over equally comparable men (Burton, Grappendorf, & Henderson, 2011). Additionally, discourse around the selection of leaders in sport organizations in Norway supported gendered images of corporate, heroic leaders (Hovden, 2010). Further, women needed to prove their ability as leaders against their male counterparts in national sport organizations as evidenced in Canada, and women experienced more challenging interviews for those leadership positions as there was an assumption that women would be less suited for such positions (Shaw & Hoeber, 2003).

Despite the indication that leadership in sport is perceived to require more stereotypical masculine attributes or is more closely linked with more stereotypical male gender roles, findings examining leadership in the US intercollegiate athletic administration context do not support a preference for male leaders. Athletic administrators perceived that both male and female leaders would provide positive organizational outcomes when leading athletic departments (Burton & Welty Peachey, 2009; Welty Peachey & Burton, 2011).

Access and treatment discrimination

Other factors to consider at the organizational level are access and treatment discrimination. Both types of discrimination can and do negatively impact women in leadership positions in sport organizations. Access discrimination excludes members of certain groups from entering the organization, while treatment discrimination occurs when individuals from certain groups receive fewer organizational resources than they would legitimately deserve (Greenhaus, Parasuraman, & Wormley, 1990). Homologous reproduction, a form of access discrimination, occurs when those in power in the organization maintain influence by allowing only those with similar characteristics to them, namely, the ability to access positions of power and influence within the organization (Kanter, 1977). Women have been excluded from the hiring process in sport by being denied access as a result of the 'old boys' network and homologous reproduction (Aicher & Sagas, 2009; Hoffman, 2011; Lovett & Lowry, 1988; Regan & Cunningham, 2012; Stangl & Kane, 1991; Whisenant, 2008; Whisenant, Miller, & Pedersen, 2005; Whisenant & Mulane, 2007).

There is also evidence in sport organizations that women are impacted by treatment discrimination as they are denied access to resources, rewards, or on the job opportunities that they legitimately deserved (Aicher & Sagas, 2009; Cunningham & Sagas, 2007). In intercollegiate athletics in the United States, women in the Senior Woman Administrator position were denied opportunities to engage in important oversight roles in budgeting and leading men's sports programs, which negatively impacted their abilities to build skill sets toward positions of athletic director (Claussen & Lehr, 2002; Grappendorf, Pent, Burton, & Henderson, 2008; Pent, Grappendorf, & Henderson, 2007; Tiell, Dixon, & Lin, 2012). Further, when examining the experiences of minority women in sport leadership, Palmer and Masters (2010) noted that Māori women were marginalized due to their ethno-cultural and gendered identities.

Individual (micro-)level research on women in leadership

At the individual or micro-level of analysis, researchers have focused on how individuals understand and make meaning of their experiences, expectations, and understandings of power, policies, and procedures operating at the organizational level. We can also examine the assumptions made by individuals in how they interact within an organization, and the self-limiting behaviors individuals engage in within their work.

Scholars have used discourse analysis to help understand women's experiences in leadership and explore forces that keep women from advancement in sport organizations. This includes a focus on how "constructions of gender are embedded in organizational discourses instead of primarily in structures or the human or social capital of individual women themselves" in research at the individual level (Claringbould & Knoppers, 2012, p. 405). When examining sport organizations in Canada, discourse analysis was used to understand perceptions of women's and men's abilities to lead and manage in sport organizations (Shaw & Hoeber, 2003). In these sport organizations, senior management and leadership roles were dominated by discourses of masculinity, and employment roles that were less valued in sport organizations were associated with women and discourses of femininity.

Human and social capital

Research has examined the human and social capital of women working in sport organizations. An individual develops human capital through education, job training, on the job experiences, and the like, and accrues social capital resources through a network of relationships with peers, supervisors, and subordinates (Sagas & Cunningham, 2004). The experiences of women in intercollegiate athletic administration in the United States revealed that social capital was more influential for men advancing in sport organizations than it was for women (Sagas & Cunningham, 2004). Also, based on other research regarding intercollegiate athletic administrators in the United States, differences on the impacts of social capital for men's and women's careers can negatively impact women's career aspirations and intentions to advance in sport organizations (Cunningham & Sagas, 2002).

Self-limiting behaviors

Frameworks to understand the lack of women in leadership in sport organizations have failed to address "the emotional and cognitive processes of women as they encounter disparate acceptance and treatment within the male-dominated sport domain" (Sartore & Cunningham, 2007, p. 245). Their framework described how "ideological gender beliefs may serve to inhibit women within sport organizations through internal identity comparison processes that may subsequently result in the unconscious manifestation of self-limiting behaviors" (p. 259). Aside from examining the experiences of women coaches in the US sports system, we are not aware of research to date that has explored self-limiting behaviors of women in sport leadership positions. This is an area that scholars should take up in the future.

Conclusion

As detailed by the depth and breadth of research explored in this chapter, understanding the continued underrepresentation of women in sport

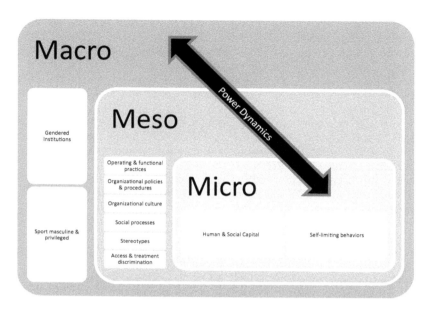

Figure 2.1 Multilevel perspective and power within sport leadership © Sarah Leberman and Laura J. Burton

leadership is a complex issue. Figure 2.1 summarizes the interaction between the three levels and illustrates how power has an impact on all levels.

Within each level the factors affecting the numbers of women in leadership positions are highlighted. It is encouraging to see scholars taking up more complex examinations of how gender is operating within sport organizations (e.g., Adriaanse & Schofield, 2013; Kihl et al., 2013; Walker & Sartore-Baldwin, 2013). However, we must also continue to recognize that gender as an organizing principle in sport needs to be considered along with other forms of identity, including race, sexual orientation, class, and ability (Burton, 2015; Fink, 2008).

References

Acker, J. (1990). Hierarchies, jobs, bodies: A theory of gendered organizations. *Gender & Society*, 4(2), 139–158.

Acker, J. (1992). From sex roles to gendered institutions. *Contemporary Sociology*, 21(5), 565–569.

Acosta, R. V., & Carpenter, L. J. (2014). Women in intercollegiate sport. A longitudinal, national study, thirty-seven year update 1977–2014. Retrieved from www.acostacarpenter.org/

Adriaanse, J. (2015). Gender diversity in the governance of sport associations: The Sydney Scoreboard Global Index of Participation. *Journal of Business Ethics*, 1–12. http://doi.org/10.1007/s10551-015-2550-3

Adriaanse, J. A., & Claringbould, I. (2016). Gender equality in sport leadership: From the Brighton Declaration to the Sydney Scoreboard. *International Review for the Sociology of Sport*, 51(5), 547–566.

Adriaanse, J. A., & Schofield, T. (2013). Analysing gender dynamics in sport governance: A new regimes-based approach. *Sport Management Review*, 14, 498–513.

Aicher, T. J. & Sagas, M. (2009). An examination of homologous reproduction and the effects of sexism. *Journal for the Study of Sports and Athletes in Education*, 3(3), 375–386.

Allison, R. (2016). From oversight to autonomy gendered organizational change in women's soccer. *Social Currents*. doi: 10.1177/2329496516651637

Anderson, E. D. (2009). The maintenance of masculinity among the stakeholders of sport. *Sport Management Review*, 12(1), 3–14.

Auster, E. R., & Prasad, A. (2016). Why do women still not make it to the top? Dominant organizational ideologies and biases by promotion committees limit opportunities to destination positions. *Sex Roles*, 75, 177–196.

Britton, D. M. & Logan, L. (2008). Gendered organizations: Progress and prospects. *Sociology Compass*, 2(1), 107–121.

Bruening, J. E. & Dixon, M. A. (2007). Work-family conflict in coaching II: Managing role conflict. *Journal of Sport Management*, 21(4), 471.

Bruening, J. E. & Dixon, M. A. (2008). Situating work–family negotiations within a life course perspective: Insights on the gendered experiences of NCAA division I head coaching mothers. *Sex Roles*, 58, 10–23.

Burton, L. J. (2015). Underrepresentation of women in sport leadership: A review of research. *Sport Management Review*, 18, 155–165.

Burton, L. J., Barr, C. A., Fink, J. S., & Bruening, J. E. (2009). "Think athletic director, think masculine?": Examination of the gender typing of managerial subroles within athletic administration positions. *Sex Roles*, 61, 416–426.

Burton, L. J., Grappendorf, H., & Henderson, A. (2011). Perceptions of gender in athletic administration: Utilizing role congruity to examine (potential) prejudice against women. *Journal of Sport Management*, 25, 36–45.

Burton, L. J., & LaVoi, N. M. (2016). An ecological/multisystem approach to understanding and examining women coaches. In N. M. LaVoi (ed.) *Women in Sports Coaching* (pp. 49–62). Oxford: Routledge.

Burton, L., & Welty Peachey, J. (2009). Transactional or transformational? Leadership preferences of division III athletic administrators. *Journal of Intercollegiate Sport*, 2(2), 245–259.

Claringbould, I., & Knoppers, A. (2007). Finding a "normal" woman: Selection processes for board membership. *Sex Roles*, 56, 495–507.

Claringbould, I., & Knoppers, A. (2008). Doing and undoing gender in sport governance. *Sex Roles*, 58, 81–92.

Claringbould, I., & Knoppers, A. (2012). Paradoxical practices of gender in sport-related organizations. *Journal of Sport Management*, 26(5), 404–416.

Claussen, C. L., & Lehr, C. (2002). Decision-making authority of senior woman administrators. *International Journal of Sport Management*, 3, 215–228.

Connell, R. W. (1995). *Masculinities*. Berkeley, CA: University of California Press.

Connell, R. (2009). *Gender*. Cambridge, UK: Polity.

Cunningham, G. B. (2008). Creating and sustaining gender diversity in sport organizations. *Sex Roles*, 58, 136–145.

Cunningham, G. B. (2010). Understanding the under-representation of African American coaches: A multilevel perspective. *Sport Management Review*, *13*(4), 395–406.

Cunningham, G. B., & Fink, J. S. (2006). Diversity issues in sport and leisure: Introduction to a special issue. *Journal of Sport Management*, *20*, 455–465.

Cunningham, G. B., & Sagas, M. (2002). The differential effects of human capital for male and female division I basketball coaches. *Research Quarterly for Exercise and Sport*, *73*(4), 489–495.

Cunningham, G. B., & Sagas, M. (2007). Examining potential differences between men and women in the impact of treatment discrimination. *Journal of Applied Social Psychology*, *37*(12), 3010–3024.

Dixon, M. A., & Bruening, J. E. (2005). Perspectives on work-family conflict in sport: An integrated approach. *Sport Management Review*, *8*(3), 227–253.

Dixon, M. A., & Bruening, J. E. (2007). Work-family conflict in coaching I: A top-down perspective. *Journal of Sport Management*, *21*(3), 377.

Dixon, M. A., & Cunningham, G. B. (2006). Data aggregation in multilevel analysis: A review of conceptual and statistical issues. *Measurement in Physical Education and Exercise Science*, *10*(2), 85–107.

Dixon, M. A., & Sagas, M. (2007). The relationship between organizational support, work-family conflict, and the job-life satisfaction of university coaches. *Research Quarterly for Exercise and Sport*, *78*(3), 236–247.

Dixon, M., Tiell, B., Lough, N., Sweeney, K., Osborne, B., & Bruening, J. (2008). The work/life interface in intercollegiate athletics: An examination of policies, programs, and institutional climate. *Journal for the Study of Sports and Athletes in Education*, *2*(2), 137–159.

Eagly, A. H., & Karau, S. J. (2002). Role congruity theory of prejudice toward female leaders. *Psychological Review*, *109*(3), 573–598.

Ely, R., & Padavic, I. (2007). A feminist analysis of organizational research on sex differences. *Academy of Management Review*, *32*(4), 1121–1143.

Fink, J. S. (2008). Gender and sex diversity in sport organizations: Concluding comments. *Sex Roles*, *58*, 146–147.

Fink, J. S. (2016). Hiding in plain sight: The embedded nature of sexism in sport. *Journal of Sport Management*, *30*(1), 1–7.

Fink, J. S., Pastore, D. L., & Riemer, H. (2001). Do differences make a difference? Managing diversity in division IA intercollegiate athletics. *Journal of Sport Management*, *15*(1), 10–50.

Grappendorf, H., & Lough, N. (2006). An endangered species: Characteristics and perspectives from female NCAA division I athletic directors of both separate and merged athletic departments. *The Sport Management and Related Topics Journal*, *2*(2), 6–20.

Grappendorf, H., Pent, A., Burton, L., & Henderson, A. (2008). Gender role stereotyping: A qualitative analysis of senior woman administrators' perceptions regarding financial decision making. *Journal of Issues in Intercollegiate Athletics*, *1*, 26–45.

Greenhaus, J. H., Parasuraman, S., & Wormley, W. M. (1990). Effects of race on organizational experience, job performance evaluations, and career outcomes. *Academy of Management Journal*, *33*(1), 64–86.

Guest, K. (2016). While women triumph at Rio 2016, the media is competing to see who can demean them the most. August 9. Retrieved from www.independent.

co.uk/voices/rio-2016-women-sexism-female-gold-medal-athletes-treatment-by-media-bbc-nbc-a7180476.html

Hoffman, J. L. (2011). The old boys' network. *Journal for the Study of Sports and Athletes in Education*, 5(1), 9–28.

Hovden, J. (2010). Female top leaders–prisoners of gender? The gendering of leadership discourses in Norwegian sports organizations. *International Journal of Sport Policy*, 2(2), 189–203.

Inglis, S., Danylchuk, K., & Pastore, D. (2000). Multiple realities of women's work experiences in coaching and athletic management. *Women's Sport and Physical Activity Journal*, 9(2), 1–27.

International Olympic Committee. (2016). Fact sheet. Retrieved from https://stillmed.olympic.org/media/Document%20Library/OlympicOrg/Documents/Reference-Documents-Factsheets/Women-in-Olympic-Movement.pdf

International Working Group on Women and Sport. (2014). Retrieved from www.sydneyscoreboard.com/

Kane, G. (2015). Leadership theories. In J. F. Borland, G. M. Kane, & L. J. Burton (eds.) *Sport Leadership in the 21st Century*. Burlington, MA: Jones & Bartlett.

Kane, M. J. (1995). Resistance/transformation of the oppositional binary: Exposing sport as a continuum. *Journal of Sport and Social Issues*, 19(2), 191–218.

Kanter, R. M. (1977). *Men and Women of the Corporation*. New York: Basic Books.

Kihl, L. A., Shaw, S., & Schull, V. (2013). Fear, anxiety, and loss of control: Analyzing an athletic department merger as a gendered political process. *Journal of Sport Management*, 27(2), 146–157.

Lapchick, R. (2015). The racial and gender report card. Retrieved from www.tidesport.org/racialgenderreportcard.html

Lapchick, R. (2016). The racial and gender report card. Retrieved from www.tidesport.org/racialgenderreportcard.html

LaVoi, N. M., & Dutove, J. K. (2012). Barriers and supports for female coaches: An ecological model. *Sports Coaching Review*, 1(1), 17–37.

Leberman, S. I., & Palmer, F. R. (2009). Motherhood, sport leadership and domain theory: Experiences from New Zealand. *Journal of Sport Management*, 23(3), 303–334.

Leberman, S. I., & Shaw, S. (2015) "Let's be honest most people in the sporting industry are still males": Female graduate employability in the sport sector. *Journal of Vocational Education & Training*, 67(3), 349–366.

Lovett, D., & Lowry, C. (1988). The role of gender in leadership positions in female sport programs in Texas colleges. *Journal of Sport Management*, 2(2), 106–117.

Martin, P. Y. (2003). "Said and done" versus "Saying and doing" gendering practices, practicing gender at work. *Gender & Society*, 17(3), 342–366.

Palmer, F. R., & Masters, T. M. (2010). Māori feminism and sport leadership: Exploring Māori women's experiences. *Sport Management Review*, 13, 331–344.

Pent, A., Grappendorf, H., & Henderson, A. (2007). Do they want more?: An analysis of NCAA senior woman administrators' participation in financial decision making. *Journal for the Study of Sports and Athletes in Education*, 1(2), 157–174.

Regan, M., & Cunningham, G. (2012). Analysis of homologous reproduction in community college athletics. *Journal for the Study of Sports and Athletes in Education*, 6(2), 161–172.

Sagas, M., & Cunningham, G. B. (2004). Does having "the right stuff" matter? Gender differences in the determinants of career success among intercollegiate athletic administrators. *Sex Roles, 50*(5), 411–421.

Sartore, M. L., & Cunningham, G. B. (2007). Explaining the under-representation of women in leadership positions of sport organizations: A symbolic interactionist perspective. *Quest, 59*(2), 244–265.

Schein, E. H. (1996). Culture: The missing concept in organization studies. *Administrative Science Quarterly, 41*, 229–240.

Schull, V., Shaw, S., & Kihl, L. A. (2013). "If a woman came in ... she would have been eaten up alive": Analyzing gendered political processes in the search for an athletic director. *Gender & Society, 27*, 56–81.

Shaw, S. (2006). Scratching the Back of "Mr X": Analyzing gendered social processes in sport organizations. *Journal of Sport Management, 20*, 510–534.

Shaw, S., & Frisby, W. (2006). Can gender equity be more equitable?: Promoting an alternative frame for sport management research, education, and practice. *Journal of Sport Management, 20*, 483–509.

Shaw, S., & Hoeber, L. (2003). "A strong man is direct and a direct woman is a bitch": Gendered discourses and their influence on employment roles in sport organizations. *Journal of Sport Management, 17*(4), 347–375.

Sibson, R. (2010). I was banging my head against a brick wall: Exclusionary power and the gendering of sport organizations. *Journal of Sport Management, 24*, 379–399.

Smith, M., & Wrynn, A. (2013). Women in the 2012 Olympic and Paralympic Games: An Analysis of Participation and Leadership Opportunities. Ann Arbor, MI: SHARP Center for Women and Girls. Retrieved from www.womenssportsfoundation.org/en/home/research/sharp-center

Spoor, J. R., & Hoye, R. (2013). Perceived support and women's intentions to stay at a sport organization. *British Journal of Management, 25*(3), 407–424.

Stangl, J. M., & Kane, M. J. (1991). Structural variables that offer explanatory power for the underrepresentation of women coaches since title IX: The case of homologous reproduction. *Sociology of Sport Journal, 8*(1), 47–60.

Tiell, B. S., Dixon, M. A., & Lin, Y. (2012). Roles and tasks of the senior woman administrator in role congruity theory perspective: A longitudinal progress report. *Journal of Issues in Intercollegiate Athletics, 5*, 247–268.

Walker, N., & Sartore-Baldwin, M. (2013). Hegemonic masculinity and the institutionalized bias toward women in men's collegiate basketball: What do men think? *Journal of Sport Management, 27*, 303–315.

Welty Peachey, J., & Burton, L. J. (2011). Male or female athletic director? Exploring perceptions of leader effectiveness and a (potential) female leadership advantage with intercollegiate athletic directors. *Sex Roles, 64*(5), 416–425.

Whisenant, W. A. (2008). Sustaining male dominance in interscholastic athletics: A case of homologous reproduction ... or not? *Sex Roles, 58*(11–12), 768–775.

Whisenant, W., Miller, J., & Pedersen, P. M. (2005). Systemic barriers in athletic administration: An analysis of job descriptions for interscholastic athletic directors. *Sex Roles, 53*, 911–918.

Whisenant, W. A., & Mullane, S. P. (2007). Sport information directors and homologous reproduction. *International Journal of Sport Management and Marketing, 2*(3), 252–263.

Whisenant, W. A., Pedersen, P. M., & Obenour, B. L. (2002). Success and gender: Determining the rate of advancement for intercollegiate athletic directors. *Sex Roles, 47,* 485–491.

Women on Boards. (2016). Gender balance in global sport report. Retrieved from www.womenonboards.net/Impact-Media/News/Sportswomen-win-gold,-but-still-paid-in-bronze

Yiamouyiannis, A., & Osborne, B. (2012). Addressing gender inequities in collegiate sport examining female leadership representation within NCAA sport governance. *SAGE Open, 2*(2), 1–13.

Chapter 3

Institutionalized practices in sport leadership

Nefertiti A. Walker, Claire Schaeperkoetter, and Lindsey Darvin

Introduction

This chapter will examine how the overrepresentation of male leadership of sport organizations has become an institutionalized practice that disadvantages women from gaining access to such positions. Institutionalized practices within sport organizations have valued male ideals, provided men with unquestioned power, and devalued women's contributions to sport leadership. This chapter will question those values, norms, and behaviors that have privileged men and masculinity in sport leadership.

Institutionalization defined

In order to understand how gender bias in sport leadership has been institutionalized, we will begin with discussion of the process of institutionalization. An institution refers to "more-or-less taken for granted repetitive social behavior that is underpinned by normative systems and cognitive understandings that give meaning to social exchange and thus enable self-reproducing social order" (Greenwood, Oliver, Sahlin, & Suddaby, 2012, pp. 4–5). These institutions are supported through norms, values, and beliefs that manifest in how one behaves. This process of establishing an institution happens over time as the norms, values, and beliefs become so ingrained into the culture that they become the taken-for-granted way of life. Institutions can form at the individual level, such as how the high-five has become a micro-level institutional norm of playing sports. It can happen at the meso level, such as how data analytics has become an extra source of information many sport organizations use to make decisions. Finally, institutions can form at the macro level, such as how our expectation of rules and officials or referees to manage the integrity of sport competitions has become part of the institution of sport. All of these concepts represent institutional ideals that were once a belief, that became a norm, and are now intricate parts of the institution of sport. Similarly, institutionalization is the process of these ideals becoming permanent, rule-like fixtures in the institution. As an example, at the end of sport competitions, competitors engage in a hand-shake or high-five. This is usually not a written rule, but an intricate part of the institution of sport competition. In many sports, to not engage with your competitor after the game is unfathomable and seen as a direct defiance of the institution of sport. Through the use of examples from sport, we will explain how the institution of sport has developed an institutionalized bias against women in leadership.

In her review examining the underrepresentation of women in leadership positions in the sport management workplace, Burton (2015) emphasized, "it is important to situate sport as a gendered space ... Therefore, any dis-cussion of women's leadership experiences in sport must include position-ing gender as a fundamental aspect of organizational and social processes" (p. 156). Acknowledging, therefore the gendered space of sport workplace settings combined with the notion that women are largely underrepresented in the sport workplace (Sartore & Cunningham, 2007), we need to under-stand how the underrepresentation came to be and why it continues to persist. Acker (1992) argued, "gender has become ... part of the everyday language of social science, largely as a consequence of the feminist move-ment and the accompanying intellectual efforts to better understand the systematic and widespread subordination of women and their domination by men" (p. 565). In detailing the importance of examining this intersection of social relations and domination/subordination in the sport setting in par-ticular, Theberge (1985) lamented that sport is often seen as a "static fact, rather than as a dynamic social practice" (p. 193). By instead viewing sport as a dynamic institutionalized male preserve, we can better understand the patriarchal control of women in the sport setting (Theberge, 1985).

The institutionalization of men as leaders

In 1972, the United States enacted Title IX to increase gender equality in government-funded entities such as intercollegiate sport. This policy sought to increase the opportunities for girls and women to participate in amateur sports. Whilst in most cases representation of girls and women as participants in amateur sports has increased, women as head coaches, athletic directors, and other leadership positions are significantly lower (Acosta & Carpenter, 2014). For example, before 1972 and the enactment of Title IX, women coached 90% of women's teams; currently, women coach only 43.4% of women's team (Acosta & Carpenter, 2014). Meanwhile, the percentage of women coaching men's teams has remained just about fixed at a measly 2–3% since 1972 (Acosta & Carpenter, 2014). This is a prime example of how gender bias has been institutionalized in sport leadership. Women were leaders of the majority of women's amateur sports programs before 1972 because most of these programs were in all-women's leagues. The leagues received less commercialization and funding, and were not completely included in the commercialized institution of sport as we know it. However, once Title IX was introduced and sport organizations were forced to include women into the male-dominated institution of sport through funding and access, men also began to take over the leadership roles that women held for years. The more women's sports became a part of the normative system of the institution of sport, the more leadership positions were *normalized* by the belief that men should occupy them. This is why today, in American amateur sports, men hold the majority of leadership positions. That is, the more normalized a sport institution becomes, the more it will relegate itself to the systematic and normalized gender bias in leadership that has been perpetuated for years.

A similar trend is apparent when considering international sport. In 2016, 90 committee members made up the International Olympic Committee (IOC), the governing body of the Olympic movement. Of those 90 members, only 22 (24.4%) were female (Lapchick, Davison, Grant, & Quirarte, 2016). Additionally, of the 15 executive board members, only four were women. This trend continues within the international federations. In 2016 women held 117 (14.5%) of the 805 leadership roles for international federations, 101 (14%) for summer sports and 16 (19.3%) for winter sports (Lapchick et. al., 2016). Further, the gender composition of coaches at the Olympic level follows a similar pattern. For example, the 2012 London Olympic Games hosted a total of 3,225 accredited Olympic coaches. Of that 3,225, only 358 (11%) were female (ICCE, 2014). South America had the lowest proportion of female Olympic coaches (2%), while the United States represented the highest proportion (16%) (ICCE, 2014). Examining international women's leagues, we see comparable institutionalized bias developed in the Women's Tennis Association (WTA). The WTA was founded and lead in its early years by all women, as stated on the WTA website:

> In September 1970, the birth of women's professional tennis was launched when nine players signed $1 contracts with World Tennis publisher Gladys Heldman to compete in a new women's tour, the Virginia Slims Series. The Original 9, as they were called, included Billie Jean King, Rosie Casals, Nancy Richey, Kerry Melville, Peaches Bartkowicz, Kristy Pigeon, Judy Dalton, Valerie Ziegenfuss and Julie Heldman.
>
> (WTA, 2016)

Now, men routinely dominate the WTA leadership. Currently, three of the top four WTA leadership positions are held by men (i.e., Chief Executive Officer, Steve Simon; President, Micky Lawler; Executive Vice President, Laurence Applebaum; and Chief Operating Officer, Matthew Cenedella). Again, signifying that once the sport moves toward institutionalization as part of the normative sport system, gender bias in leadership begins to take place. Netball, which is rarely competitively played by men, has an

International Netball Federation Board of Directors that is entirely female. While the International Cricket Council, which is much more commercialized and played by both women and men, has the vast majority of its leadership positions held by men. The more women's sports become a part of the commercialized, widely followed and accepted institution of sport, the more men become normalized as leaders and the less women leaders we see.

Institutionalized barriers

In order to examine the different ways in which male leadership in sport organizations has been institutionalized, we will detail several different frameworks for the institutionalization process. We will discuss the various conceptual frameworks that have been developed in order to either examine or attempt to explain how underrepresentation of women in leadership in sport has become institutionalized. Specifically, we will briefly discuss the following concepts: the glass wall, hegemonic masculinity, capital, role congruity and the relevance of each of these concepts to the institutionalized bias of women as leaders in sport.

The glass wall

The term 'glass wall' was introduced to the workplace literature in 1999 by Miller, Kerr, and Reid, highlighting the horizontal rather than vertical barriers to women progressing into certain leadership roles. Although sparse, there are a few studies that have examined the glass wall phenomenon as an institutionalized barrier in sport. The glass wall is often used as a metaphor for institutionalized barriers to women in men's sport, whereas the much more familiar term 'the glass ceiling' refers to the lack of access women have to moving up the organizational hierarchy to leadership positions and was originally mentioned in the *Wall Street Journal* in 1986 (Weyer, 2007). Specifically, the glass wall as described in sport management has thus far referred to the lack of access women have to working in men's sports. To our knowledge, Walker and Bopp first applied this term in the sport management literature in their research published in 2011. This is problematic because many of the highest paying and most visible leadership position in sports, are in men's sports. Also, we would assume at least half of women leadership opportunities would be lost by not having access to men's sports. Walker, Bopp, and Sagas (2011) examined gender bias toward women in the hiring process for a men's college basketball coach. In-basket scenarios were used in a quasi-experimental study in which the variables of hiring recommendation, capability, and job-fit were assessed for potential candidates of both genders. Participants were given a job description from a university with a pseudonym. They were then given the resume of a qualified male candidate, qualified female candidate, or an overqualified female candidate. As their names suggest, the qualified male candidate and the qualified female candidate both had identical qualifications. The overqualified female candidate qualifications were significantly better than both the qualified male candidate and the qualified female candidate. Finally, participants were instructed to rate the candidate based upon capability and job-fit, and to give a hiring recommendation. Results suggest that although women were scored relatively equal to men on capability and job-fit to coach men's college basketball, women were rated significantly lower than men on the variable of hiring recommendation (Walker et al., 2011). This result suggests that although participants deem women just as qualified as men, participants were less likely to recommend hiring females, solely because the candidate was a woman. This particular example shows how this institutionalized barrier, the glass wall, perpetuates itself at the macro level (i.e., society).

To better understand whether the institutionalization of the glass wall manifests itself at the meso level (i.e., organization), Walker and Bopp (2011) examined the perceptions of women who have worked as coaches in men's sports. Results provide evidence that gendered opportunities, male-exclusive social networks, and pressures to over-compensate for being female were strongly influential on the intentions of women to pursue leadership roles in men's sports (Walker & Bopp, 2011). It was broadly echoed that much would have to change at the organizational level to break down the barriers to women as leaders in men's sports. Particularly, sexist attitudes toward women in sport would have to be addressed, transparency in hiring decisions become the norm, and organizational support for the inclusion of women in the hiring process for positions in men's sports. The next section will highlight the sexist and hyper-masculine culture of men's sports, which supports the glass wall phenomenon.

To support previous work examining the institutionalization of the glass wall acting as a barrier to women as leaders in sport, Walker and Sartore-Baldwin (2013) examined this phenomenon of women working in men's sports through qualitative interviews with men. By talking with men who have coached with women in men's sports, they sought the perspective of men who are deeply entrenched in the institution of men's sports. Their results suggest that men's college basketball in particular and men's sports generally speaking are "hyper-masculine, gender exclusive, and resistant to change" (p. 308). Further, this study suggests that change may come from the core stakeholders, which include both men and women in sport leadership positions. The findings are particularly enlightening for understanding the glass wall phenomenon in sport because they suggested that change would come when leaders working in the trenches of sport, which are mostly men, consider women as viable candidates for leadership roles in men's sports. In essence, male leaders in men's sports suggest that their fellow male sport leaders become more inclusive and accepting of qualified women as leaders in sport. It is also important to note that, given so much of the research takes place in the coaching context, much more research needs to take place examining the glass wall phenomenon at the professional, administrative, and staff level of sport organizations.

Homologous reproduction

Numerous investigations dedicated to examining the decline of female head coaches have employed the homologous reproduction framework (Darvin & Sagas, 2016; Regan & Cunningham, 2012; Whisenant, 2008; Whisenant & Mullane, 2007). In their study examining the prevalence of homologous reproduction, defined as the idea that those in charge of hiring are more prone to hire those who are "similar" to themselves, Regan and Cunningham (2012) found that most athletics directors were men. By looking at the association between gender of the athletics director and gender of the head coaches of women's basketball, softball, and volleyball, results indicated that the gender of the athletics director was associated with the gender of the women's basketball and softball head coaches. Further, there were statistically significant associations between the gender of the athletics director and having all of the three coaches being the same gender as the athletics director. Similar examinations have been conducted at the interscholastic level. In a study conducted by Whisenant (2008), it was determined that homologous reproduction was prevalent within girls' basketball and softball. More specifically, under a male athletic director, male coaches were represented at a higher rate (65.1%) than female coaches for girls' basketball. Under a female athletic director for that same sport, it was determined that female head coaches were represented at a higher rate (54.1%). This same trend was found within the sport of softball. When the athletic director was female, female head coaches were represented at a higher rate (67.3%), while under a male athletic director, male head coaches were represented at a higher rate (57.2%) than were females. Beyond coaching, the homologous reproduction framework has been applied to hiring practices within athletic departments. Whisenant and Mullane (2007) examined whether the athletic director's gender influenced the gender composition of the sports information directors, finding that athletic directors did engage in homologous reproduction practices.

While administrative and head coach hiring practices often perpetuate male dominance within sport organizations, the same has not been found when considering head coaches and their staff hiring practices. Darvin and Sagas (2016) examined head coach gender and the subsequent gender composition of their staff members for four NCAA sports (women's basketball, women's soccer, softball, and volleyball) across all three divisions. Results indicated that while female head coaches for these sports were more likely to hire female assistant coaches, male head coaches were not reproducing themselves as frequently. Although these results suggest a positive trend for females in coaching and run counter to other studies within the homologous reproduction framework, these higher percentages of female assistant coaches for women's teams have not, to this point, impacted the overall number of women in head coaching roles, as that percentage has remained relatively steady over the past ten years (43%) (Acosta & Carpenter, 2014). Overall these studies suggest that male leaders hire other men for leadership positions. Again, enabling the institution of sport that prefers men as leaders as opposed to women. This supports the work of Anderson (2009) which sought to examine how the stakeholders, hiring managers, and leading decision-makers in sport continue patterns of male representation in sport management positions at the top of the organizational hierarchy. It was emphasized that, "they [those in charge of hiring] would seek similar qualities in people they hire – appointing clones to reproduce the masculinized nature of their sport" (Anderson, 2009, p. 7). The best person for the job may indeed be the person that least threatens the current structure in the sport management setting (Anderson, 2009). As such, men as leader becomes institutionalized.

Human capital and social capital

Numerous scholars have lauded the importance of human capital and its relationship with career development (Sagas & Cunningham, 2004). Specifically, Sagas and Cunningham (2004) examined differences in human capital and social capital between males and females in sport. Athletic administrators completed a questionnaire to determine if human capital and/or social capital served as a determinant in promotions in sport management. Results indicated that social capital (but not human capital) did have a greater impact for men than women. Further, they posited, "recent researchers have also noted a form of discrimination in managerial advancement in that women often receive differential returns for their investments" (Sagas & Cunningham, 2004, p. 414). Such differential returns may be a byproduct of the proverbial glass ceiling that can occur for women in the sport management workplace setting (Galloway, 2012). The glass ceiling has been described as "a metaphor for examining gender disparities between men and women in the workplace ... Such disparities are not explained by job-related characteristics of the employee, but by gender differences" (Galloway, 2012, p. 53). Despite past work experience and accrued knowledge (i.e., varying forms of human capital and social capital), the female sport management employee may still face barriers to employment at the senior leadership level. The female sport management employee is therefore stunted by the aforementioned glass ceiling (Galloway, 2012). Specifically, the glass ceiling serves as a metaphor for the lack of access women have to leadership positions in sports, generally speaking. As opposed to the before mentioned glass wall, which usually refers to women's lack of access to leadership positions in men's sports.

Role congruity theory

Another lens that may be helpful in examining the institutionalized bias against women in leadership is through role congruity theory. Eagly and Karau (2002) developed a theory to explain prejudice against female leaders in order to explain why females struggle with attaining and maintaining leadership roles. It is argued that people have dissimilar ideas of male and female leaders. Specifically, "prejudice can arise when perceivers judge women as actual or potential occupants of leader roles because of inconsistency between the predominantly communal qualities that perceivers associate with women and the predominantly agentic qualities they believe are required to succeed as a leader" (Eagly & Karau, 2002, p. 575). Consequences of such inconsistencies are threefold: (1) more favorable attitudes toward male leaders in comparison to female leaders, (2) more difficulty for women to advance to leadership positions, and (3) more difficulty for women to maintain their leadership positions if and when they attain them (Eagly & Karau, 2002). Such difficulty in maintaining leadership positions for women aligns with the glass cliff—the idea that women may be promoted to leadership positions, but those positions may inherently involve a higher level of risk and resultant failure for women (Ryan & Haslan, 2005).

Acknowledging that stereotypes may exist about the qualities an athletic director should embody, Burton, Barr, Fink, and Bruening (2009) studied gender typing of sport management administrators' managerial sub roles. It was found that when compared to the positions of life skills coordinator and compliance coordinator, the "masculine sub roles (i.e., allocating resources, delegating, managing conflict, strategic decision making, and motivating and inspiring) were considered significantly more important" for the athletic director position (Burton et al., 2009, p. 423). Although women can possess such characteristics, they are not perceived to be capable of consistently exemplifying these skills. When they do engage in such behaviors, they are considered incongruent with how a woman should act. Women are not perceived as successful as their male counterparts even though they may engage in the same behaviors and may therefore struggle with retaining their leadership roles (Burton et al., 2009). In another study similarly examining perceptions of gender in different types of management positions in intercollegiate athletics, the most salient finding from their study was that female candidates "were evaluated as significantly less likely to be offered the athletic director position when compared with the male candidate" (Burton, Grappendorf, & Henderson, 2011, p. 36). Discussing their results through the lens of role congruity theory, it was argued that females were less likely to be offered the athletic director position because female traits (e.g., helpful, kind, sympathetic, sensitive, gentle) were deemed to be incongruent with agentic characteristics more typically used to describe successful male leaders (Burton et al., 2011). We argue this is a demonstration of the continued institutionalized gender bias of leadership positions in the sport management setting. These characteristics associated with each gender are congruent with the institutionalized belief of what a leader looks like in a way that disenfranchises women to lesser leadership roles, and positions men as the norm for leadership.

When describing why such institutionalization persists, Dufur (2006) bemoaned, "since sport symbols are linked so intimately with masculinity, women's display of those symbols does not mesh well with the dominant femininity that defines women as physically attractive, petite, demure, weak, and supportive rather than aggressive" (p. 587). This quote circles back to the norms, values, and beliefs that enable institutionalized bias. As such, women face gender-based barriers to employment in sport management settings (Dufur, 2006). Martin (2003) emphasized that men need not overtly or knowingly engage in gendered practice. Rather, by continuing as "the way it's always been," social closure and oppression continues to exist in ways that are "consistent with institutionalized norms and stereotypes of masculinity" (Martin, 2003, p. 361). Similarly, Shaw and Hoeber (2003) suggest varying forms of discourse influence the differing roles found in sport organizations. Their findings indicate that senior-level management roles were most commonly linked to men and that discourses of masculinity were prominent, while women and more feminine discourse were linked to undervalued roles in sport organizations. We now harken back to Burton's (2015) work imploring scholars to "situate sport as a gendered space" (p. 156). In doing so, many scholars have examined the underrepresentation of females in leadership roles in sport management. Despite a better understanding for why such institutionalized underrepresentation exists, "women continue to face challenges and obstacles when seeking leadership positions in sport organizations" (Burton, 2015, p. 163). By detailing these theoretical concepts, we hope to have further illustrated the institutionalization process of men in leadership and the bias women face in sport.

Discrimination

According to Cunningham (2008), the lack of women present in sport organizations is influenced by gender discrimination. Additionally, research has determined that both access and treatment discrimination, specifically, influence the lack of women in leadership positions of sport organizations (Cunningham & Sagas, 2007). Within sport organizations, access discrimination suggests that the "old boys network," or exclusive networks in general, prevent certain individuals from entering the field (Walker & Sartore-Baldwin, 2013). Similarly, sex discrimination is one of the most common forms of discrimination seen in male-dominated professions (i.e., sports) (Knoppers, 1987). Although there may be a lack of sport research and given that it is quite difficult to obtain direct evidence of gender discrimination, the sparse representation of women as leaders for male teams (i.e., head coach, front office), while men are well represented as leaders for female teams, raises suspicions about the biased culture of sport organizations. Beyond the institutionalization of gender bias, institutionalized discrimination may be influencing the lack of women as leaders in sport. Therefore, scholars turn to methods of collecting indirect evidence of gender discrimination. Anderson and Gill (1983) found indirect evidence of gender-differentiating hiring standards when researching men who coached females and women who coached females. They determined that men who coached females had fewer years of collegiate athletic experience and had also received fewer collegiate athletic awards. Examining the practices of unfavorable evaluations of female leaders may be a fruitful setting for future inquiry into concepts of discrimination.

Conclusion: institutional change—women breaking institutionalized barriers in sports

Thus far, in this chapter we have focused the majority of the discussion on how the underrepresentation of women in sport leadership positions has manifest into an institutional norm, even in women's sports. However, we do believe there is a shift taking place in sports. Sport organizations are beginning to realize the benefits of diversity and inclusion. In a recent espnW project named Open Look, Drs. Nefertiti Walker and Nicole Melton have suggested that inclusive sport organizations boast a workplace where employees are not only more satisfied, less likely to leave, and bring their authentic self and ideas to the table, but are also more successful. Sport organizations, specifically college athletic departments, are more successful in objective measures such as team wins, as well as subjective measures evaluated by employees' feeling of success (espnW 2014). Sport organizations seek to identify and support leaders who can move them toward measures of success. Therefore, knowing that women in leadership positions help accomplish this goal has changed the way sport operates. Recently, the National Football League (NFL) has implemented a rule "that the league would now require at least one woman be interviewed for any executive position openings in the league office" (Belson, 2016, p. 1). Currently, the NFL does have a few women in important league office positions, such as Dawn Hudson, chief marketing officer; Anna Isaacson, vice president for social responsibility; and Lisa Friel, who runs investigations into player misconduct (Belson, 2016). Implementing this policy suggests the NFL values women voices, and is demanding women be included in the process of leading their organization. The NFL is the most popular and profitable sports league in the United

States, which suggests others, through mimetic pressures (i.e., copying the policies of other organizations in order to fit in to the norms set by industry leaders), may follow their lead of gender inclusion in leadership positions.

Over the years, the rate at which we see women serving in front office leadership roles of men's professional sports leagues has continued to show promise for the future state of inclusion. For example, in 2013 women occupied 21.7% of the senior executive level positions in Major League Baseball (Lapchick, 2013). Further, during the 2013 NBA season, women held 41.1% of the professional positions within the league office, and a historical high of 18.5% of vice president positions (Lapchick, 2013). The NFL has also experienced an increase in gender inclusion over the past few seasons. In 2013, 20 women occupied roles at or above the vice president level in the NBA, an increase from 17 women in 2011–2012 (Lapchick, 2013). Similarly, the National Basketball League Players Association (NBAPA) Executive Director, Michele Roberts, is the first woman to hold such a powerful and influential role in the NBA. Specifically, "she is the first woman to lead a major sports union" (Chafkin, 2015, p.1). Michele Roberts being elected as the Executive Director of the NBAPA speaks not only to the league's move toward a culture of gender inclusion, but also to the inclusive perceptions of the individual athletes in the NBA. The old ideals of men not wanting to be led by women are being challenged in some of the most masculine sport environments, such as the NFL and NBA. Even in professional coaching, women are breaking barriers as leaders. In 2014, Becky Hammon, of the NBA's San Antonio Spurs, became the first woman hired as a full-time coach in any of the American men's sport leagues. Similarly, in 2016, Kathryn Smith was hired for the Buffalo Bills, an NFL team, as the first full-time woman hired to a coaching staff in the NFL. In Europe the Ladies European Tour is led by Chair Helena Alterby Nordstrom. In Australia, New Zealander Raelene Castle was appointed as the first woman CEO to a Professional Rugby League Club—The Canterbury Bankstown Bulldogs in 2013. In Honk Kong, Chan Yuen-ting lead Eastern to the Hong Kong Premier League championship were they won their first title in 21 years. Chan suggested, "maybe I can be a good example. It depends on the culture of the region. In Hong Kong, between men and women, there is no discrimination. We are really fair. I am young and a woman and the club gave me a chance" (Duerden, 2016, p. 1). These sport organizations and the women they hire are opening doors for women in leadership.

Although most sport leagues and organizations have not implemented specific policies to address the lack of gender diversity in leadership positions, there are still women breaking through institutional barriers. Overall, the institutionalized gender bias of women in leadership positions has led to the lack of access and opportunities for women in sports. However, times are changing. Women are gaining access to leadership positions in professional and amateur sports. Norms and behaviors will begin to change and interviewing female applicants will become commonplace. The myth that men do not want to be lead by women is already being debunked by the success of women leaders such as Becky Hammon, who in 2015 lead a group of NBA rookies to the coveted NBA Summer League Championship. In this particular example, male allies in team management recognized Becky Hammon's talent and were change agents for gender inclusion. Although the norm in the NBA is to hire men, they saw the value in hiring the best person for the job, regardless of gender. This decision results in an immediate return on their investment, by Hammon leading their team to the Summer League Championship. Similarly, as mentioned in the previous section, Yuen-ting had a combination of male allies both in management and in subordinates, the players who followed her lead. However, she mentioned that Hong Kong has a much more egalitarian culture, which would be conducive to breaking down institutionalized bias. This combination of inclusive culture, coupled with male allies, produces an environment rich for women to obtain fair access to leadership positions and success. Research, inclusive policies, change agents, and male allies are all working to break down the institutionalized barriers to women in sports. Future research should examine how to encourage cultural changes and also develop and empower male allies, and explore other techniques for the de-institutionalization of barriers to women in sport leadership.

References

Acker, J. (1992). From sex roles to gendered institutions. *Contemporary Sociology: A Journal of Reviews, 21*(5), 565–569.

Acosta, R. V. & Carpenter, L. J. (2014). Women in intercollegiate sport: A longitudinal, thirty-one year update, 1977–2010. Unpublished manuscript, Brooklyn College, Brooklyn, New York.

Anderson, D. F. & Gill, K. S. (1983) Occupational socialization patterns of men's and women's interscholastic basketball coaches. *Journal of Sport Behavior, 6*, 105–116.

Anderson, E. D. (2009). The maintenance of masculinity among the stakeholders of sport. *Sport Management Review, 12*(1), 3–14.

Belson, K. (2016). N.F.L. will require interviews of women for league executive positions. *New York Times*. Retrieved from www.nytimes.com/2016/02/05/sports/football/nfl-women-rooney-rule-super-bowl.html?_r=0

Burton, L. J. (2015). Underrepresentation of women in sport leadership: A review of research. *Sport Management Review, 18*(2), 155–165.

Burton, L. J., Barr, C. A., Fink, J. S., & Bruening, J. E. (2009). "Think athletic director, think masculine?": Examination of the gender typing of managerial subroles within athletic administration positions. *Sex Roles, 61*(5–6), 416–426.

Burton, L. J., Grappendorf, H., & Henderson, A. (2011). Perceptions of gender in athletic administration: Utilizing role congruity to examine (potential) prejudice against women. *Journal of Sport Management, 25*(1), 36–45.

Chafkin, M. (2015). Outside shooter. *The Atlantic*. Retrieved from www.theatlantic.com/magazine/archive/2015/05/outside-shooter/389549/

Cunningham, G. B. (2008). Creating and sustaining gender diversity in sport organizations. *Sex Roles, 58*, 136–145.

Cunningham, G. B. & Sagas, M. (2007). Examining potential differences between men and women in the impact of treatment discrimination. *Journal of Applied Social Psychology, 37*(12), 3010–3024.

Darvin, L. & Sagas, M. (2016). An examination of homologous reproduction in the representation of assistant coaches of women's teams: A 10-year update. *Gender Issues*, 1–15.

Duerden, J. (2016). Chan Yuen-ting: The female coach who took a men's team to a national title. Retrieved from www.theguardian.com/football/blog/2016/jun/14/chan-yuen-ting-female-football-coach-hong-kong-eastern

Dufur, M. J. (2006). Gender and sport. In J. Saltzman Chafetz (ed.) *Handbook of the Sociology of Gender* (pp. 583–599). New York: Springer.

Eagly, A. H. & Karau, S. J. (2002). Role congruity theory of prejudice toward female leaders. *Psychological Review*, *109*(3), 573–598.

espnW (2014) Open look: Project 1 data summary (Research Report No. 1). December. Bristol, CT: N. A. Walker & E. N. Melton.

Galloway, B. J. (2012). The glass ceiling: Examining the advancement of women in the domain of athletic administration. *McNair Scholars Research Journal*, *5*(1), 51–62.

Greenwood, R., Oliver, C., Sahlin, K., & Suddaby, R. (2012). *The Sage Handbook of Organizational Institutionalism*. London: Sage.

ICCE women in coaching (2014). Gender and coaching report card: London 2012 Olympics. Retrieved from www.icce.ws/_assets/files/news/IWG/Leanne_NormanGender_Coaching_Report_Card.pdf

Knoppers, A. (1987). Gender and the coaching profession. *Quest 39*(1), 9–22.

Lapchick, R. (2013). Racial and gender report card. Retrieved from http://nebula.wsimg.com/728474de65f7d28b196a0fbb47c05a91?AccessKeyId=DAC3A56D8FB 782449D2A&disposition=0&alloworigin=1

Lapchick, R., Davison, E., Grant, C., & Quirarte, R. (2016). Gender report card: 2016 International sports report card on women in leadership roles. Retrieved from https://nebula.wsimg.com/0e5c5c3e23367795e9ec9e5ec49fc9b2?AccessKeyId=DAC3A56D8FB782449D2A&disposition=0&alloworigin=1

Martin, P. Y. (2003). "Said and done" versus "Saying and doing" gendering practices, practicing gender at work. *Gender & Society*, *17*(3), 342–366.

Miller, W., Kerr, B. & Reid, M. (1999). A national study of gender-based occupational segregation in municipal bureaucracies: Persistence of glass walls? *Public Administration Review*, *59*(3), 218–230.

Regan, M. & Cunningham, G. (2012). Analysis of homologous reproduction in community college athletics. *Journal for the Study of Sports and Athletes in Education*, *6*(2), 161–172.

Ryan, M. & Haslan, S. A. (2005). The glass cliff: Evidence that women are over-represented in precarious leadership positions. *British Journal of Management*, *16*(2), 81–90.

Sagas, M. & Cunningham, G. B. (2004). Does having "the right stuff" matter? Gender differences in the determinants of career success among intercollegiate athletic administrators. *Sex Roles*, *50*(5–6), 411–421.

Sartore, M. L. & Cunningham, G. B. (2007). Explaining the under-representation of women in leadership positions of sport organizations: A symbolic interactionist perspective. *Quest*, *59*(2), 244–265.

Shaw, S. & Hoeber, L. (2003). "A strong man is direct and a direct woman is a bitch": Gendered discourses and their influence on employment roles in sport organizations. *Journal of Sport Management*, *17*, 347–375.

Theberge, N. (1985). Toward a feminist alternative to sport as a male preserve. *Quest*, *37*(2), 193–202.

Walker, N. A. & Bopp, T. (2011). The underrepresentation of women in the male dominated sport workplace: Perspectives of female coaches. *Journal of Workplace Rights*, *15*(1), 47–64.

Walker, N. A., Bopp, T., & Sagas, M. (2011). Gender bias in the perception of women as collegiate men's basketball coaches. *Journal for the Study of Sports and Athletes in Education*, *5*(2), 157–176.

Walker, N. & Sartore-Baldwin, M. (2013). Hegemonic masculinity and the institutionalized bias toward women in men's collegiate basketball: What do men think? *Journal of Sport Management*, *27*, 303–315.

Weyer, B. (2007). Twenty years later: Explaining the persistence of the glass ceiling for women leaders. *Women in Management Review*, *22*(6), 482–496.

Whisenant, W. A. (2008). Sustaining male dominance in interscholastic athletics: A case of homologous reproduction... or not? *Sex Roles*, *58*(11–12), 768–775.

Whisenant, W. A. & Mullane, S. P. (2007). Sport information directors and homologous reproduction. *International Journal of Sport Management and Marketing*, *2*(3), 252–263.

Women's Tennis Association (2016). The WTA Story. Retrieved from www.wtatennis.com/scontent/article/2951989/title/about-the-wta

Chapter 4

The impact of bias in sport leadership

Heidi Grappendorf and Laura J. Burton

Introduction

Sport as a social institution has privileged heterosexual male power and domination, which is evident in all spheres, including leadership (see Burton, 2015). In addition, leadership and notions of successful leadership are consistently perceived as masculine and best embodied by men. As such, women are perceived as lacking the necessary skills to lead, most notably in the male-dominated institution of sport. When women seek access to leadership positions in sport organizations, they face biased perceptions of their ability to be successful leaders and this bias can be further damaging as women must overcome these stereotypes when exercising leadership and/or when holding leadership positions. They also face challenges for acting outside of their stereotypical gender role once in leadership roles.

This chapter will focus on the potential stereotypes and biases that women working in sport organizations may face. We will begin by introducing the concepts of social role theory, move to a discussion of gender role stereotypes and leadership stereotypes, and describe how women face a double bind when aspiring to leadership positions and/or exercising leadership in sport organizations. How stereotypes can be self-limiting to women and the impacts of stereotype threat to women in sport leadership will also be highlighted. At the close of this chapter, we will offer potential solutions that individuals working in sport organizations can consider to help minimize the impact of stereotypes for women in sport leadership.

Sport as a social institution

Exploring sport as a social institution is important to understanding some of the phenomena and theories related to bias examined in this chapter. Social institution is defined as "a set of relations, values, norms, statuses, roles, groups and establishments that are widely accepted and adopted by the society within the scope of their basic needs and that regulate the social structure" (Kaplan, Tekinay, & Ugurlu, 2013, p. 64). Sport can therefore be considered a very prominent social institution in almost all societies.

Sport has traditionally been a male-dominated domain where women's sports have been marginalized (Coakley, 2014; Schell & Rodriguez, 2000), as sport was created by and for men, and continues to be controlled and dominated by men in many ways (Acosta & Carpenter, 2014; Adriaanse, 2015). Considering it is widely accepted that men have been the dominant majority in sport and reproduce themselves through mechanisms such as networking, hiring, and promotion, it provides a challenging environment for women to attain positions of power or move up the organizational ladder (Whisenant, 2005). We need not look further than who holds leadership positions in national and international governing boards, college athletics, and professional leagues to find evidence of continued control and dominance.

To help understand the continued control and dominance by men in sport, it is important to examine the values that are held and continually reinforced. In other words, particular values can be disseminated through sport, as sport and sport organizations reproduce traditional gender roles that reify male power and dominance (Claringbould & Knoppers, 2008; Frey & Eitzen, 1991; Shaw & Hoeber; 2003). Anderson (2009) and Fink (2016) reinforce the point that sport is a powerful place where traditional values regarding masculinity are celebrated and upheld, as well as serving as a social institution organized to reinforce masculinity and reproduce hegemonic masculinity (i.e., where men maintain and reproduce power over women). Thus, sport has traditionally been utilized to serve as a medium for celebrating the achievements of men and promoting the values of masculinity, while marginalizing the status of women. As Frey and Eitzen (1991) noted "sport has been as a result largely a 'male preserve' supported by institutional practices of discrimination against women" (p. 516). Ultimately because sport values masculinity and masculine traits (Anderson, 2009; Shaw, 2006), women are seen as aberrant employees, thereby creating a dynamic where women may face negative consequences as a result of their presence in sport organizations, including in leadership positions (see Burton, 2015 for a review).

Women and leadership in sport

As previously described in the Introduction and Chapter 2 of this book, despite increased sport participation opportunities for girls and women, they are underrepresented in sport leadership (Acosta & Carpenter, 2014; Adriaanse, 2015; Lapchick, 2014). Data of women in sport management and leadership indicates that women's representation has declined in some areas, while making modest gains in others. For example, internationally, less than 1% of voters in FIFA's Congress are women, while national soccer boards have only 8% female representation (Dodd, 2015). On the International Olympic Committee (IOC) there are only 22.6% female board members

(IOC, 2016). It is evident there is an underrepresentation of women in sport management and leadership in a variety of sporting areas both nationally and internationally.

To help understand the underrepresentation of women in sport leadership, it is important to note that women working in sport organizations continue to face an array of barriers not only when entering management, but also when moving into leadership positions in those organizations (Burton, 2015). "The potential reasons for women's under-representation, and men's overrepresentation, in influential positions in sport management can be described as overwhelming" (Shaw & Hoeber, 2003, p. 348) and unfortunately, 15 years after this statement was published, it is still the case for women in sport leadership.

Gender stereotypes

To help explain what may be happening to women in sport leadership, social role theory has been utilized. Social role theory proposes that there are expectations regarding the roles that men and women occupy in society (Wood & Eagly, 2012). These expectations effect both the roles society perceives men and women should occupy (prescriptive roles) and the qualities and behavioral tendencies stereotypically demonstrated by each gender (descriptive roles). Within these socially constructed expectations women are often described as holding communal attributes such as being affectionate (emotive), helpful, and nurturing and are perceived as most appropriate for women to demonstrate (Wood & Eagly, 2012). Conversely, men are often described as holding agentic attributes such as being aggressive, dominant, and self-confident and are perceived as most appropriate for men to demonstrate (Wood & Eagly, 2012). When individuals are perceived as behaving contrary to these expectations, it can be perceived negatively by other individuals and as a result they may experience a backlash for not demonstrating perceived appropriate stereotypical gender roles (Eagly & Karau, 2002).

Stereotypes have been defined as "the unconscious or conscious application of (accurate or inaccurate) knowledge of a group in judging a member of the group" (Banaji & Greenwald, 1994, p. 58). Gender role stereotyping is forming specific expectations and assumptions regarding an individual's abilities and behavior on the basis of their gender roles (Hughes & Seta, 2003). These expectations and assumptions (e.g., stereotypes) are often accepted based upon the cultural and societal beliefs or one's own beliefs about women and women's roles in the workforce. Stereotypes are formed based on observations about social roles and also through occupational roles (Koenig & Eagly, 2014), such as woman as team mom and man as coach, woman as a nurse and man as a doctor, or man as a CEO and woman as an administrative assistant. Prescriptive gender role stereotypes indicate that women should occupy more communal roles and jobs, and men should be in more agentic roles and jobs (Eagly & Karau, 2002; Heilman, 2012). Thus, gender stereotypes are derived from shared understandings of what are considered expected and appropriate attributes and behaviors for men and women (Wood & Eagly, 2012).

The implications of social role theory and gender stereotyping are widespread, but particularly applicable to women in sport leadership. As described by Brescoll (2016) "the most influential psychological theories of gender and power have all emphasized the central role of gender stereotypes in explaining the underrepresentation of women in leadership positions (p. 416). The role stereotypes of "women take care and men take charge" (Hoyt & Burnette, 2013, p. 1307) affect how women are evaluated in leadership positions and are both pervasive and resilient. Further, emerging research by Cundiff and Vescio (2016) indicated that if individuals strongly endorse gender stereotypes (e.g., women as nurturing and men as dominant), they were less likely to attribute gender disparities in the workforce (e.g., fewer women in sport leadership positions) to gender discrimination. Conversely, those who did not strongly endorse gender stereotypes were more likely to acknowledge that discrimination plays a role in why we see gender disparities in the workforce (Cundiff & Vescio, 2016). These findings are concerning when considered in the context of sport, as women are persistently underrepresented in leadership positions in sport organizations and individuals who strongly endorse gender stereotypes will not recognize that gender discrimination is contributing to the lack of women in leadership and can hinder organizational policies which seek to minimize gender discrimination (e.g., Title IX).

Leadership stereotypes

Historically, leadership has been depicted in primarily masculine terms, and therefore many theories of leadership focus on stereotypically masculine qualities (Eagly, 2007). Leaders are consistently classified as having the characteristics of self-confidence, dominance and aggressiveness and these characteristics have been regarded as more similar to men than to women (Schein, 1973, 1979). Work by other scholars has noted that leaders are perceived to have more agentic than communal traits and characteristics (e.g., Powell & Butterfield, 1979). Additional research has supported the view that occupations that require leadership behavior are characterized as more masculine than feminine occupations (e.g., Shinar, 1975). This work has been replicated over the past 40 years using multiple diverse groups of people in the United States and internationally, and supports the perspective that leaders are consistently associated with men not women, and that leaders are perceived to be more masculine (agentic) than feminine (communal) (Koenig, Eagly, Mitchell, & Ristikari, 2011). Thus, if we continue to identify leadership behavior with men and male characteristics, it will continue to create an uphill battle for women seeking leadership positions.

Mismatch of gender stereotypes and leadership stereotypes

There are real implications for women seeking leadership positions in sport when appropriate female behavior is framed as communal, but effective leadership behavior is seen as agentic and, thus, in masculine terms. With such a framing, a perceived lack of fit between gender role stereotypes of women and stereotypes regarding the role of leader is created. There are three predominant theories that describe the intersection of gender and leader stereotypes: role congruity theory (Eagly & Karau, 2002), status incongruity theory (Rudman, Moss-Racusin, Phelan, & Nauts, 2012), and the lack of fit model (Heilman, 2012). Each of these theories explains how gender stereotypes of women are misaligned with stereotypes of effective leadership.

The lack of fit model describes a perceived lack of fit between the traits seen as typical for women and the traits required of successful leaders (Heilman, 2012). In other words, if women are traditionally viewed as being nurturing, kind, and sensitive and as having communal traits, Heilman noted there will not be a 'fit' with what one thinks of a woman when considering leadership. Related, role congruity theory describes the double bind women face in leadership as women are perceived as lacking the necessary attributes of leadership (agentic traits) and are perceived as not qualified for such positions. This framework specifically refers to the incongruity between stereotypes of women and stereotypes of leadership, and if or when women are in leadership, the potential negative consequences they face. Ultimately, when women do demonstrate agentic or communal leadership behavior, they are perceived as violating gender norms and are unfavorably evaluated for doing so (Eagly & Karau, 2002). As an extension of the double bind described in role congruity theory, work by Rudman and colleagues (2012) explain that the nature of the backlash toward women in leadership results from the defense of a gender hierarchy in leadership, where men are expected to occupy positions of leadership and retain status as leaders. In the end, the backlash occurs as leadership is not viewed as a place where women belong as it is a domain reserved for men.

Women in sport leadership: mismatch of leadership and gender stereotypes

The mismatch of effective leadership stereotypes and gender stereotypes hinder women in sport leadership. A prototypical leader of a sport organization should demonstrate more masculine managerial behavior than feminine managerial behavior (Burton, Barr, Fink, & Bruening, 2009), which is consistent with work on leadership prototypicality (Koenig et al., 2011). When evaluating leadership in intercollegiate athletics in the United States, stereotypically masculine managerial roles, including allocating resources, strategic decision-making, and punishing employees, are regarded as more appropriate roles for an intercollegiate athletic director (i.e., leader) (Burton et al., 2009). As noted previously, men hold the majority of athletic director positions in the United States (Acosta & Carpenter, 2014) and therefore perceptions of leadership as masculine and requiring more masculine managerial roles serves to disadvantage women regarding their fit with this leadership role.

Another factor at play for women in sport leadership is the leadership double bind described in role congruity theory. Using that framework, women can be perceived as having the necessary skills to be successful in sport leadership positions, but ultimately are not selected for such positions potentially due to gender stereotyping of women (Burton, Grappendorf, & Henderson, 2011). As noted in their findings, Burton and her colleagues revealed that individuals working in athletic administration in the context of US intercollegiate sport at the Division I level (the most competitive level of intercollegiate sport) evaluated comparable male and female athletic administrators as similar in their ability and their potential to be successful as athletic directors. However, despite this perceived equal competence for leadership, athletic administrators did not believe the female administrator would be selected for the position of athletic director. Further, in another study by Grappendorf and Lough (2006), female athletic directors in US intercollegiate athletic departments perceived that gender bias and discrimination contributed toward the underrepresentation of women pursuing a career such as an intercollegiate athletic director. In addition, 77% of female athletic directors believed the perception that women cannot lead men was a barrier to their overall career success (Grappendorf & Lough, 2006). Ultimately, women in sport leadership can obtain the necessary skills, be competent in their jobs, and yet still not be viewed as a viable candidate for a leadership position, highlighting that the double bind still exists.

Another facet related to the mismatch of leadership and gender stereotypes focuses on the discourse regarding leadership and selection for leadership in sport organizations. In Norway, work by Hovden (2010) revealed that discourses regarding the selection of leaders to sport governing bodies supported gender stereotypical imagery of heroic and masculine leaders. In other work, within a national sport organization in England, women reported having to prove their ability to lead against their male counterparts as a result of stereotypes of leadership as masculine. They were also subject to more challenging interviews for leadership positions because those managers of the organization conducting the interviews made gendered stereotypical assumptions that women would be less suited for those positions (Shaw & Hoeber, 2003).

In an effort to counter stereotypes regarding their abilities to lead in national sport organizations, women in leadership positions on national sport governing boards felt pressure to avoid what they perceived to be female gender stereotypical behavior and tried to adopt behaviors that were more stereotypically masculine (Claringbould & Knoppers, 2008). Further, "paradoxically, this pressure to behave in or associate with gender-neutral ways limited what women could do" (Claringbould & Knoppers, 2008, p. 408), evidencing the double bind women face within sport leadership positions. Similar findings were reported when exploring the recruitment and selection process of board members for Dutch national sport organizations. Women indicated that they faced a double bind in being selected as a board member, stating that they had to be "like one of the men" (Claringbould & Knoppers, 2007, p. 501) with regard to work experience, but were expected to not act like the men with regard to behavior, by being ambitious or aggressive (i.e., agentic) (Knoppers & Anthonissen, 2008). Ultimately, gender role stereotyping can be a significant challenge for women seeking to be hired and equitably treated and rewarded, as well as a major barrier for companies and organizations wanting to hire, maintain, and promote fairly. Given the preceding discussion it is not surprising that leadership can be "psychologically burdensome for women and [stereotyping and bias] can contribute to their underrepresentation" (Hoyt & Murphy, 2016, p. 388).

The impact of gender stereotypes on women in leadership has also been evaluated with regard to the context within which women are selected for leadership positions. An emerging line of inquiry has explored whether and how stereotypes of leadership and gender may place women in precarious leadership positions. This notion, termed the 'glass cliff,' describes how women are more likely to be selected for leadership positions in organizations that are declining or have experienced a crisis (Ryan & Haslam, 2005). The underlying mechanism used to explain this phenomenon is based on stereotypes of leadership and gender stereotypes, as women are perceived as non-prototypical leaders and therefore may be viewed as a different type of leader to help navigate the failing organization out of trouble (Kulich, Lorenzi-Cioldi, Iacoviello, Faniko, & Ryan, 2015). The glass cliff has not been examined empirically in the field of sport management, but may provide an interesting avenue to explore women's experiences in sport leadership.

The impact of stereotype threat is another critical concern that needs to be considered in the context of women's experiences in sport leadership. In the following section we describe the concept of stereotype threat and discuss how this threat impacts women in leadership.

Stereotype threat

Gender based stereotypes create disadvantages, and have real consequences for women in leadership, including sport leadership (Hoyt & Murphy,

2016). The concept of stereotype threat, first explored by Steele and Aronson (1995) in the context of racial stereotypes, is also applicable to gender stereotypes in sport leadership. Stereotype threat is "the concrete, real-time threat of being judged and treated poorly in settings where a negative stereotype about one's group applies" (Steele, Spencer, & Aronson, 2002, p. 385). Stereotype threat is a complex process in which the type of threat experienced by the individual depends on the source of the threat (who judges the action—self, in-group, out-group) and on the target of the threat (who one's actions reflect upon) (Shapiro & Neuberg, 2007).

The impacts or outcomes associated with stereotype threat are equally complex, including declining performance and avoidance of situations in which these stereotypes may manifest. Within the context of sport leadership, the outcome of stereotype threat for women may include a decreased motivation to take on leadership roles and/or decreased engagement in leadership positions. Sport organizations may well contribute to female leaders experiencing increased stereotype threat, as those threats are increased in "organizations where women are scarce, in contexts where gender stereotypes are made salient through the media or physical environments, or in organizational cultures extolling the virtues of competition or innate brilliance for success" (Hoyt & Murphy, 2016, p. 390).

Addressing bias and stereotypes

We now turn the discussion to ways of addressing the impact of stereotypes, stereotype threat and biases. Before we discuss specific steps, we will introduce the concept of second-generation bias to understand how gender stereotypes operate within organizations to impede women's experiences in attaining leadership positions and exercising leadership. Then we will discuss both individual and organizational-level steps that can be taken to help mitigate the impact of gender stereotyping and stereotype threat on women in sport leadership, and finally we highlight strategies to assist in reducing stereotyping and stereotype threat at the individual level.

Second-generation bias

An understanding of why women continue to face barriers in accessing leadership positions and exercising leadership in the workplace has shifted from explicit gender discrimination to an understanding of more implicit and subtle forms of gender bias, as we have described in this chapter. This subtle form of gender bias impacting women is described as second-generation bias, "the powerful but subtle and often invisible barriers for women that arise from cultural assumptions, organizational structures, practices, and patterns of interaction that inadvertently benefit men while putting women at a disadvantage" (Ibarra, Ely, & Kolb, 2013, p. 60). In other words, second-generation bias is deeply entrenched in organizations and practices where masculine values are reflected, thus creating gendered stereotypes that put women at a disadvantage. These subtle and invisible barriers described by second-generation bias include the limited number of role models for women aspiring to leadership positions and a lack of access to networks and sponsors to help women as they seek to advance into positions of leadership. Another challenge addressed in second-generation bias is the structure of careers paths and work that appear to be gender neutral, but are actually based on structures and practices that benefit men's lives. This can include expectations that it is easy to move to another position in a different state or country to enhance your career. Finally, the notion of the double bind also contributes to second-generation bias. As we have described earlier in the chapter, this double bind manifests as women are not expected to possess leadership skills and are therefore not seen as a 'good' fit for such positions, and conversely women are disliked when they are in leadership positions or demonstrate leadership behavior (Ibarra et al., 2013).

Recommendations to reduce second-generation bias

Based on the concepts of second-generation bias, we provide recommendations that can be implemented in sport organizations to help mitigate the impact of this subtle form of bias. One of the first steps that can be taken is to educate members of the organization regarding the components of second-generation bias and how this bias impacts individuals in the organization. This includes discussion of the concepts of gender-role stereotypes and leadership stereotypes and how these stereotypes influence women's experiences in sport organizations, including how they are evaluated for leadership positions in those organizations. There are online evaluation tools available to help individuals understand and examine their own gender biases (e.g., Project Implicit). It is important to note that even with an understanding of gender stereotypes and biases, recognition alone will not mitigate their influence on individual behaviors or change organizational policies. Compelling new research has discovered that in order to minimize the impacts of stereotypes it might be more useful to not merely identify that individuals hold stereotypes, but more importantly, organizations are "highlighting the pervasiveness of individuals' willingness to exert effort against their unconscious stereotypes" (Duguid & Thomas-Hunt, 2015, p. 354).

Naming gender bias and the double bind women face in leadership is important at the organizational level, and organizations should provide spaces and/or opportunities for women to come together to discuss and interpret messages they receive in their organizations (e.g., evaluations, feedback), as all messages should be evaluated through the lens of gender stereotypes. By recognizing and naming biases and stereotypes, women can gain "a more nuanced understanding of the subtle and pervasive effects of gender bias, how it may be playing out in their development as leaders, and what they can do to counter it" (Ely, Ibarra, & Kolb, 2011, p. 486). This can also help women be less susceptible to the negative outcomes of these challenges.

Other organizational-level changes that can be implemented to help mitigate gender bias include changes to the hiring process. Gender blind evaluation of resumes, by removing information that reveals the gender of the applicant has increased the number of women interviewed for positions in other fields (Aslund & Skans, 2012; Krause, Rinne, Zimmermann, 2012). Further, there are training programs such as Situational Attribution Training (Steward, Latu, Kawakami, & Myers, 2010) that have been developed to minimize racial bias during the interview process. This type of training program may be adapted to minimize gender bias (Latu, Mast, & Stewart, 2015).

Recommendations to reduce stereotype threat

There are ways in which the threat of stereotypes can be moderated to reduce negative outcomes for women. These intervening factors can be established at the organizational level and can also occur at the individual level. At the individual level, women with high levels of leadership self-efficacy suffer fewer negative consequences from stereotype threats. In addition, women who hold the belief that characteristics are malleable, can change or adapt over time, and have a growth mindset (Dweck, 1999), also appear to minimize the consequences of stereotype threat. Interpersonal factors, beyond individual differences among women, can have significant effects on women's experiences of stereotype threat. Female role models, in particular, can help protect women from negative threats to their leadership identity (Simon & Hoyt, 2013).

At the organizational level, there are steps that can be taken to reduce stereotype threat for women in sport leadership. The first, and one quite relevant to the context of sport organizations, is the creation of identity-safe environments that challenge the acceptance of negative stereotypes linked to minority identities (e.g., race, gender, sexual identity) (Davies, Spencer & Steele, 2005). Sport organizations that supported an organizational culture described as having community and cohesion, respect and inclusion, and were success oriented, resulted in more positive outcomes for LGBT employees and for the organizations overall (Cunningham, 2015). The organizational culture described in Cunningham's (2015) work would likely also reduce stereotype threat for other minority identities. Another important step that sport organizations can take to minimize stereotype threat is to encourage entry-level female employees, and/or those without leadership experience to take up leadership roles and foster a growth mindset in the organization, which endorses employee growth, "by advocating the belief that everyone can expand their intelligence and abilities can foster identity safety and combat stereotype threat" (Hoyt & Murphy, 2016, p. 394).

There has been limited research to examine how stereotype threat contributes to the lack of women in sport leadership. However, Sartore and Cunningham (2007) provided a conceptual model to explain how the influence of gender stereotypes can be attributed to self-limiting behavior for women in sport leadership. Newly emerging work on how stereotype threat influences women in leadership, as detailed above, provides interesting new avenues for research and support for programs to help minimize this threat for women in sport leadership.

Ultimately, it is important to educate and empower women to recognize the biases they face in their pursuit of leadership, and how to overcome them as they aspire to leadership in sport organizations. As Ibarra, Ely, and Kolb (2013) found, when women were empowered and had support, they would take steps to off-set negative biases. Therefore it is important for women to find support, build networks, and seek a mentor.

Additionally, Ibarra and colleagues (2013) noted that we must stop sending messages to women that they are the problem and need 'fixing' and that they must stop being 'too nice,' or 'too sensitive' or even 'too aggressive' or 'too assertive.' In other words, we cannot keep blaming women for being who they are and penalizing them for whatever characteristic they demonstrate. Women in leadership must stop being put into this bind and the 'catch-22' of leadership of no matter who they are or what they do, they are penalized. Blaming women for systematic bias accomplishes nothing, except to further impede them.

Providing opportunities through leadership development and training that specifically help women to consider, describe, and anchor their leadership purpose is critical. When women are able to firmly establish (i.e., anchor) their purpose(s) for leading, they are able to redirect their attention toward shared goals and to consider who they need to be and what they need to learn in order to achieve those goals. Women need to be encouraged to not define themselves relative to gender stereotypes, whether that may manifest as a rejection of stereotypical masculine approaches to leadership because they feel inauthentic to women, or by rejecting stereotypically feminine leadership behaviors for fear that those behaviors convey incompetence, women in leadership can focus on behaving in ways that advance the purposes upon which they stand (Ibarra et al., 2013).

Conclusion

It is clear that women face challenges when seeking leadership positions within the sport realm. This chapter identified some of the major biases and stereotypes that women encounter, as well as some recommendations as to how to address them. The problem of the underrepresentation of women in sport leadership is a complex one. However, with knowledge of biases and the impact stereotypes can have, steps can be taken to best support women and alleviate the challenges that create their underrepresentation.

References

Acosta, R.V., & Carpenter, L.J. (2014). Women in intercollegiate sport: A longitudinal study—thirty-seven-year update (1977–2014). Unpublished manuscript. Brooklyn College, Brooklyn, NY. Retrieved from http.://webpages.charter.net/womeninsport/

Adriaanse, J. (2015). Gender diversity in the governance of sport associations: The Sydney Scoreboard Global Index of Participation. *Journal of Business Ethics*, *137*(1), 149–160.

Anderson, E.D. (2009). The maintenance of masculinity among the stakeholders of sport. *Sport Management Review*, *12*(1), 3–14.

Aslund, O., & Skans, O.N. (2012). Do anonymous job application procedures level the playing field? *ILR Review*, *65*, 82–107.

Banaji, M.R., & Greenwald, A.G. (1994). Implicit stereotyping and prejudice. In M. P. Zanna & J. M. Olson (eds.) *The Psychology of Prejudice: The Ontario Symposium,* vol. 7 (pp. 55–76). Hillsdale, NJ: Erlbaum.

Brescoll, V.L. (2016). Leading with their hearts? How gender stereotypes of emotion lead to biased evaluations of female leaders. *The Leadership Quarterly*, *27*, 415–428.

Burton, L.J. (2015). Underrepresentation of women in sport leadership: A review of research. *Sport Management Review*, *18*(2), 155–165.

Burton. L.J., Barr, C.A., Fink, J.S., & Bruening, J.E. (2009). "Think athletic director, think masculine?" Examination of the gender typing of managerial subroles within athletic administration positions. *Sex Roles*, *5–6*, 416–426.

Burton, L.J., Grappendorf, H., & Henderson, A. (2011). Perceptions of gender in athletic administration: Utilizing role congruity theory to examine (potential) prejudice against women. *Journal of Sport Management*, *25*, 36–45.

Claringbould, I., & Knoppers, A. (2007). Finding a "normal" woman: Selection processes for board membership. *Sex Roles*, *56*(7–8), 495–507.

Claringbould, I., & Knoppers, A. (2008). Doing and undoing gender in sport governance. *Sex Roles*, *58*(1–2), 404–416.

Coakley, J. (2014) *Sports in Society: Issues and Controversies*. New York: McGraw-Hill.

Cundiff, J.L., & Vescio, T.K. (2016). Gender stereotypes influence how people explain gender disparities in the workplace. *Sex Roles*, *75*(3–4), 126–138.

Cunningham, G. (2015). Creating and sustaining workplace cultures supportive of LGBT employees in college athletics, *Journal of Sport Management*, *29*, 426–442.

Davies, P., Spencer, S., & Steele, C. (2005). Clearing the air: Identity safety moderates the effects of stereotype threat on women's leadership aspirations. *Journal of Personality and Social Psychology*, *88*(2), 276–287.

Dodd, M. (2015). FIFA needs more women. November 19. Retrieved from www.nytimes.com/2015/11/20/opinion/fifa-needs-more-women.html?_r=0

Duguid, M.M., & Thomas-Hunt, M.C. (2015). Condoning stereotyping?: How awareness of stereotyping prevalence impacts expression of stereotypes. *Journal of Applied Psychology*, 100(2), 343–359.

Dweck, C.S. (1999). *Self-Theories: Their Role in Motivation, Personality and Development*. Philadelphia, PA: Psychology Press.

Eagly, A.H. (2007). Female leadership advantage and disadvantage: Resolving the contradictions. *Psychology of Women Quarterly*, 31, 1–12.

Eagly, A.H., & Karau, S.J. (2002). Role congruity theory of prejudice toward female leaders. *Psychological Review*, 109, 573–598.

Ely, R.J., Ibarra, H., & Kolb, D.M. (2011). Taking gender into account: Theory and design for women's leadership development programs. *Academy of Management Learning & Education*, 10(3), 474–493.

Fink, J.S. (2016). Hiding in plain sight: The embedded nature of sexism in sport. *Journal of Sport Management*, 30(1), 1–7.

Frey, J.H., & Eitzen, D.S. (1991). Sport and society, *Annual Review of Sociology*, 17, 503–522.

Grappendorf, H., & Lough, N. (2006). An endangered species: Characteristics and perspectives from female NCAA Division I athletic directors of both separate and merged athletic departments. *The Sport Management and Related Topics Journal*, 2, 6–20.

Heilman, M.E. (2012). Gender stereotypes and workplace bias. *Research in Organizational Behavior*, 32, 113–135.

Hovden, J. (2010). Female top leaders–prisoners of gender? The gendering of leadership discourses in Norwegian sports organizations. *International Journal of Sport Policy*, 2(2), 189–203.

Hoyt, C.L., & Burnette, J.L. (2013). Gender bias in leader evaluations merging implicit theories and role congruity perspectives. *Personality and Social Psychology Bulletin*, 39(10), 1306–1319.

Hoyt, C.L., & Murphy, S.E. (2016). Managing to clear the air: Stereotype threat, women, and leadership. *The Leadership Quarterly*, 27, 387–399.

Hughes, F.N., & Seta, C.E. (2003). Gender stereotypes: Children's perceptions of future compensatory behavior following violations of gender roles, *Sex Roles*, 49, 685–691.

Ibarra, H., Ely, R., & Kolb, D. (2013). Women rising: The unseen barriers. *Harvard Business Review*, 91(9), 60–66.

International Olympic Committee. (2016). Women in the Olympic movement. Retrieved from www.olympic.org/Documents/Reference_documents_Factsheets/Women_in_Olympic_Movement.pdf

Kaplan, Y., Tekinay, D., & Ugurlu, A. (2013). Social status of sport: Sport as a social event, phenomenon and institution. *International Journal of Science Culture and Sport*, 1, 64–69.

Knoppers, A., & Anthonissen, A. (2008). Gendered managerial discourses in sport organizations: Multiplicity and complexity. *Sex Roles*, 58(1–2), 93–103.

Koenig, A.M., & Eagly, A.H. (2014). Evidence for the social role theory of stereotype content: Observations of groups' roles shape stereotypes. *Journal of Personality and Social Psychology*, 107(3), 371–392.

Koenig, A.M., Eagly, A.H., Mitchell, A.A., & Ristikari, T. (2011). Are leader stereotypes masculine? A meta-analysis of three research paradigms. *Psychological Bulletin*, 137(4), 616–642.

Krause, A., Rinne, U., & Zimmerman, K. F. (2012). Anonymous job applications in Europe. *IZA Journal of European Labor Studies*, *1*, 1–20.

Kulich, C., Lorenzi-Cioldi, F., Iacoviello, V., Faniko, K., & Ryan, M. K. (2015). Signaling change during a crisis: Refining conditions for the glass cliff. *Journal of Experimental Social Psychology*, *61*, 96–103.

Lapchick, R. (2014). Race and Gender Report Cards. Retrieved from www.tidesport.org/racialgenderreportcard.html

Latu, I. M., Mast, M. S., & Stewart, T. L. (2015). Gender biases in (inter) action the role of interviewers' and applicants' implicit and explicit stereotypes in predicting women's job interview outcomes. *Psychology of Women Quarterly*, *39*(4), 539–552.

Powell, G. N., & Butterfield, D. A. (1979). The "good manager": Masculine or androgynous? *Academy of Management Journal*, *22*(2), 395–403.

Project Implicit. (nd). Retrieved from https://implicit.harvard.edu/implicit/takeatest.html

Rudman, L. A., Moss-Racusin, C. A., Phelan, J. E., & Nauts, S. (2012). Status incongruity and backlash effects: Defending the gender hierarchy motivates prejudice against female leaders. *Journal of Experimental Social Psychology*, *48*, 165–179.

Ryan, M. K., & Haslam, S. A. (2005). The glass cliff: Evidence that women are over-represented in precarious leadership positions. *British Journal of Management*, *16*(2), 81–90.

Sartore, M. L., & Cunningham, G. B. (2007). Explaining the under-representation of women in leadership positions of sport organizations: A symbolic interactionist perspective. *Quest*, *59*(2), 244–265.

Schein, V. (1973). The relationship between sex role stereotypes and requisite management characteristics. *Journal of Applied Psychology*, *57*, 95–100.

Schein, V. E. (1979). Examining an illusion. *Human Relations*, *32*, 287–295.

Schell, L. A., & Rodriguez, S. (2000). Our sporting sisters: How male hegemony stratifies women in sport. *Women in Sport & Physical Activity Journal*, *9*(1), 15–35.

Shapiro, J. R., & Neuberg, S. L. (2007). From stereotype threat to stereotype threats: Implications of a multi-threat framework for causes, moderators, mediators, consequences, and interventions. *Personality and Social Psychology Review*, *11*(2), 107–130.

Shaw, S. (2006). Scratching the back of "Mr X": Analyzing gendered social processes in sport organizations. *Journal of Sport Management*, *20*(4), 510–534.

Shaw, S., & Hoeber, L. (2003). "A strong man is direct and a strong woman is a bitch": Gendered discourses and their influence on employment relations in sports organizations. *Journal of Sport Management*, *17*, 347–375.

Shinar, E. H. (1975). Sexual stereotypes of occupations. *Journal of Vocational Behavior*, *7*(1), 99–111.

Simon, S., & Hoyt, C. L. (2013). Exploring the effect of media images on women's leadership self-perceptions and aspirations. *Group Processes & Intergroup Relations*, *16*, 232–245.

Steele, C. M., & Aronson, J. (1995). Stereotype threat and the intellectual test performance of African Americans. *Journal of Personality and Social Psychology*, *69*(5), 797–811.

Steele, C. M., Spencer, S. J., & Aronson, J. (2002). Contending with group image: The psychology of stereotype and social identity threat. *Advances in Experimental Social Psychology*, *34*, 379–440.

Stewart, T. L., Latu, I. M., Kawakami, K., & Myers, A. C. (2010). Consider the situation: Reducing automatic stereotyping through situational attribution training. *Journal of Experimental Social Psychology*, *46*(1), 221–225.

Whisenant, W. (2005). Organizational justice and commitment in interscholastic sports. *Sport, Education and Society*, *10*(3), 343–357.

Wood, W., & Eagly, A. (2012). Social role theory. In P. Van Lange, A. Kruglanski, & E. Higgins (eds.), *Handbook of Theories of Social Psychology* (pp. 458–478). London: Sage.

Chapter 5

Intersectionality: the impact of negotiating multiple identities for women in sport leadership

E. Nicole Melton and Michael J. Bryant

Introduction

In many cases, people discuss diversity in terms of singular diversity dimensions. Consider recent media stories about athletes who have publically disclosed their sexual orientation. Articles and news segments tend to focus exclusively on the athlete's sexual orientation, while devoting relatively little attention to their racial identity or other relevant social identities that might influence their opportunities or experiences in sport. Such a narrow emphasis not only misrepresents a person's identity, but also fails to acknowledge how multiple diverse identities operate simultaneously.

To shed light on the impact and importance of recognizing people's multiple identities, WNBA player Layshia Clarendon recently shared her story of living at the center of various intersections. When discussing her reaction to the prejudice and discrimination she encounters, Clarendon (2016)—who identifies as black, gay, female, non-cisgender, and Christian—writes:

> What's most upsetting is not simply being misidentified ... What's upsetting is that it is a constant reminder that binaries rule our society. There is no space for the in-between. You have to be either male or female, gay or straight. When you don't fit those rigid molds, you are confronted everywhere you go that *there is no space for you.* The larger issue at play here is our limited view on gender, our antiquated definition of what it means to be a man and what it means to be a woman. *We don't often think critically about how patriarchy, sexism, and racism intersect.* (emphasis added)

Clarendon's comments highlight how when people do not neatly fit into a box based on a singular diversity dimension, they are treated differently, or not accepted, in many sport spaces.

Adopting a more critical approach, and recognizing how marginalized identities intersect, may help explain why Serena Williams has not always been loved or enthusiastically embraced by those within the traditionally white, upper-class world of tennis. Crouch (2014), for instance, suggests the "dueling–isms of American prejudice" manifest each time viewers (predominantly males) feel compelled to comment on Williams' body or style of play, which does not mesh with societal expectations for how a (white) female athlete should look and act. He notes how some concluded her "toned arms made her look more like a male boxer or linebacker than like a women's tennis player," while others criticized her tennis outfits as being "flashy, unserious, and self-absorbed" (Crouch, 2014, p. 2). Meanwhile, viewers are less critical of Maria Sharapova's mini-dresses and admired Roger Federer when he wore a familiar suave white blazer at Wimbledon in 2016 (Roger Federer is getting serious at Wimbledon, 2016). Commentators even suggested Federer was sending a message to competitors to "Look at me (Federer), I'm the seven-time champion," I'm confident, and ready to win. And, while it is okay for men to exude confidence, or anger challenging the chair umpire (something John McEnroe was beloved for doing), female athletes are constantly reminded that they are guests in the white, male-dominated sport institution, and are expected to behave in ways that conform to its hegemonic traditions and ideals.

The tendency to concentrate on one diversity dimension, or assume that those who share a specific diversity dimension (e.g., African American) experience similar challenges and opportunities, is also evident in discussions related to women in sport leadership. In a recent espnW article, for example, journalist Jim Caple (2015) investigated the possibility of Major League Baseball (MLB) hiring its first female general manager (GM). To understand how this barrier might be broken, he decided to examine the knowledge, skills, and abilities of Kim Ng. Ng is the current senior vice president of baseball operations for the MLB, previously served as assistant general manager for both the New York Yankees and Los Angles Dodgers, and is the highest ranking woman in baseball.

After conducting interviews with Ng and several people within her personal and professional network, he identified core reasons she might be the first female GM in the MLB. According to the article, Ng's keys to success include her (a) expertise in baseball analytics, (b) personal demeanor, (c) tenacious work ethic, (d) willingness to sacrifice work–life balance, (e) competitive nature, (f) exceptional communication and negotiation skills, (g) deep understanding of the game, (h) business acumen, (i) athletic background, and (j) ability to be "one of the guys." In fact, Joe Torre (MLB's executive vice president for baseball operations) insists Ng has all the qualifications needed to be a GM, and Dan Evans (former White Sox and Dodgers general manager) states, "there is no one in the game who could question her ability to be that person" (Caple, 2015).

While the majority of the article highlights Ng's abilities and qualifications, it did provide three reasons a team has not offered her a GM position. Jim Boden (ESPN analyst and former Cincinnati Reds GM), for instance, was confident gender was not a factor, but thinks Ng might have a slight weakness in scouting talent—even though the article frequently referenced her proficiency in scouting analytics. Dan Evans, on the other hand, simply felt poor timing or lack of fit may hinder Ng's opportunities. While both men quickly dismissed the idea of a gender bias, it is difficult to follow the fit argument, especially since Ng seems to display all the traits men traditionally value. The article even suggested the launching point of her career came a few weeks into her first job with the MLB. During a chance golf outing, she was able to gain the respect of her male colleagues after they witnessed her competitive drive on the course, and her desire to play from the same tees as the men.

There is no question people need to celebrate and share Kim Ng's story of immense success. However, Caple framed his article in a way that raises a number of concerns. First, while Ng's story provides one example of how a woman with multiple identities (e.g., woman, Asian-American) traversed the gendered sport landscape, it certainly does not reflect the challenges and opportunities all women face.

Second, Caple primarily draws from interviews with Ng's male colleagues and mentors to tell her story. As a result, these male voices shape the narrative and the reader learns more about their opinions and values than Ng's perspectives. For instance, Ng's baseball career began when she accepted an unpaid internship position with the Chicago White Sox. Those interviewed suggest Ng's willingness to forgo more lucrative job prospects in order to break into the industry demonstrates her dedication, passion for the game, and motivation to succeed. While this may be true, the article neglects to consider how her family's support—both emotional and financial—allowed her to pursue this opportunity. Similarly, her colleagues never mention her ethnic identity. However, Ng described how her parents, who are of Chinese decent, instilled the importance of a strong work ethic and expected an unwavering commitment to excellence (Caple, 2015). Thus, while Ng acknowledges the role her culture and upbringing played in her career, the article tends to downplay factors associated with her social class and ethnicity.

Finally, the narratives Caple emphasized or deemphasized maintain the status quo and reinforce the gendered assumption that women must act like men in order to succeed in sport. For example, he assured readers Ng is a real sports fan by describing the sports paraphilia in her office, noted how she gained respect by playing golf from the *men's* (gendered language used in article) tees, and made several references to how she fits in with the guys. What's more infuriating—though Caple spends the majority of the article documenting Ng's notable qualifications—he remains silent when two former MLB executives assert gender bias has no impact on hiring decisions. At this point, he had objective evidence that she is undoubtedly qualified for the position, had the support of Joe Torre, and was writing for a socially conscious, espnW audience. He had all the tools to take a stand. Yet when it was his moment to hit a homerun for equality, he failed to even step up to the plate.

The Kim Ng article demonstrates how those in the sports media typically represent individuals with multiple identities. They focus on one diversity dimension (e.g., Ng's identity as a woman), and allow dominant male discourses to frame the narrative. As a result, we do not learn the person's unique perspectives because her voice remains in the background of the story (unless the article was written by the women with multiple identities, see Clarendon, 2016). Unfortunately, sport management scholars provide few insights into the experiences of people with multiple identities. Most of the extant research focuses on institutional structures and organizational practices that limit women's leadership potential (see Burton, 2015). Less work, however, addresses the "emotional and cognitive processes of women as they encounter disparate acceptance and treatment within the male-dominated sport domain" (Sartore & Cunningham, 2007, p. 245)—particularly from the perspective of women with multiple marginalized identities.

The purpose of this chapter, therefore, is to further our understanding of how the intersection of multiple marginalized social identities impacts women's experiences and opportunities in sport. To do so, we will review the tenets of intersectionality theory and then discuss outcomes related to multiple marginalized identities, such as minority stress and identity management techniques. Next, we will present sport industry perspectives from women with diverse identities. Finally, we will suggest ways to create more welcoming and supportive sport spaces for women with intersecting identities.

Intersectionality

Much of the literature within sport and general management focuses on the unique effects of singular diversity dimensions. For instance, researchers might examine how race, gender, and sexual orientation affect people's salary or opportunities for professional development within a sport organization. Although this approach is appropriate and helpful in creating baseline data, people do not have a single identity, and it is difficult if not impossible to compartmentalize the various aspects of their identity. As such, research designs must use methods that capture the unique, lived experiences of people who have multiple identities (e.g., multiple diversity dimensions) that operate simultaneously.

Recognizing this need, Crenshaw (1991) developed the idea of intersectionality. This concept informed her original work examining race and gender, and highlighted the unique inequities black women encounter. Using an intersectionality approach, researchers can uncover multiple forms of prejudice women of color face due to structural and systematic pressures. More recent applications of intersectionality research also investigate issues related to sexual orientation (Walker & Melton, 2015), social class (McDowell & Cunningham, 2009), and ability (Norman, 2016). As LaVoi (2016) notes, "intersectionality forwards understanding that one's identity (e.g., race, gender, sexuality, age, class, ability, and ethnicity) interacts on multiple, interdependent, and often simultaneous levels with racism, sexism, homophobia, and belief-based bigotry, which contributes to 'intersecting' forms of systemic injustice, oppression, and social inequality" (p. 16). It is also important to note, intersectionality (or intersectionality theory) is a critical theory. Scholars using this approach do not attempt to quantify the additive effects of various identities; instead, they focus on the qualitative effects of multiple points of difference.

To further enhance understanding of the challenges women with multiple identities face within institutions, Crenshaw (1991) also outlines three constructs within intersectionality theory. They include (a) representational intersectionality, (b) political intersectionality, and (c) structural intersectionality. Representational intersectionality refers to the presence of stereotypes in cultural presentations, such as sports media or film that affects individuals with multiple identities. The visible overrepresentation of white men in leadership positions, for instance, perpetuates the notion that these individuals possess superior leadership abilities compared to their counterparts. As mentioned in the opening example, media messages praising the masculine traits of successful women in sport may also reinforce leadership stereotypes. Carter-Francique and Olushola (2016), on the other hand, note how increased representations of black female coaches in basketball counters the notion that only men, or white women, can hold the head coach position.

Structural intersectionality, refers to how hierarchical power structures and people's social categorizations intersect, and negatively influence the treatment and experiences of people with marginalized identities. Much of the extant sport management research draws from the social categorization framework (Tajfel & Turner, 1979; Turner, Hogg, Oakes, Reicher, & Wetherell, 1987) to explain why white, heterosexual men maintain their power within sport organizations. According to this framework, people (a) identify themselves in terms of social groups, (b) subconsciously make social comparisons, and (c) generally form more positive attitudes toward, and prefer to interact with, people similar to self (i.e., intergroup bias, see Ferguson & Porter, 2013). Illustrative of these dynamics, members of the privileged social group in sport (white, heterosexual men) continue to hire and promote people who look and act like them.

Finally, political intersectionality refers to when competing political agendas among social groups discourage individuals with multiple social identities from expressing their views. For instance, an African American executive may be hesitant to advocate for pro-LGBT policies for fear she might offend her other social groups. Recent actions by the WNBA allude to the pressure athletes face. For example, during the 2014 season, the WNBA created a marketing campaign directly targeting the LGBT community. As part of the Pride campaign, players were asked to wear warm-up shirts picturing a rainbow basketball on their team's Pride night. However, members of the Indian Fever were told not to wear the shirts because certain players, who held leadership roles, refused to support the campaign (Clarendon, 2016). Political pressure also played a role in 2016, when WNBA players (70% of whom are African American) were fined for wearing 'Black Lives Matter' t-shirts (the fines were later rescinded). The league-imposed fines were surprising for two reasons. First, NBA players were not fined for similar actions in 2014. Second, the league had players wear 'Orlando Strong' shirts after 49 people were murdered in a mass shooting at the Pulse night club in Orlando, Florida, USA. This league-endorsed show of solidarity took place a mere 10 days before players wore 'Black Lives Matter' shirts to raise awareness around racial injustice (Gibbs, 2016).

Exposure to inaccurate cultural representations, encountering organizational structures and systems that limit one's experiences and opportunities, and feeling conflicting pressures from different social groups adversely affects minority members in several ways. Specifically, the combined effect of these negative occurrences creates unique social stressors (i.e., minority stress) that majority group members do not experience—oftentimes compeling minority members to adopt identity management techniques to evade prejudice and discriminatory treatment. In the next section we will discuss the minority stress model and the outcomes related to experiencing this form of stress.

Minority stress

Meyer's (2003) minority stress model provides a framework for understanding the distinct and chronic stressors minorities experience because of their marginalized identities. The model describes stress processes, consequences associated with stressful events, and coping mechanisms minorities use to lessen their stress and enhance mental health. The three stress processes minorities encounter include (a) experiencing prejudice and discrimination (b) expecting or fearing that one will experience disparate treatment; and (c) internalizing negative stereotypes associated with their marginalized identities. Though Meyer originally developed the model to examine sexual minorities, it has been applied to other populations, including women, immigrants, the poor, and racial and ethnic minorities.

With respect to multiple diverse identities, Meyer (2003) suggests having multiple marginalized identities increases one's likelihood of experiencing prejudice or discrimination. The low number of women of color in sport leadership positions perhaps most visibly reflects the increased access discrimination people with multiple diverse identities face. These individuals also have to exert considerable mental effort in negotiating their identities (see Borland & Bruening, 2010). For example, they balance being a woman, racial minority, and lesbian while working in male-dominated, predominantly white, heterosexist sport organizations. Women in sport leadership roles may experience additional strain if their values—ones that are deeply connected to their salient cultural identities—conflict with traditional leadership styles or organizational objectives. Māori (indigenous people of New Zealand) women sport leaders, for instance, note that sexism, racism, and classism negatively affect their sport leadership experiences. However, they also describe how their cultural understanding of leadership, which emphasizes leaders' responsibility to give back to the community, can conflict with sport organizations that focus solely on economic or athletic success (Palmer & Masters, 2010).

With regard to the consequences of multiple minority stress, research suggests experiencing several forms of discrimination (i.e., race, gender, and sexual orientation), combined with the need to negotiate multiple marginalized identities, negatively relates to a number of mental, physical, and professional outcomes. Within the sport management literature, for instance, qualitative investigations reveal that athletes and sport administrators of color, who also identify as lesbian, tend to be socially isolated within sport organizations and feel forced to conceal parts of their identity (Melton & Cunningham, 2012; Walker & Melton, 2015). At times, the mental and professional toll of being "othered" has motivated many of these women to pursue career opportunities in more inclusive, non-sport industries (Walker & Melton, 2015).

However, not all people with multiple identities report higher instances of stress, and many successfully cope with their stress (Herek & Garnets, 2007). According to Herek and Garnets (2007), this occurs because "integrating multiple identities may enhance a minority individual's overall psychological resilience and increase one's available resources for coping with stigma" (p. 363). Specifically, recourses (e.g., social support, positive evaluations) individuals receive from other social group affiliations help them manage, and excel in spite of, experiencing various forms of discrimination. Though Herek and Garnets (2007) make a compelling argument, it is still unclear if having a multiple minority status is beneficial. In fact, lesbian athletes and administrators of color, who have experienced discriminatory treatment because of their devalued sexual identity, have reported increased anxiety and feelings of shame (Melton & Cunningham, 2012).

Sport management researchers have identified three factors that influence minority stress. First, Sartore and Cunningham (2009) proposed that the level of stigma consciousness, or "the degree to which women focus on their stereotyped social identity within the sport context" (p. 298), can reduce the negative psychological effects related to one's marginalized identify. Thus, women of color with high levels of stigma consciousness are more likely to anticipate that they will experience negative stereotyping, prejudice, and discrimination. Second, these authors suggest that one's role with a sport organization can impact their stress. For instance, women who hold low-status positions may feel more pressure to downplay their marginalized identities.

Melton and Walker's (2015) study with athletic administrators in the United States provides additional insights into these dynamics. Specifically, their findings suggest one's position within the organization positively related to psychological safety (feel contributions are valued and safe to be authentic self) at work. However, this relationship was moderated by one's sex and sexual orientation, such that top-level female administrators reported lower levels of psychological safety than male administrators, and high-ranking LGBT administrators reported lower psychological safety than their heterosexual counterparts. Furthermore, lesbian administrators reported the lowest level of psychological safety.

Finally, perceived social support can also influence one's level of minority stress. Lack of support was frequently mentioned in Walker and Melton's (2015) qualitative investigation with black lesbians working in college sport. Participants expressed how they felt isolated within their athletic departments because they were not welcomed into the predominantly white lesbian community or the black coaches' and administrators' community. Though support groups are not always available for women with multiple identities, some research describes how these women create their support system to handle the stain of being "othered" within their sport organizations. For instance, Māori women in sport leadership positions organized a 'team' of people within their organization who shared similar values (Palmer & Masters, 2010).

Identity management techniques

As previously mentioned, people with multiple identities often engage in a variety of identity management techniques in order to gain acceptance or avoid discriminatory treatment. Goffman (1963) uses the term "covering" to describe when people with stigmatized identities make considerable efforts to downplay parts of their identity that are devalued in society. The strategies people use to cover their marginalized identities has been observed in a number of diversity-related research in sport. For example, black female administrators may straighten their hair to de-emphasize their race (McDowell, 2008), and openly gay and lesbian sport employees might emphasize their shared sport fan identity to connect with heterosexual coworkers (Melton & Cunningham, 2014a). In these examples people are not hiding their identity, rather they use various identity management tactics to ensure their stigmatized identity remains in the background during social interactions.

Yoshino and Smith (2013) expanded Goffman's (1963) concept of covering by identifying four forms of covering: appearance, affiliation, advocacy, and association. Appearance-based covering refers to how people present themselves in social settings, which includes mannerisms they use, how they dress, and grooming preferences. Affiliation-based covering is when people avoid behaviors that may confirm negative stereotypes associated with their identity. For instance, a woman may not mention her children at work for fear her colleagues will think she is less committed to the job. Association-based covering, on the other hand, is when people with marginalized social identities limit contact with other group members. A lesbian athletic director, for example, may not bring her partner (spouse) to work gatherings. Finally, advocacy-based covering concerns one's willingness to support his or her social group. This form of covering occurs when a woman is hesitant to challenge a sexist remark or joke.

Similar to association-based and affiliation-based cover, research suggests that women, particularly when participating or working in sports viewed as more masculine, will engage in "defensive othering"—the process in which subordinate group members distance themselves from other subordinates by displaying attitudes and behaviors that reinforce and legitimize their devalued status (Ezzell, 2009, p. 111). Specifically, women will take on the views of dominant group members (i.e., emphasizing the notion that men's sport is superior to women's sport, support the view that women should not appear too muscular or masculine, or reinforce the belief that heterosexuality is and should be the norm) in response to the lesbian stigma and backlash women encounter in sport settings. When relying on this strategy, women cast themselves as the exception to the stereotype, thereby unintentionally reinforcing masculine hegemony and heteronormative ideology in sport.

Organizational performance

Manifestations of minority stress at the individual level (e.g., depression, low self-esteem, low job satisfaction) can also significantly influence group, team, or organizational outcomes. For instance, research suggests employees who report high levels of work-related stress are more likely to experience poor physical and psychological well-being, which limits their performance and/or production at work (Cryer, McCraty, & Childre, 2003). However, when diverse employees feel valued and included in the workplace, they are more likely to experience high job satisfaction, which relates to positive organizational outcomes (Milliken & Martins, 1996). Walker and Melton (2015) observed this in their qualitative investigation with female athletic administrators. The women of color in non-inclusive work environments were more likely to express low job satisfaction and intention to leave the organization than those who worked in inclusive environments.

Research also suggests inclusive climates relate to performance gains at the organizational level. For instance, Cunningham (2011b) examined performance outcomes related to sexual orientation diversity in NCAA Division I athletic programs. In his study, athletic departments that combined high sexual orientation diversity with a proactive diversity strategy (i.e., a strategy that values diversity and emphasizes inclusion and positively relates to job satisfaction among minorities) were able to significantly outperform other programs—in some instances, these programs earned almost seven times the NACDA points of their peers. In a follow-up study with athletic departments from all NCAA divisions (Cunningham, 2011a), findings indicated high sexual orientation diversity positively related to a creative work environment when the organization had a strong commitment to diversity.

Sport industry perspectives

Considering the limited amount of sport management research examining the experiences of women with multiple identities, we interviewed 11 sport industry professionals—from diverse backgrounds and who are at different points in their careers—to further our understanding of how the intersection of multiple marginalized social identities impacts their experiences and opportunities in sport (see Table 5.1, pseudonyms have been used).

While some are at the top of their fields, others are just beginning their careers in sport. Collecting such an array of perspectives allowed us to develop a more authentic understanding of the challenges and opportunities women face when holding, or pursuing, leadership positions in sport. Below we first present their perceptions of the barriers women with multiple identities face in the sport industry, and then discuss strategies for creating more accepting and welcoming sport environments for minorities.

Challenges

Lack of diversity in positions of power

When discussing the main challenges women with multiple identities face, many of the industry professionals we interviewed discussed how the low percentage of diversity at the top of sport organizations limits girls' and women's expectations of what careers they can and should pursue. It is not surprising the women expressed this concern given that men continue to hold the majority of leadership positions in sport organizations, both in the United States and internationally (Acosta & Carpenter, 2012; International Working Group on Women and Sport, 2012; Lapchick, 2015; Smith & Wrynn, 2013). In fact, when comparing the diversity of hiring practices in sport to the hiring practices in Fortune 500 companies, sport organizations continue to lag behind. While 5% of Fortune 500, and 8% of Fortune 50, companies have female CEOs, there are only two women who hold

Table 5.1 Sport industry perspectives: participant profiles

Pseudonym	Position	Sport Tenure	Racial Identity	Number of Children	Marital Status	Sexual Orientation	College Athlete	Citizenship
Alice	Former President and CEO of WNBA Team	19	Asian, Native American, Caucasian	1	Married	Lesbian	Yes, DI Basketball	USA
Kia	Senior Associate AD for Internal Operations at DI program	12	African American	0	Single	Heterosexual	Yes, DI Basketball	USA
Mona	Deputy Director of Athletics at DI program	26	African American	2	Married	Heterosexual	Yes, DI Track & Field	USA
Maci	Assistant Coach	2	Caucasian	0	Single	Lesbian	Yes, DI Field Hockey	Canadian
Astin	Founder and Director of Non-profit sport organization	5	Cuban and African American	0	Married	Lesbian	Yes, DI Soccer	USA
Lucy	International business affairs for professional league	1	Asian	0	Single	Heterosexual	Yes, DI Tennis	China
Sabari	International business affairs for professional league	1	Indian	0	Single	Heterosexual	Yes, Tennis	India

Elizabeth	Assistant Athletics Director for DI program	8	Caucasian	0	Single	Lesbian	Yes, DI Basketball	USA
Lilliana	Sports Agent	3	Latina	0	Single	Heterosexual	No	Chile
Skylar	Assistant Director for College Recreation Department	4	Caucasian	0	Single	Non-gender conforming lesbian	No	USA
Becca	Non-managerial position in sports marketing firm	1	Non-white	0	Single	Heterosexual	No	Italy

this position on a professional men's team—Jeanie Buss of the Los Angeles Lakers and Gillian Zucker of the Los Angeles Clippers. Furthermore, there are only two women of color who hold the president or CEO position in the WNBA, and they both work for teams not affiliated with an NBA franchise—Alisha Valavanis (Seattle Storm) and Christine Simmons (Los Angeles Sparks). These sentiments were reflected by the participants. For examples Alice indicated that

> It's hard to aspire to something you can't see. A little boy can dream of being anything because he sees himself everywhere. Considering all the other social pressures girls face that undermines their confidence, it takes a very rare and special girl to believe she can do something that no other woman has done.

Similarly, Skylar observed:

> I think it's hard to trust that people will really accept women who might look different than what they are accustomed to seeing. Most women in leadership positions typically look pretty feminine. You don't see many, if any, women at the top who aren't gender conforming.

Limited opportunities to develop valuable skills

According to Ely and Padavic (2007), the current positions minorities hold within an organization can also influence one's idea of what roles are appropriate and attainable for certain people. Such attitudes can lead to occupational segregation, which refers to "the clustering of people into particular roles based on their demographic characteristics" and "can limit career choices and opportunities and create wage disparities" (Cunningham, 2015, p. 75). Data from the 2014–2015 Racial and Gender Report Card (Lapchick, 2015) highlights how racial minorities are often pigeonholed into certain jobs within intercollegiate athletes. For example, many contend fundraising and development experiences are prerequisites to becoming an athletic director, yet racial minorities hold less than 6% of those positions. The opinions conveyed during the interviews support these dynamics. Specifically, participants expressed that men who control hiring decisions often believe women lack certain sport business-related abilities (e.g., scouting or player development), and only add value in specific areas of the organization (e.g., corporate social responsibility, public relations, international business). The following participant comments reflect this.

> Women get hired, but they aren't always given any responsibility or opportunity to make decisions that matter. If I think back on why I've

been successful, I can't stress enough how valuable my first job was. I was given real responsibilities; I had a budget and deadlines and had to coordinate with a lot of different groups to get the job done.

(Alice)

If I'm given an opportunity, I take it. Even if I'm not sure how to do it, I'm confident I can figure it out or I know someone who can give me some advice on how to solve the problem. When you're starting out, you have to seize the few opportunities you have to show people you have what it takes.

(Kia)

Since I speak Spanish they might think that I could maybe add value in some way. Maybe in player relations or customer services.

(Lilliana)

Organizational culture in sport

According to Schein (1996), organizational culture refers to the "the set of shared, taken-for-granted implicit assumptions that a group holds and that determines how it perceives, thinks about, and reacts to its various environments" (p. 236). The organization's culture serves to direct behaviors and is taught to newcomers as a model for what is valid and appropriate. Past research demonstrates how hegemonic masculine norms have shaped organizational culture within the sport industry—promoting practices that privilege sport's prototypical members (males who are able-bodied, white, protestant, and heterosexual) and marginalize people, values, and behaviors that challenge hegemonic masculinity (Cunningham, 2008). Over time, these social processes, activities, and mindsets have become institutionalized, such that people unquestionably accept them as legitimate.

When reflecting on their experiences in sport, all the women spoke about how prevailing norms within sport organizations influence women's leadership opportunities. For instance, they described how the sport culture rewards those who display great passion, embrace traditional sport values, and are willing to sacrifice work–life, and pay, to help the team. Employees are required to work long hours and weekends, constantly entertain clients, and socialize with coworkers after work—particularly during the early stages of their careers. Such a demanding schedule may not be feasible for women who have responsibilities outside of work.

In addition, women with multiple identities are "othered" in sport (Collins, 2000), which means they do not easily fit in dominant binary categorizations (e.g., male/female, white/black, lesbian/heterosexual, rich/poor). Their othered status can make it difficult to connect with peers and lead to feelings of isolation within sport organizations (Walker & Melton, 2015). Alice observed:

> Sport has a very social culture, which blurs the line between work and play. You're working all the time, nights and weekends. There's a lot of entertaining. After work you're hanging out with coworkers. You don't have time for a personal life, you're always working. But, I knew I had to keep the pace and stay out to show I was committed ... It was also during these time where I was able to form friendships with my coworkers ... When they got to know me on a personal level, I felt my gender or sexuality was less of an issue. Sport prides itself on passion and hard work, it doesn't pride itself on new ideas or welcome people from different backgrounds. They like to do things like they've always been done I became bored with this. Other industries emphasize innovation and value divergent thinking. Their business models excite me ... The sport industry has a lot of guys who seem content with the current mode of operation and refuse to adopt new strategies or incorporate cutting-edge technology.

Lilliana indicated that:

> The jobs that are available in the sport industry offer very low pay. So you have to have a lot of passion to first work in an industry where the cards are stacked against you, and be willing to earn less money. Economically speaking, I'm not able to make that sacrifice.

Constant pressure to perform

The women also recognized that sports' institutionalized values and practices reinforced gender and racial stereotypes related to leadership abilities. For instance, people in sport are more likely to associate leadership with men or masculine traits (Burton, Barr, Fink, & Bruening, 2009). According to the women we interviewed, men also believe women lack the necessary skills, abilities, or commitment to be effective sport leaders. As such, all of the women constantly felt the need to prove their competence and focus exclusively on producing quantifiable results for their sport organization. Sabari reflected:

> I think you're always aware that you're different. You don't look like everyone else and you stand out because of it. You don't want people to judge you or think you're not good enough. So I try to show my expertise and what I've done because people assume I don't really belong.

Lucy suggested that:

> Women have to always make sure their contributions make the team better. I also think it's important to be a good team member. So I try to not be conformational because I see how that has hurt other women. If you push your point too much or you're too argumentative people won't listen or won't want to work with you.

Managing multiple identities

All of the women described ways they negotiated or covered various parts of their identities. Those who were just starting their careers in sport, and held relatively little power or status in the organization, tended to be more concerned about how others perceived them at work. As such, they would use various techniques to downplay parts of their identity, such as their gender or sexuality. With respect to the women who had worked in the industry longer or held more prestigious positions, they were comfortable bringing their authentic self to the workplace, but did monitor the way they communicated with certain audiences. In general, all of the women managed their multiple identities so that they could best "fit" or connect with a certain group of people in their organization. This was highlighted in the following comments:

> If I'm talking to a group of African American girls, I draw from my experiences as a racial minority. I use a different approach if I'm talking as a You Can Play ambassador, and probably draw more from my experiences as a lesbian to connect with that audience. I think it all depends on your audience and figuring out the best way to get your message across. I'm naturally an introvert so I consciously try to be more outgoing and talkative when I'm around clients or people at work. But, I think people are expanding their idea of what it takes to be good leader. More and more companies are now appreciating a variety of leadership traits and styles.
>
> (Astin)

> It's all about finding a connection point with your audience. I think you are always trying to emphasize parts of your identity or downplay parts to connect with someone. It's a constant force you have to deal with, but it's also a skill you need to have, everyone needs to have. You need to be able to read people and know how to frame your argument in a way that resonates with them.
>
> (Alice)

> I'm always cognizant of how I'm being perceived by others, and I know my gender and race play into that perception ... I know I can't act in ways my male colleagues can.
>
> (Mona)

Suggested strategies for success

While all of the women we interviewed recognized the barriers women face when working in the sport industry, they were optimistic not only that the sport culture could change, but also that women holding sport leadership positions would soon be the norm rather than the exception. To achieve this goal, they suggested a number of strategies to enhance the experiences and opportunities for women in sport. First, several of the women who held top positions within the industry emphasized the need to celebrate and share women's success stories. According to those interviewed, increasing public awareness of powerful women serves as one way to challenge biased assumptions that men are the only ones equipped to be effective sport leaders, and also provides women and girls with visible role models. It is important, however, to ensure that the stories of women from all backgrounds receive attention, as failure to provide a diverse set of perspectives will not address the issues related to representational intersectionality. As such, sport leaders must be mindful of who they choose to highlight and how they portray these successful women in the sport industry.

Second, to change the culture of sport it is necessary for leaders to champion diversity and inclusion efforts. Leaders have the potential and power to influence others' perceptions of the value of diversity and inclusion, as they provide the example of appropriate behaviors and interactions, such as equitable treatment, promoting diverse hiring practices, fostering collaboration among diverse teams, and productively managing conflict (Ferdman, 2014; see also Avery, 2011). Furthermore, Smith and Smith (2016) argue that no diversity and inclusion initiative will ever be successful without leadership support. Social learning theory (Bandura, 1986) aids in understanding the importance of leader behaviors, as Bandura states, "virtually all learning phenomena, resulting from direct experience, can occur vicariously by observing other people's behaviors and the consequences for them" (p. 19). To illustrate these effects, consider past research demonstrating that employees will engage in inclusive behaviors when their leaders expect them to (Umphress, Simmons, Boswell, & Triana, 2008), and that when sport leaders challenge prejudice, their supportive behaviors can enhance feelings of inclusiveness among minority employees (Melton & Cunningham, 2014b).

Third, sport leaders must also provide skill-enhancing opportunities for women and girls from diverse backgrounds. Many of those we interviewed argued that minority women will never succeed if sport organizations do not give them real responsibility and assign them tasks that make a meaningful impact in the organization. In addition, all of the women stressed the need to provide minority girls ample opportunities to participate in sport. They felt sport participation can expose girls to strong, female role models and help them develop the necessary skills to be effective sport leaders.

Alice expressed how sport "hard wires you to not only set goals, but to then develop strategies to achieve those goals," while Astin suggested, "you learn that it takes all types of people, with different abilities and backgrounds, to succeed. You learn the importance of working through conflict and finding common ground with people who are different from you." Several of the women also noted how sport participation increased their confidence and self-esteem, taught them how to deal with failure, and how to celebrate their successes. In addition, they discussed how early co-ed sport experiences helped them learn how to effectively interact and negotiate with men. Given the many positive outcomes of sport participation, sport leaders need to create an array of competitive and recreational sport opportunities that are accessible and attract girls from all backgrounds—regardless of their race, ethnicity, religion, nationality, social class, athletic background, or mental and physical ability (Aspen Institute Project Play, 2016; Cohen, Melton, & Welty Peachy, 2014; Walseth, 2015; With-Nielsen & Pfister, 2011).

Finally, the women explained that having a strong support system is essential to ensuring success in the sport industry. Mona described this as forming a "dream team" that can comprise a variety of people (e.g., friends, family members, mentors, sponsors, colleagues) who provide professional support and emotional support. All of the women felt building their professional network was key to accessing various positions or opportunities in sport. However, many also noted that emotional support is particularly important for women with multiple identities, as they often encounter unique social stress because of their minority status. Astin stated, for instance, "it's important to stay physically and mentally healthy. It's difficult to work in a sport environment that usually isn't welcoming for people who are different. You need your team of people you trust to help you stay sane."

Conclusion

The purpose of this chapter was to further our knowledge of how the intersection of multiple marginalized social identities impacts women's experiences and opportunities in sport. We hope the review of past literature, combined with current perspectives of women working in the sport industry, inspires both researchers and practitioners to continue to explore ways we can create more accepting sport environments for women with multiple diverse identities. While there are certainly challenges to overcome, the stories of these women demonstrate success is possible.

References

Acosta, R. V., & Carpenter, L. J. (2012). Women in intercollegiate sport. A longitudinal, national study, thirty-five year update 1977–2012. Retrieved from www.acostacarpenter.org/

Aspen Institute Project Play. (2016). State of play 2016: Trends and developments. Retrieved from www.aspenprojectplay.org/sites/default/files/StateofPlay_2016_FINAL.pdf

Avery, D. R. (2011). Support for diversity in organizations. *Organizational Psychology Review*, *1*, 239–256.

Bandura, A. (1986). *Social Foundations for Thought and Action: A Social Cognitive Theory*. Englewood Cliffs, NJ: Prentice-Hall.

Borland, J. F., & Bruening, J. E. (2010). Navigating barriers: A qualitative examination of the under-representation of Black females as head coaches in collegiate basketball. *Sport Management Review*, *13*, 407–420.

Burton, L. J. (2015). Underrepresentation of women in sport leadership: A review of research. *Sport Management Review*, *18*, 155–165.

Burton, L. J., Barr, C. A., Fink, J. S., & Bruening, J. E. (2009). Think athletic director, think masculine? Examination of the gender typing of managerial subroles within athletic administration positions. *Sex Roles*, *61*, 416–426.

Caple, J. (2015). Will Kim Ng be MLB's first female GM? Retrieved from http://espn.go.com/espnw/news-commentary/article/13371785/will-kim-ng-mlb-first-female-gm

Carter-Francique, A. R., & Olushola, J. (2016). Women coaches of color: Examining the effects of intersectionality. In N. M. LaVoi (ed.) *Women in Sports Coaching* (pp. 81–94). London: Routledge.

Clarendon, L. (2016). Layshia Clarendon on how LGB too often leaves off the T. Retrieved from www.esquire.com/news-politics/a45824/layshia-clarendon-gender-binaries/

Cohen, A., Melton, E. N., & Welty Peachey, J. (2014). Using coed sport's ability to encourage inclusion and equality. *Journal of Sport Management*, *28*, 220–235.

Collins, P. H. (2000). Gender, black feminism, and black political economy. *The Annals of the American Academy of Political and Social Science*, *568*(1), 41–53.

Crouch, I. (2014). Serena Williams is America's greatest athlete. Retrieved from www.newyorker.com/news/sporting-scene/serena-williams-americas-greatest-athlete

Crenshaw, K. (1991). Mapping the margins: Intersectionality, identity, politics, and violence against women of color. *Stanford Law Review*, *43*(6), 1241–1299.

Cryer, B., McCraty, R., & Childre, D. (2003). Pull the plug on stress. *Harvard Business Review*, *81*(7), 102–107.

Cunningham, G. B. (2008). Creating and sustaining gender diversity in sport organizations. *Sex Roles*, *58*(1–2), 136–145.

Cunningham, G. B. (2011a). Creative work environments in sport organizations: The influence of sexual Orientation diversity and commitment to diversity. *Journal of Homosexuality*, *58*, 1041–1057.

Cunningham, G. B. (2011b). The LGBT advantage: Examining the relationship among sexual orientation diversity, diversity strategy, and performance. *Sport Management Review*, *14*(4), 453–461.

Cunningham, G. B. (2015). *Diversity and Inclusion in Sport Organizations* (3rd ed.). Scottsdale, AZ: Holcomb-Hathaway.

Ely, R., & Padavic, I. (2007). A feminist analysis of organizational research on sex differences. *Academy of Management Review*, *32*(4), 1121–1143.

Ezzell, M. B. (2009). "Barbie dolls" on the pitch: Identity work, defensive othering, and inequality in women's rugby. *Social Problems*, 56(1), 111–131.

Ferdman, B. M. (2014). The practice of inclusion in diverse organizations: Toward a systemic and inclusive framework. In B. M. Ferdman & B. R. Deane (eds.) *Diversity at Work: The Practice of Inclusion* (pp. 3–54). San Francisco, CA: Jossey-Bass.

Ferguson, M., & Porter, S. C. (2013). An Examination of categorization processes in organizations: The root of intergroup bias and a route to prejudice reduction. In Q. Roberson (ed.) *The Oxford Handbook of Diversity and Work* (pp. 98–114). Oxford: Oxford University Press.

Gibbs, L. (2016). Punished by the league for "Black Lives Matter" activism, WNBA players fight back. Retrieved from http://thinkprogress.org/sports/2016/07/25/3801601/wnba-black-lives-matter/

Goffman, E. (1963) *Stigma*. New York: Prentice-Hall.

Herek, G. M., & Garnets, L. D. (2007). Sexual orientation and mental health. *Annual Review of Clinical Psychology*, 3, 353–375.

International Working Group on Women and Sport. (2012). Retrieved from www.sydneyscoreboard.com

Lapchick, R. (2015). The racial and gender report card. Retrieved from www.tidesport.org/racialgenderreportcard.html

LaVoi, N. (2016). A framework to understand experiences of women coaches around the globe: The ecological-intersectional model. In N. M. LaVoi (ed.) *Women in Sports Coaching* (pp. 13–34). London: Routledge.

McDowell, J. (2008). Head Black woman in charge: An investigation of Black female athletic directors' negotiation of their gender, race, and class identities. *Dissertations Abstract International*, 69(7), 3210.

McDowell, J., & Cunningham, G. B. (2009). The influence of diversity perspectives on Black female athletic administrators' identity negotiations outcomes. *Quest*, 61, 202–222.

Melton, E. N., & Cunningham, G. B. (2012). When identities collide: Exploring multiple minority stress and resilience among college athletes. *Journal for the Study of Sports and Athletics in Education*, 6, 45–66.

Melton, E. N., & Cunningham, G. B. (2014a). The experiences of LGBT sport employees: A social categorization perspective. *Journal of Sport Management*, 28, 21–33.

Melton, E. N., & Cunningham, G. B. (2014b). Who are the champions? Using a multilevel model to examine perceptions of employee support for LGBT-inclusion in sport organizations. *Journal of Sport Management*, 28, 189–206.

Melton, E. N., & Walker, N. A. (2015). Psychological safety among women in sport: The influence of status, gender, and sexual orientation. Paper presented at the North American Society for Sport Management 2015 Conference, Ottawa, Ontario, Canada.

Meyer, I. H. (2003). Prejudice, social stress, and mental health in lesbian, gay, and bisexual populations: Conceptual issues and research evidence. *Psychological Bulletin*, 129, 674–697.

Milliken, F. J., & Martins, L. L. (1996). Searching for common threads: Understanding the multiple effects of diversity in organizational groups. *Academy of Management Review*, 21(2), 402–433.

Norman, L. (2016). Lesbian coaches and homophobia. In N. M. LaVoi (ed.), *Women in Sports Coaching* (pp. 65–80). London: Routledge.

Palmer, F. R., & Masters, T. M. (2010). Māori feminism and sport leadership: Exploring Māori women's experiences. *Sport Management Review, 13*, 331–344.

Roger Federer is getting serious at Wimbledon. (2016). Retrieved from www.news. com.au/sport/tennis/roger-federer-is-getting-serious-at-wimbledon/news-story/3dc b851b71700a715c2cc516a4b0998e

Sartore, M. L., & Cunningham, G. B. (2007). Explaining the under-representation of women in leadership positions of sport organizations: A symbolic interactionist perspective. *Quest, 59*, 244–265.

Sartore, M. L., & Cunningham, G. B. (2009). The lesbian label as a component of women's stigmatization in sport organizations: An exploration of two health and kinesiology departments. *Quest, 61*(3), 289–305.

Schein, E. H. (1996). Culture: The missing concept in organization studies. *Administrative Science Quarterly, 41*(2), 229–240.

Smith, G. A., & Smith J. C. (2016). Diversity and inclusion: Insights and lessons learned from world-class organizations. Paper presented at the NCAA Inclusion Forum, Indianapolis, Indiana.

Smith, M., & Wrynn, A. (2013). *Women in the 2012 Olympic and Paralympic Games: An Analysis of Participation and Leadership Opportunities.* Ann Arbor, MI: SHARP Center for Women and Girls. Retrieved from www. womenssportsfoundation.org/en/home/research/sharp-center

Tajfel, H., & Turner J. C. (1979). An integrative theory of intergroup conflict. In W. G. Austin & S. Worchel (eds.) *The Social Psychology of Intergroup Relations* (pp. 33–47). Monterey, CA: Brooks/Cole.

Turner, J. T., Hogg, M. A., Oakes, P. J., Reicher, S. D., & Wetherell, M. S. (1987). *Rediscovering the Social Group. A Self-categorization Theory.* Oxford, UK: Blackwell.

Umphress, E. E., Simmons, A. L., Boswell, W. R., & Triana, M. (2008). Managing discrimination in selection: The influence of directives from an authority and social dominance orientation. *Journal of Applied Psychology, 93*, 982–993.

Walker, N. A., & Melton, E. N. (2015). The triple threat: Examining the intersection of gender, race, and sexual orientation in sport organizations. *Journal of Sport Management, 29*, 257–271.

Walseth, K. (2015). Muslim girls' experiences in physical education in Norway: What role does religiosity play? *Sport, Education & Society, 20*, 304–323.

With-Nielsen, N., & Pfister, G. (2011). Gender constructions and negotiation in physical education: Case studies. *Sport, Education & Society, 16*, 645–665.

Yoshino, K., & Smith, C. (2013). Uncovering talent: A new model of inclusion. Retrieved from www2.deloitte.com/content/dam/Deloitte/us/Documents/about-deloitte/us-inclusion-uncovering-talent-paper.pdf

Chapter 6

Quotas to accelerate gender equity in sport leadership: do they work?

Johanna A. Adriaanse

Introduction

Since 2008 Marisol Casado, a Spanish woman, has been the elected president of the International Triathlon Union, the global governing body of that sport (International Triathlon Union, 2016). Her position is unique as she is one of only six women occupying the role of president of an international sport federation (International Working Group on Women and Sport, 2016c). Throughout the world women and girls have embraced playing sport but there has been no significant increase in the number of women in organizational leadership roles. Although a substantial body of research has investigated the underrepresentation of women in sport leadership (Adriaanse & Schofield, 2013; Burton, 2015; Claringbould & Knoppers, 2008, 2012; Hovden, 2010; Pfister & Radtke, 2009; Schull, Shaw, & Kihl, 2013; Shaw & Hoeber, 2003; Shaw & Penney, 2003; Shaw & Slack, 2002), increasing women's presence at the executive table remains a challenge. Yet the benefits of gender diversity in leadership are widely acknowledged. A review of scholarship on women directors on corporate boards, for example, was informed by more than 400 publications spanning the past 30 years (Terjesen, Sealy, & Singh, 2009).

This chapter explores the use of gender quotas as a strategy to accelerate the growth of women in sport leadership, particularly in the governance of national sport organisations (NSOs) and international federations (IFs). First, I present an overview of the current global status of women's participation in sport governance based on the Sydney Scoreboard, a global index for women in sport leadership. This provides compelling evidence that only limited progress has been made to date and gender equity in sport governance remains elusive. Second, I discuss several strategies for disrupting the status quo at an international level, including the *Brighton Plus Helsinki Declaration* and an important initiative by the United Nations (Adriaanse & Claringbould, 2016), as well as the introduction of gender quotas. The latter is controversial. Many organizations oppose this type of intervention, although quotas can be effective in bringing about positive change. Third, I explore the use of quotas in the public, corporate, and sport sectors. Drawing on examples from Norway (Skirstad, 2009; Torchia, Calabro, & Huse, 2011) and the International Olympic Committee (IOC) (Henry, Radzi, Rich, Shelton, Theodoraki, & White, 2004; Henry & Robinson, 2010), I compare the effectiveness of targets versus quotas. I also discuss the impact of quotas in sport governance based on a recent study of Australian sport organizations. Finally, I draw conclusions about the use of quotas as a strategy to accelerate gender equity in sport governance.

Current status of women's participation in sport governance globally

Data from the Sydney Scoreboard global index for women in sport leadership indicate that women's representation in the governance of sport has increased in recent years (International Working Group on Women and Sport, 2016c). The Sydney Scoreboard, a legacy of the 5th IWG World Conference on Women and Sport, monitors women's presence on sport boards using three key indicators: board directors, board chairs, and chief executives. At a national level, based on data from 38 countries and 1599 NSOs, the average representation of women directors increased from 19.7% in 2010 to 20.7% in 2014 (International Working Group on Women and Sport, 2016c). Further, while the average for women chairs remained the same at 10.6% during this period, the average for women chief executives rose from 17.3% in 2010 to 19.8 % in 2014. See Table 6.1 for a summary of the findings.

At an international level, based on data from 76 IFs, the average representation of women directors went up from 12% in 2012 to 13.3% in 2014. In addition, women occupying the position of chair or president of an international federation increased from 7% to 8% and those in the role of chief executive or secretary-general from 9% to 21% in the same time period. Table 6.2 shows a summary of these results.

It should be noted, however, that, in a number of IFs, women's participation rates in leadership were markedly below the average (International Working Group on Women and Sport, 2016c). Some 24 of 76 IFs had no women on their board in 2014, including several that govern popular global

Table 6.1 Percentage of women as director/chair/chief executive of national sport organisations (NSOs) in 2010 and 2014

Leadership Position	2010	2014	Change
Women directors	19.7	20.7	+1
Women chairs	10.6	10.6	0
Women chief executives	17.3	19.8	+2.5

Note: based on 38 countries and 1599 NSOs – see sydneyscoreboard.com

Table 6.2 Percentage of women as director/chair/chief executive of international federations (IFs) in 2012 and 2014

Leadership Position	2012	2014	Change
Women directors	12	13.3	+1.3
Women chairs	7	8	+1
Women chief executives	9	21	+12

Note: based on 76 IFs – see sydneyscoreboard.com

sports such as tennis, cricket, rugby, handball, and baseball. In a case of 'reverse' gender inequity, the IF that governs the popular sport of netball had 0% men's participation on its board. FIFA, the international governing body of the world's most popular sport, football, had only one woman among its 24 executive members (4%) in 2014.

Although average results show an increase, albeit small, in women's representation in sport governance globally, in all cases women remain markedly underrepresented; none of the indicators has yet reached 40%. As a measure of gender equity, a minimum of 40% representation of men and women is often regarded as evidence of gender balance or gender parity in groups. This target is adopted by researchers (Joecks, Pull, & Vetter, 2013; Kanter, 1977) and is also recommended by public policy makers in governance such as the Australian Human Rights Commission (2010) and the European Parliament (Whelan & Wood, 2012). The consequences of a lack of gender balance in board composition are twofold. First, important stakeholders of the organization are excluded from participation in decision-making. Board directors play a critical role in developing strategy and decision-making as they represent the source of values and objectives that develop and sustain an organization (Clarke, 2007). For example, hundreds of thousands of girls and women play tennis and football worldwide; nevertheless they are represented minimally if at all at the highest level of the sport's governance. This means that their voice is excluded from the shaping of core organizational values and the creation of a strategic vision for the sport. Second, a substantial body of research has demonstrated the advantages of a gender-balanced board (Bilimoria & Wheeler, 2000; Nielsen & Huse, 2010; Terjesen et al., 2009; Torchia et al., 2011; van der Walt & Ingley, 2003). These include greater sensitivity to different perspectives, which bodes well for innovation and better decision-making and problem-solving. In addition, boards with three or more women directors have been shown to be more inclined to consider non-financial performance measures such as CSR involvement and stakeholder satisfaction (Terjesen et al., 2009). These types of performance measures are increasingly essential for the sustainability of contemporary organizations. In other words, a lack of gender balance in board composition suggests that the governance of global sport is not reaching its full potential (Adriaanse, 2016).

Disrupting the status quo

Several international strategies designed to address gender inequality in sport governance have been implemented since the 1990s. The *Brighton Declaration* was the first international declaration which specifically identified the aim of increasing women's participation in sport leadership, with the goal of empowering women and advancing sport. This declaration was informed by key UN documents such as the *Charter of the United Nations* (United Nations, 1945), the *Universal Declaration of Human Rights* (United Nations, 1948) and the *Convention on the Elimination of all Forms of Discrimination Against Women* (CEDAW) (United Nations, 1979). Representing a global voice, delegates from 82 countries adopted the *Brighton Declaration* at the 1st IWG World Conference on Women and Sport in Brighton in 1994 (International Working Group on Women and Sport, 2016b). An updated version, the *Brighton plus Helsinki Declaration*, was adopted by participants from almost 100 nations at the 6th IWG World Conference on Women and Sport in Helsinki in 2014 (International Working Group on Women and Sport, 2016b). One of the ten principles in this declaration focuses on leadership in sport:

> Women remain under-represented in the leadership and decision making of all sport and sport-related organisations. Those responsible for these areas should develop policies and programmes and design structures which increase the number of women coaches, advisers, decision makers, officials, administrators and sports personnel at all levels with special attention given to recruitment, mentoring, empowerment, reward and retention of women leaders.
>
> (International Working Group on Women and Sport, 2016b, p. 10)

So far 441 organizations have signed the *Brighton Declaration* or updated *Brighton Plus Helsinki Declaration*, including the most prestigious and influential sport bodies: the International Olympic Committee, the International Paralympic Committee, and FIFA (International Working Group on Women and Sport, 2016a). Other international signatories include the Association of Summer Olympic International Federations, the Commonwealth Games Federation, the International University Sports Federation and SportAccord. Some 28 IFs and 66 National Olympic Committees have also signed the declaration, as well as many government organizations such as ministries for sport and sport councils. A list of all signatories can be viewed at http://iwg-gti.org/iwg-signatories-2/. In summary, many organizations worldwide have committed to the advancement of women and sport at all levels, including women's representation in sport leadership.

Another important strategy for disrupting the status quo in the governance of sport globally was the UN publication *Women 2000 and Beyond:*

Women, Gender Equality and Sport (United Nations Division for the Advancement of Women, 2007). It was developed in collaboration with the International Working Group on Women and Sport (IWG) and WomenSport International and launched by the UN at the 52nd Session of the Commission on the Status of Women at the UN Headquarters in New York in 2008. This was the first time in the history of the United Nations that an entire publication was devoted to women and sport. It urges a range of bodies, including governments, UN entities, sporting institutions and non-government organizations, to take further action to address discrimination against women and girls in sport. One of the specific issues it addressed was the under-representation of women in decision-making bodies of sport organizations at local, national, regional, and international level. In order to accelerate the process of change in sport governance it recommended:

> Establishing higher targets for women's participation in decision making and leadership … Monitoring and evaluation of the impact of initiatives, such as the use of targets and quotas, need to be significantly strengthened. Reliable and comparable data are required, both as an advocacy and awareness tool.
> (United Nations Division for the Advancement
> of Women, 2007, pp. 29–30)

In line with this recommendation, the IWG decided that the legacy of its next conference, the 5th IWG World Conference on Women and Sport, would be the Sydney Scoreboard. Its purpose was to increase "within the context of the achievement of the *UN Millennium Development Goals* … the number of women on the boards/management committees of all sport organisations at international, regional, national and local level" (International Working Group on Women and Sport, 2016c). The Sydney Scoreboard, an online tool, has since developed into a global index for women in sport leadership which has collected and displayed data on boards of national sport organizations and international federations since 2010. People active in the global women sport movement in approximately 50 countries have contributed data with the aim of raising awareness and promoting a new level of transparency and accountability around gender equity in sport leadership. Essentially, the tool was conceptualized as a catalyst for change. As previously noted, however, change has been extremely modest to date and gender balance in sport governance has not yet been achieved. What other initiatives or strategies have been or can be used?

Gender quotas

A common strategy for accelerating women's participation in leadership has been the adoption of gender quotas, also referred to as affirmative or positive action. Gender quotas need to be distinguished from gender targets.

While both quotas and targets refer to a minimum number or percentage of women in specific positions, quotas are mandated through legislation or some other form of regulatory requirement (Whelan & Wood, 2012). In the realm of sport, quotas can be embedded as a clause in the organization's constitution or by-laws. Quotas are not negotiable and often need to be achieved within a specified timeframe. Non-compliance results in sanctions or penalties for the organization. Gender targets, on the other hand, are more voluntary in nature, reflecting aspirational goals that the organization hopes to achieve. They cannot be legally enforced and usually do not carry sanctions if not achieved. Nevertheless, managers can receive performance rewards if their organization does reach the targets. Because of their voluntary nature, targets are more widely accepted by organizations than are quotas.

The main objection to gender quotas is the perception that women are appointed simply to fulfil the quota, even if they lack the required qualifications and competency for the position. There is, however, no research evidence that women appointed under quotas are less competent or perform less effectively. Whelan and Wood (2012) provide a useful list of examples of common arguments for and against the use of quotas. They identify the following key arguments in favor of the introduction of quotas. After decades of aspirational programs and initiatives that have largely failed, quotas are an effective temporary measure to achieve greater gender equity. Only quotas can enforce the attainment of a critical mass of women in leadership roles. In addition, quotas encourage organizations to be innovative, to identify talented women and to work harder to provide development opportunities for them. In contrast, those against quotas often argue that they undermine the principle that merit and meritocracy should take priority over diversity in business. Further, quotas lead to additional regulation, which increases costs and inefficiencies for organizations. Finally, many women themselves do not like to be appointed through quotas because they believe that their appointment will be viewed as tokenistic and not based on their qualities.

Use of gender quotas in the public, corporate, and sport sectors

Although gender quotas are controversial, they were first used extensively in the political realm to increase women's representation in government. Subsequently, the corporate sector also adopted this strategy to increase gender balance on its boards. One of the more notable examples was the case in Norway. In 2005, the Norwegian government introduced a quota law that called for a minimum of 40% representation of men and women on the boards of its public limited-liability companies (Torchia et al., 2011). Interestingly, this law was passed after companies had been given the opportunity in 2002 to voluntary implement a 40% target. When insufficient progress had been made after several years, the law was passed in 2005. Sanctions for non-compliance included dissolution of the company. Enforcement of the law began in 2008, by which time the majority of companies had already met the requirements. As a result of the quota law, women's participation on these Norwegian boards increased from 7% in 2003 to 40.3% in 2010. This example clearly demonstrates that quotas enforced by law are more effective than voluntary targets in achieving gender balance on boards.

The sport sector has been reluctant to adopt quotas. Even in Norway, sport organizations perceived a 40% gender quota as too radical (Skirstad, 2009). Following a consultation process on the strategic direction of Norwegian sport, participants agreed that women's representation in leadership positions should increase, but they did not support the implementation of a 40% gender quota. Nevertheless, women's representation in the General Assembly of Norwegian sport, the highest decision-making body for sport, increased from 8% to 39% between 1971 and 2007. Skirstad (2009) attributed this dramatic improvement to evolutionary changes in the internal and external contexts. The internal context refers to the structure and culture within the sport organization, while the external context refers to the wider political, social, and economic environment. Gender equity measures in Norwegian society at large influenced measures in the sport sector such as the adoption of a modest target of a minimum of two male and two female representatives. Despite this modest target, women's participation in the governance of Norwegian sport achieved a relatively high proportion (39%). This was largely facilitated by the broader environment—the external context—which promoted a positive approach to gender equity. The positive change toward gender equity on sport boards in Norway is continuing. In 2014 based on data from 51 Norwegian NSOs, the average representation of women directors was 37.4% (International Working Group on Women and Sport, 2016c). In terms of representation of women directors in sport governance, Norway was placed second highest in the list of 38 countries on the Sydney Scoreboard global index for women in sport leadership.

In 2016, FIFA, one of the most influential global sport organizations, voted to replace the current executive committee with a new 36-member council that included a gender quota (FIFA, 2016). The statutory reform stated that the members of each confederation must ensure that they elect at least one female member to the council. There are six confederations, which means that a minimum of six of the 36 members or 16.7% must be women. This is an improvement on women's representation in its leadership; however, from 4% in 2014 to 16.7% in the new council means that gender balance will not yet be achieved. The IOC, another influential and prestigious global sport organization, has also used positive action to increase women's presence on boards of Olympic bodies. In 1996, the IOC adopted targets for women's representation on executive committees of National Olympic Committees (NOC) and those International Sport Federations that are part of the Olympic movement (Henry et al., 2004). The targets were for women to occupy a minimum of 10% of executive positions by the end of 2001, increasing to a minimum of 20% by the end of 2005. A key finding of research (Henry et al., 2004) into the success of these targets is that they have had a clear positive impact on raising awareness of gender inequities and bringing talented women into Olympic executive positions. Nevertheless, the targets were not achieved since, overall, women's presence on executives of NOCs had only risen to 17.6% and on IFs to 18.3% in 2009 (Henry & Robinson, 2010). Some continents achieved better women's representation on its NOC executive committees than others. The average women's presence on NOCs was well below the target of 20% in Asia (12.5%) and Europe (14.1%), while Africa (19.5%) was close to the target. By contrast, NOCs in both the Americas (20.5%) and Oceania (26.1%) exceeded the target. Researchers attributed this higher level of women's representation to the fact that NOCs in Oceania had been established relatively recently and thus were less influenced by traditional patterns of male domination in sport governance. In relation to the IFs, women's overall representation (18.3%) is actually skewed by the presence of a small number of women—sometimes only one—on some small boards. Therefore the results are even more sobering; more than half (55.3%) of the IFs had only one or no women executives.

Regardless of whether or not the target was achieved, it should be noted that, in terms of gender balance, a target of 20% is very modest; a minimum of 40% is usually regarded as a measure of gender equity. There were no penalties or sanctions for failing to achieve the targets. Unlike quotas, they were not compulsory or legally binding. Henry and Robinson (2010) concluded that even those NOCs and IFs that had achieved the minimum target had not necessarily adopted new policies which would enhance women's participation in sport organizations. This raises another important issue, namely, that the adoption of targets and quotas is not necessarily sufficient to achieve true gender equity in the governance of sport. This requires transcending numbers and ensuring that women and men exercise equal influence in strategic decision-making and resource allocation. The next section further explores this issue in relation to the impact of gender quotas, including the issue of how we can ensure sustainable change to achieve gender equity.

The impact of gender quotas

A recent study examined the impact of gender quotas on gender equity in the governance of National Sport Organizations in Australia (Adriaanse & Schofield, 2014). It was part of a larger study into gender dynamics on the boards of these organizations. The theoretical concept of a *gender regime*

(Connell, 2009) was central to the study. A gender regime refers to a pattern of gender relations characterized by four interwoven dimensions of social life: production relations, power relations, emotional relations, and symbolic relations. According to Connell, the first dimension—production relations—is about the way in which production or work is divided along gender lines. In the context of sport governance, it involves the way in which roles and tasks are allocated to men and women on the board. The second dimension, power relations, refers to the manner in which power, authority, and control are divided along gender lines. In sport governance, this relates to who exerts influence on the board and makes important decisions. As previously discussed, men often outnumber and outrank women on sport boards and therefore wield more power and influence. The third dimension of a gender regime is emotional relations, which refer to attachment and antagonism between people along gender lines. In the case of sport boards, this concerns patterns of attachment and hostility between and among men and women board members. This can be observed when, for example, they support or, alternatively, undermine each other in their work. The fourth dimension, symbolic relations, involves the prevailing beliefs and attitudes about gender. In the realm of sport governance, this refers to the way in which men and women understand and value gender and gender equity. It includes board members' beliefs about gender equity and the use of gender quotas. An overview of the four-dimensional gender model applied to the context of sport governance is presented in Table 6.3.

Although these four dimensions can be examined separately for heuristic purposes, it is important to emphasize that they are interwoven and constantly interact with each other. Overall, the four dimensions produce a gender pattern or regime which provides a better understanding of how gender works in organizations or on a board. Further, it allows an analysis of the prospects for gender equity in the organization or, in this case, the governance of a sport organization (Connell, 2005; Schofield & Goodwin, 2005).

Table 6.3 Four-dimensional gender model applied to sport governance

Gender dimension	Application to sport governance
Production relations	How roles and tasks are allocated to men and women on the board
Power relations	How power, authority, and control are divided between and among men and women board members
Emotional relations	Patterns of attachment and hostility between and among men and women board members
Symbolic relations	How men and women understand and value gender and gender equity

The study investigated the gender regime on boards of three Australian NSOs which had adopted gender quotas that were specified in their respective constitutions. Board D was the national governing body of a popular non-Olympic individual and team sport. Using the four-dimensional model, Adriaanse and Schofield's (2014) analysis showed that this board represented a gender regime that could best be characterized as one of *masculine hegemony*. It had introduced a gender quota of one, which meant that at least one director must be male and at least one female. There were seven male and two female directors on the board. In terms of production relations, men assumed most of the tasks because they were in the majority. Men also prevailed in power relations because they occupied the most influential positions, such as president and chief executive. In terms of emotional relations, men and women worked cooperatively and there was no evidence of explicit affection or hostility between them. In terms of symbolic relations, most directors understood gender equity as providing equal opportunity for all. Interviews with the board members disclosed that several male directors did not agree with the use of gender quotas. One male director said: "There should be more (women) … (but) it shouldn't be mandated … I am not interested in 'you must have that and you must have (this).'" They stated that the lack of gender balance on the board was mainly because not enough women were willing to 'step up' and be nominated for leadership positions. One of the women directors commented that women often lacked governance skills and experience. The board agreed that gender inequity was essentially a problem within women themselves. The chief executive, nevertheless, felt that the board had an obligation to actively address the issue. Given that he was a minority of one, the prospects for achieving gender equity on this board were very limited.

Board C was the Australian governing body of a popular Olympic individual sport. The gender relations on this board shaped a gender regime of *masculine hegemony in transition* (Adriaanse & Schofield, 2014). The constitution included a gender clause of a minimum of two directors of each gender. At the time of the study, the board consisted of four men and two women; therefore women's representation was 33%. Production and power relations were dominated by men because they outnumbered women, assumed the majority of tasks and had a strong influence in the decision-making process. An interesting dynamic emerged, however, because a woman occupied the president's role and she was committed to promoting gender equity in the sport. In terms of emotional relations, she was strongly supported by a close group of two directors and the male chief executive. On the other hand, she was fiercely resisted by one male director who felt that she was not a good leader due to her uncompromising rational approach and her lack of knowledge of the sport itself. Regarding the symbolic relations, there was ambivalence about the gender quota clause. Most directors felt that getting the "best" people on the board had priority over achieving a gender-balanced board. One male director said: "I just believe you get the best people, whoever the best people are, that's what you need for the organization." On the other hand, the chief executive strongly supported gender balance by arguing that the presence of more diverse perspectives would actually enhance the board's decision-making and problem-solving capacity. Overall, as in the previous gender regime, prospects for gender equity on this board were limited, but could be viewed more positively mainly due to the influence of the female president and the supportive attitude of the chief executive.

Board E was the governing body of a prominent Olympic team sport in Australia. The gender regime on this board was characterized as one of *gender mainstreaming in progress* (Adriaanse & Schofield, 2014). The gender quota set for this board was a minimum of three members of each gender. There were nine directors, six men and three women, or a 33% representation of women. Although men dominated production and power relations merely through numbers, the minority of three women had significant influence through their specific portfolios, which included finance and high performance. The women were strongly supported in their role by the chair and the chief executive, both of whom were male. It was evident that the emotional relations among board members were supportive and collaborative; the board formed a cohesive team. In terms of symbolic relations, none of the directors expressed resistance to the gender quota clause. They were committed to gender equity. The CEO said: "The organisation … very much embraces the ethos of equality across a whole range of areas, and that is true for the board as well." Directors also understood that gender equity needs to go beyond gender balance in numbers on the board. They mentioned that it involves equitable contributions and participation by men and women at every level of the sport. As one of the women directors explained, it meant considering a gender perspective on all issues such as board composition, policy development and resource allocation, which reflects a gender mainstreaming approach (Rees, 2002). Gender equity had not yet been achieved but, in comparison with the previous two sport boards, this gender regime demonstrated conditions that were the most conducive to accelerated positive change.

The key finding of the study was that a quota of a minimum of three women was fundamental for advancing gender equity in sport governance. It is important to emphasize that a minimum percentage is insufficient; the quota needs to extend to specify a minimum number of three. Both boards C and E had 33% women's representation but only Board E had three women members. It was this, I argue, that contributed to its ongoing gender regime of gender mainstreaming with its promise of advancing gender equity. This finding supports other research in corporate governance which found that the appointment of three or more women is necessary to form a critical mass which is essential to change boardroom dynamics (Konrad,

Kramer, & Erkut, 2008; Torchia et al., 2011). The study also showed that the establishment of a quota with a minimum of three was only the first condition for advancing gender equity. In relation to the four-dimensional gender model, the other conditions were: i) board members' understanding of and commitment to gender equity across all activities of the sport organization (symbolic relations); ii) the allocation of women directors to key portfolios or roles on the board (production and power relations); and iii) a collaborative, supportive environment among board members (emotional relations).

Conclusion

This chapter has explored the use of gender quotas to improve gender equity in sport leadership, in particular in the governance of national sport organizations and international federations. Gender quotas are often introduced after other initiatives have failed to achieve gender equity as seen, for example, in the Norwegian case study discussed above (Torchia et al., 2011). Establishing quotas, however, is controversial. Proponents argue strongly that quotas are an effective strategy for identifying and promoting talented women, which benefits the organization. Opponents, including some women, are equally passionate in their view that quotas undermine appointments based on merit. The study of boards of Australian sport organizations provides evidence of this ambivalence toward gender quotas; while some board members (on Board E) embraced this measure, others (on Boards C and D) clearly did not.

Several global initiatives other than quotas have been introduced to address gender equity in sport leadership. The first international declaration to advance women and sport—the *Brighton Declaration*, which was updated in 2014 to the *Brighton plus Helsinki Declaration* and signed by more than 400 organizations worldwide—includes a clause on increasing the number of women in sport leadership positions (International Working Group on Women and Sport, 2016b). Another key initiative was the publication and wide distribution of the UN document *Women 2000 and Beyond: Women, Gender Equality and Sport* (United Nations Division for the Advancement of Women, 2007). It emphasized the need to address the underrepresentation of women in decision-making bodies of sport organizations from local to international level and included a range of recommendations on ways of achieving gender equity in sport leadership. Despite these important initiatives, data from the Sydney Scoreboard show that gender equity has not yet been achieved. Although considerable progress has been made, women remain markedly underrepresented: none of the three key indicators of women's participation as directors, chairs, and chief executives has yet reached 40%. The introduction of targets to improve gender balance in sport governance has had limited success due to the voluntary nature of this strategy. This was evident when the use of gender targets for Olympic governing bodies was evaluated (Henry et al., 2004; Henry & Robinson, 2010).

The limited progress made so far suggests that the use of gender quotas warrants consideration as a strategy to accelerate women's representation in sport governance. But do they work? A key finding of a study into the impact of quotas on gender equity in Australian sport was that a minimum of three women who made up a third or more of board members contributed to gender equity. However, this is only a first step because quotas needed to operate with other gender dimensions to move toward gender equity, that is, equal participation by men and women in board decision-making. Based on the four-dimensional gender model (Connell, 2005, 2009), the other conditions were: adopting gender equity as an organizational value by all board members; sharing of influential roles on the board, with both men and women taking responsibility for significant portfolios; and creating a cohesive, supportive team of board members. Overall, gender quotas are best perceived as part of a suite of strategies to achieve gender equity in sport leadership. International declarations and publications on women, sport and gender equity are valuable in creating awareness of and sensitivity to the issue, but it is clear that additional efforts are required to achieve equal participation by men and women on sport boards. Gender quotas can add value and work effectively provided they occur in conjunction with the other three conditions on the board. Ultimately, when gender balance in the composition of the board is achieved, global sport governance can reach its full potential.

References

Adriaanse, J. (2016). Gender diversity in the governance of sport associations: The Sydney Scoreboard global index of participation. *Journal of Business Ethics*, *137*(1), 149–160.

Adriaanse, J. A., & Claringbould, I. (2016). Gender equality in sport leadership: From the Brighton Declaration to the Sydney Scoreboard. *International Review for the Sociology of Sport*, *51*(5), 547–566.

Adriaanse, J. A., & Schofield, T. (2013). Analysing gender dynamics in sport governance: A new regimes-based approach. *Sport Management Review*, *16*, 498–513.

Adriaanse, J. A., & Schofield, T. (2014). The impact of gender quotas on gender equality in sport governance. *Journal of Sport Management*, *28*(5), 485–497.

Australian Human Rights Commission. (2010). *Gender Equality Blueprint*. Sydney: Australian Human Rights Commission.

Bilimoria, D., & Wheeler, J. V. (2000). Women corporate directors: Current research and future directions. In R. J. Burke & M. C. Mattis (eds.) *Women in Management: Current Research Issues* (vol. II, pp. 138–163). London: Sage.

Burton, L. J. (2015). Underrepresentation of women in sport leadership: A review of research. *Sport Management Review*, *18*(2), 155–165.

Claringbould, I., & Knoppers, A. (2008). Doing and undoing gender in sport governance. *Sex Roles*, *58*, 81–92.

Claringbould, I., & Knoppers, A. (2012). Paradoxical practices of gender in sport-related organisations. *Journal of Sport Management*, 26(5), 404–416.

Clarke, T. (2007). *International Corporate Governance: A Comparative Approach*. London: Routledge.

Connell, R. (2005). Advancing gender reform in large-scale organisations: A new approach for practioners and researchers. *Policy and Society*, 24(4), 5–24.

Connell, R. (2009). *Gender*. Cambridge, UK: Polity.

FIFA. (2016). FIFA Congress. Retrieved 8 from www.fifa.com/about-fifa/fifa-congress/index.html?intcmp=fifacom_hp_module_extracongress

Henry, I., Radzi, W., Rich, E., Shelton, C., Theodoraki, E., & White, A. (2004). *Women, Leadership and the Olympic Movement*. Loughborough: Institute of Sport & Leisure Policy, Loughborough University and the International Olympic Committee.

Henry, I., & Robinson, L. (2010). *Gender Equity and Leadership in Olympic Bodies*. Loughborough: Centre for Olympic Studies and Research, Loughborough University and International Olympic Committee.

Hovden, J. (2010). Female top leaders – prisoners of gender? The gendering of leadership discourses in Norwegian sports organizations. *International Journal of Sport Policy and Politics*, 2(2), 189–203.

International Triathlon Union. (2016). About. Retrieved from www.triathlon.org/about

International Working Group on Women and Sport. (2016a). IWG signatories. Retrieved from http://iwg-gti.org/iwg-signatories-2/

International Working Group on Women and Sport. (2016b). Past IWG World Conference and their legacies. Retrieved 29 February 2016, from http://iwg-gti.org/past-iwg-world-conferences-and-their-legacies/

International Working Group on Women and Sport. (2016c). The Sydney Scoreboard: A global index for women in sport leadership. Retrieved from www.sydneyscoreboard.com/

Joecks, J., Pull, K., & Vetter, K. (2013). Gender diversity in the boardroom and firm performance: What exactly constitutes a "critical mass"? *Journal of Business Ethics*, *118*, 61–72.

Kanter, R. M. (1977). *Men and Women of the Corporation*. New York: Basic Books.

Konrad, A.M., Kramer, V., & Erkut, S. (2008). Critical mass: The impact of three or more women on corporate boards. *Organizational Dynamics*, *37*(2), 145–164.

Nielsen, S., & Huse, M. (2010). The contribution of women on boards of directors: Going beyond the surface. *Corporate Governance: An International Review*, *18*(2), 136–148.

Pfister, G., & Radtke, S. (2009). Sport, women and leadership: Results of a project on executives in German sports organisations. *European Journal of Sport Science*, *9*(4), 229–243.

Rees, T. (2002). A new strategy: Gender mainstreaming. Paper presented at the 5th European Women and Sport Conference, Berlin.

Schofield, T., & Goodwin, S. (2005). Gender politics and public policy making: Prospects for advancing gender equality. *Policy and Society*, 24(4), 25–44.

Schull, V., Shaw, S., & Kihl, I. A. (2013). If a woman came in ... she would have been eaten up alive: Analyzing gendered political processes in the search for an athletic director. *Gender and Society*, 27(1), 56–81.

Shaw, S., & Hoeber, L. (2003). "A strong man is direct and a direct woman is a bitch": Gendered discourses and their influence on employment roles in sport organisations. *Journal of Sport Management*, 17, 347–375.

Shaw, S., & Penney, D. (2003). Gender equity policies in national governing bodies: An oxymoron or a vehicle for change? *European Sport Management Quarterly*, 3(2), 78–102.

Shaw, S., & Slack, T. (2002). "It's been like that for donkey's years": The construction of gender relations and the cultures of sports organisations. *Culture, Sport, Society*, 5(1), 86–106.

Skirstad, B. (2009). Gender policy and organisational change: A contextual approach. *Sport Management Review*, 12(4), 202–216.

Terjesen, S., Sealy, R., & Singh, V. (2009). Women directors on corporate boards: A review and research agenda. *Corporate Governance: An International Review*, 17(3), 320–337.

Torchia, M., Calabro, A., & Huse, M. (2011). Women directors on corporate boards: From tokenism to critical mass. *Journal of Business Ethics*, 102(2), 299–317.

United Nations. (1945) Charter of the United Nations. Retrieved from www.un.org/en/charter-united-nations/

United Nations. (1948). Universal Declaration of Human Rights. Retrieved from www.un.org/en/universal-declaration-human-rights/

United Nations. (1979). Convention on the elimination of all forms of discrimination against women. Retrieved from www.un.org/womenwatch/daw/cedaw/cedaw.htm

United Nations Division for the Advancement of Women. (2007). *Women 2000 and Beyond: Women, Gender Equality and Sport*. New York: United Nations Division for the Advancement of Women.

van der Walt, N., & Ingley, C. (2003). Board dynamics and the influence of professional background, gender and ethnic diversity of directors. *Corporate Governance: An International Review*, 11(3), 218–234.

Whelan, J., & Wood, R. (2012). *Targets and Quotas for Women in Leadership: A Global Review of Policy, Practice and Psychological Research*. Melbourne: Centre for Ethical Leadership, Melbourne Business School.

Chapter 7

Young women in sport: understanding leadership in sport

Vicki D. Schull

Introduction

Sport participation rates for girls and women have increased dramatically over the last four decades. In the United States, nearly 3.2 million girls participate in high school sports (NFHS, 2013), while over 200,000 women participate in sport at the college level (Acosta & Carpenter, 2014). The increased participation rates bode well for women in leadership, given the popular anecdote that *sport participation builds leadership*. In fact, women have increased their representation in leadership positions across a variety of employment and business sectors, and many women in upper-level leadership positions attribute their success to their participation in sports (EY & espnW, 2015). Yet the belief that sport builds leadership does not seem to apply to women in sport, and despite these record participation rates, the underrepresentation and continued decline of women in leadership positions persists at all levels of sport (Acosta & Carpenter, 2014; Lapchick, 2012; LaVoi, 2013; Smith & Wrynn, 2013).

The continued decline of women in sport leadership and coaching positions was underscored in the 2016 National Collegiate Athletic Association (NCAA) Women's Basketball Final Four where, for the first time in its 35-year history (and the first time in the 44-year history of women's college basketball championships) all four teams were coached by men (Walters, 2016). The NCAA Women's Final Four basketball championship is one of the most watched women's sporting events in the United States, and historically at least one of the four teams playing for the championship was coached by a women. Women's college basketball in the United States also features a higher percentage of women head coaches at 59.2% (Acosta & Carpenter, 2014), and yet the figure is still deficient.

The underrepresentation and continued decline of women holding leadership positions is somewhat surprising when framed by: 1) the dramatic increase in sport participation opportunities for girls and women; 2) the belief that sport participation builds leaders and associated skills; and 3) the knowledge that a logical career progression to sport leadership positions begins with sport participation (Everhart & Chelladurai, 1998; Lough & Grappendorf, 2007). Put another way, former athletes are more likely to enter the sport leadership pipeline and move into coaching and sport management positions; however, this logic does not seem to translate to women in sport leadership, despite their increased participation rates. This begs the question that if girls and women are participating in sports at record levels, why then are so few women rising through the ranks to obtain and/or maintain sport leadership positions?

This chapter examines how young women conceptualize leadership in sport by focusing specifically on the sport leadership perceptions of female athletes. Sport and gender scholars have examined women's underrepresentation in sport leadership by focusing on women who currently hold or have recently held leadership positions within various sport organizations (for a review, see Burton, 2015). However, female athletes represent a large and often overlooked pool of qualified candidates who are a critical piece of the puzzle with perhaps the most promise to increase women's representation in leadership positions across all levels of sport (Madsen, 2010; Schull, 2014). For example, Drago, Hennighausen, Rogers, Vescio, and Stauffer (2005) found that many female athletes are not pursuing leadership positions in college sports when their athletic careers have concluded. By examining their understandings of leadership and leadership narratives, we can recognize perceptions of leadership, develop strategies to support leadership development from a multilevel perspective, and provide useful knowledge to practitioners in the coaching and mentoring of young women in sport leadership. Highlighting female athletes' perceptions of leadership in sport can also contribute new insights and broader sociological understandings of leadership practices (Elliot & Stead, 2008), which can go some way to disrupting the dominant forms of masculinity associated with sport leadership.

Peer leadership in sport

It is well established that leadership is a very important practice within the context of sport teams. A coach, by the nature of his or her position, leads a team, and the majority of scholars have thus focused their attention on the coach leadership construct. However, the focus of this chapter is on peer or athlete leadership. Peer leadership is defined as the behaviors and attributes displayed by and among team members intended to influence group members to achieve common goals (Loughead, Hardy, & Eys, 2006). Peer leadership includes both formal and informal roles—that is to say, anyone can display leadership regardless of title or position within the group or team. While there have been numerous studies focusing on peer leadership in sport, few have focused specifically on young women's leadership perceptions in the context of sport. Women's leadership experiences remain marginalized and excluded in masculine-oriented cultures (Elliott & Stead, 2008), and sport is certainly a culture and social institution with a strong

Table 7.1 Peer leadership in sport: young women's perceptions

Authors	Participants	Findings/Conclusions
Price & Weiss, 2011	Adolescent girls participating in soccer (14–18 years old)	(a) Higher levels of perceived sport competence, intrinsic motivation, and behavioral conduct were positively linked to peer leadership behaviors (b) Peer leadership behaviors are important to team outcomes such as cohesion, goal attainment, and efficacy
Price & Weiss, 2013	Adolescent girls participating in soccer (14–18 years old)	(a) Peer and coach transformational leadership behaviors were related to positive athlete and team outcomes (b) Peer transformational leadership behaviors were more influential than coach leadership to social cohesion (b) Coach transformational leadership behaviors were more influential than peer leadership related to individual athlete outcomes (d) Both peer and coach transformational behaviors were influential on task outcomes
Loughead & Hardy, 2005	Women (94) and men (144) Canadian athletes in a variety of competitive levels (Mean age: 20.39)	(a) Coach and peer leaders displayed different leadership behaviors (b) Peer leaders displayed more positive feedback, social support, and democratic behaviors, while coaches displayed more autocratic behaviors and behaviors related to training and instruction (c) Peer leadership was displayed by both team captains and other team members
Loughead, Hardy, & Eys, 2006	Women (118) and men (140) varsity student-athletes from two Canadian universities (Mean age: 20.6)	(a) Formal team leaders more likely identified as team leaders and serve as liaisons to coaches while informal leaders were more often viewed as peer leaders; the majority of players identified as leaders were third and fourth year players and starters (b) Fewer athletes occupied external leadership roles compared to social and task leadership (c) Team and peer leadership was stable over the course of a season

Study	Sample	Findings
Eys, Loughead, & Hardy, 2007	Women (115) and men (103) varsity student-athletes from two Canadian universities (Mean age: 20.6)	(a) Athletes who perceived a balance between the three leadership functions (i.e., task, social, and external) were more satisfied with their team's performance and integration than those athletes who perceived an imbalance in the three functions
Holmes, McNeil, Adorna, & Procaccino, 2008	Women (46) and men (33) student-athletes from a US university (Mean age: 19.32 [women] and 19.58[men])	(a) Men athletes preferred peer leaders to display more autocratic behaviors compared to women athletes (b) Both men and women participants believed peer leaders should work hard and set an example; however, men participants placed more value on work ethic and performance leadership behaviors while women participants placed more value on vocal and encouraging leadership behaviors
Holmes, McNeil, & Adorna, 2010	Women (17) and men (16) student athletes from a US university (18–21 years old)	(a) Certain perceptions of peer sport leadership behaviors and characteristics are common for both men and women (e.g., vocal, trustworthy, lead by example, role model, interpersonal skills) (b) Leadership perceptions more important for women athletes included being vocal, sensitive, and interpersonal skills (c) Leadership perceptions more important for men athletes included being trustworthy and having athletic/sport experience
Glen & Horn, 1993	Female (106) high school soccer athletes	Peer leaders rely on both instrumental and expressive behaviors
Schull, 2014	Women (23) student athletes at a US university (19–22 years old)	(a) Female athletes' perceptions of peer leadership including communication, being an example, and social leadership (b) Participants' perceptions of peer leadership draw on both masculine and feminine leadership styles (c) Participants' leadership perceptions include gendered assumptions related to leadership

history of favoring men and featuring dominant forms of masculinity. So the lack of attention to women's leadership experiences is not necessarily surprising. It is, however, problematic, as we know research informs practice.

Nine studies were identified that examined athlete peer leadership in sport including the leadership experiences, behaviors, and or conceptions of young women in sport. Only four of those studies focused exclusively on female athletes' peer leadership perceptions and experiences, while five included both female and male athletes. One recent study examined the leadership perceptions of female athletes in US college sport utilizing a gendered social process approach (Schull, 2014). Table 7.1 provides a summary of these studies.

Gender and leadership in sport

In order to explore and analyze the leadership perceptions of young women in sport, it is important to understand the integral links between gender, leadership, and the sport context. Briefly, leadership and gender are both inherently social products and influenced by socio-cultural factors within a specific context. Sport is a decidedly gendered context where common leadership conceptions and narratives feature forms of dominant masculinity (Hovden, 2000; Shaw, 2006; Shaw & Hoeber, 2003), and where sport leadership positions are quantitatively dominated and controlled by men (Acosta & Carpenter, 2014; Lapchick, 2012; LaVoi, 2013; Smith & Wrynn, 2013). Gender, leadership, and sport thus comprise a powerful and dominant trio (Schull, 2016), and as such, potentially make sport leadership positions difficult for some women to successfully navigate (Madsen, 2010).

Gender is positioned as a set of social relations where beliefs around what it means to be a man or woman, male or female, and masculine or feminine are created, expressed, and reproduced through complex social processes (Britton & Logan, 2008; Ely & Meyerson, 2000). Gender relations play out in ways in which masculinity/femininity, male/female are defined and described in relation to the other. As gendered distinctions and differences are made, gender inequality is created, sustained, and in some cases, challenged. While there are several categories of gendered social processes, those related to leadership conceptions include: 1) narratives, cultures, and ideologies; and 2) gender appropriate behaviors and expectations (Britton & Logan, 2008; Ely & Meyerson, 2000). For example, dominant masculine values and ideologies such as aggression, physicality, and power are endemic in general sport narratives and therefore define the culture of sport as a masculine space. Sport leadership narratives also feature masculine values such as heroic individualism, authority, and paternalism (Hovden, 2000, 2010; Knoppers & Anthonissen, 2005; 2008; Schull, 2014, 2016). Masculine leadership narratives contribute to a state of play in sport contexts and cultures that favor certain men as sport leaders more so than women and similarly value expressions of masculinities over forms of femininity.

Gender-appropriate behaviors and expectations also influence notions of leadership in many contexts—especially male-dominated positions and cultures found in sport contexts. For example, gendered leadership expectations and stereotypes are associated with sport leadership including senior management positions in sport organizations (Hovden, 2000; Knoppers & Anthonissen, 2005, 2008; Shaw, 2006; Shaw & Hoeber, 2003), as well as expectations for male and female coaches (Fasting & Pfister, 2000; Messner, 2009; Schull, 2014, 2016). Gender-appropriate behaviors and expectations in sport, like other masculine-dominated contexts, often place women in "double-binds," where feminine styles of leadership are expected of women, yet not rewarded and valued equally (Eagly, 2007). While at the same time, if women display the masculine leadership styles compatible with the context, they are penalized because others may perceive this to be incompatible with their identities as women.

Leadership is also a social process constructed and embedded in a context where prevailing assumptions, beliefs, and history matter (Osborn, Hunt, & Jauch, 2002). Perceptions of leadership are thus influenced by an individual's experiences—both past and present—and are shaped by collective beliefs within a specific socio-historic context. For example, socio-cultural factors that influence sport leadership conceptions include the competition level and setting, the high task-focused orientation of sport, individuals' past sport experiences, as well as leader-focused attributes such as communication, sport skill/competence, and class/age (Holmes et al., 2008; Holmes et al., 2010; Price & Weiss, 2011, 2013). Leadership is thus conceptualized and practiced differently in sport compared to other settings and influenced by the gendered sport culture where men and masculine values have been historically embedded and continue to persist.

Gender-specific leadership styles

Noteworthy to the study of leadership is a recent shift in leadership practices and ideals from traditional conceptions featuring authoritative, command, and control styles to more egalitarian, collaborative, and relational styles (Fletcher, 2004). Gender is also implicated in this shift as leadership and gender scholars contend that traditional leadership styles are conceived of in terms of masculine traits and values. For example, traits commonly associated with traditional leadership include authority, heroic individualism, control, and 'power over' subordinates. While both men and women can display these traits and characteristics, they are socially constructed as masculine and more often assigned to men. Contemporary leadership styles featuring egalitarian, collaborative, relational, and 'power with' styles are socially constructed as feminine. Here again, both men and women can display these traits, but they are more commonly assigned to women. Despite the shift in leadership practices, conceptions and everyday narratives of leadership remain stuck in the outdated styles and approaches (Fletcher, 2004). That is to say that leadership narratives and attributes remain firmly grounded in masculine values—especially in male-dominated contexts such as sport (Drago et al., 2005; Hanold, 2011; Schull, 2014).

Gender-specific leadership styles (e.g., authoritarian/masculine and relational/feminine) emerged in examinations of the differences between men and women related to the way they lead and the associated leadership attributes. While it is widely disputed whether or not men and women truly lead differently, the gendered ideologies and stereotypes that have emerged from such inquiries are no doubt part of the greater leadership narratives. There is also some criticism around gender-specific leadership styles as it can be seen as an oversimplification based on its gender binary approach (Hovden, 2010). This is an important critique given that gender binaries highlight gender differences and could be perceived as prescriptive in nature. That is, stating that all men lead in authoritative ways, while all women are relational leaders is clearly a generalization and thus perpetuates gender stereotypes and biases. While recognizing this important critique, gender-specific leadership is a useful frame through which to examine leadership conceptions of young women in sport. A gender-specific approach can enhance understandings of gendered leadership conceptions within social processes (e.g., narratives, ideologies, cultures, and gender-appropriate behaviors) by examining how gendered categories associated with leadership acquire meaning. Furthermore, sport scholars have utilized gender-specific leadership styles to examine women's perceptions of their own leadership work in sport (Brown & Light, 2012), as well as conceptions of female leadership in sport (Hovden, 2010). The focus on women's leadership perceptions, experiences, and constructions of female leadership can also serve to dismantle the gender binary and gendered assumptions and beliefs by highlighting variations and contradictions to gender-specific leadership styles. It is with this approach in mind that I next discuss and analyze female athletes' perceptions of leadership in sport, while paying close attention to the gendered nature of leadership.

Female athletes' perceptions of leadership and gender implications

Young women in sport conceptualize peer leadership as a multidimensional construct of leader-focused behaviors including task-oriented behaviors, social-oriented behaviors, communication, and external behaviors. Peer leadership was also often described as positional or hierarchical in nature, although many female athletes do believe that anyone can be a leader and contribute to the leadership process within their athletic teams. Many of the leadership dimensions highlighted are reflective of the behavioral leadership approach (Yukl, 2012). There are also some subtle gender implications associated with the multiple dimensions of peer leadership. More broadly, a behavioral approach by definition is focused on the leader's behaviors drawing attention to agentic qualities and 'heroic individualism' which are considered masculine in nature (Eagly, 2007; Eagly & Johannesen-Schmidt, 2001; Fletcher, 2004). The multiple dimensions are further outlined in this section and the gender implications of each dimension are woven into the discussion.

Task-oriented leadership

Task-oriented peer leadership for female adolescent soccer players included a variety of sport-related leadership behaviors such as developing team cohesiveness and confidence, guiding team tasks, and goal attainment (Price & Weiss, 2013). Female athletes in college sport also believed that peer leaders should demonstrate a strong work ethic, serve as an example within their team, and provide positive feedback and motivation, as these functions relate to team goals and performance outcomes (Holmes et al., 2008, 2010; Loughead & Hardy, 2005; Schull, 2014). One female athlete described leadership in task-oriented terms: "Leadership is somebody who can command a presence within a team … they're very objective, they can look over the entire situation, and what's going on and see the best possible answer to the problem" (Schull, 2014). In terms of serving as an example, another female athlete stated: "That's what leadership is, taking initiative, going out on a limb, and you do things without being told to do it" (Schull, 2014).

Team task completion and goal achievement is often associated with a transactional leadership style (Peachy & Burton, 2011; Yukl, 2012). Given the high-task and goal-oriented nature of sport teams, transactional styles are seemingly a good match for sport contexts. Transactional leadership styles often feature autocratic behaviors and are therefore more often affiliated with men and perceived to be masculine in nature (Eagly, 2007; Eagly & Johannesen-Schmidt, 2001; Fletcher, 2004). The first quote above, for example, highlights the autocratic and transactional (i.e., masculine) leadership style—in particular the way a leader is described as "commanding a presence within a team." Other masculinized leadership traits implicit within transactional leadership are agency with a team/group, assertiveness, and heroic individualism (Eagly, 2007; Fletcher, 2004; Hovden, 2000). For example, the second quote above highlights, not only the heroic and individual nature of leadership, but also how leaders demonstrate agency, or the capacity to act for a group or team. Such leadership perceptions that laud the behaviors of an individual leader as solely responsible for leadership within a team or group are in contrast to the more collective and collaborative leadership practices, which again are socially constructed as feminine (Fletcher, 2004).

The connection between transactional leadership and masculinity suggests that perhaps some female athletes believe masculine leadership styles are better suited for athletic contexts. The connection between masculine leadership traits and transactional leadership in sport could also help to explain why some female athletes prefer men coaches in a variety of settings, including US college sport. For example, Drago et al. (2005) found that female athletes preferred a coach who was able to command respect, was authoritarian, and kept their personal lives private, while Frey, Czech, Kent, and Johnson (2006) found that nine out of twelve female athletes expressed explicit preferences for male coaches, because they believed men were better able to enforce discipline and garner respect.

Gendered leadership expectations of coaches and preferences for male coaches could also be influential to female athletes' career aspirations to obtain sport leadership positions. For example, young women in sport may internalize the gendered and masculinized leadership assumptions and expectations and perhaps feel that their own leadership styles are not compatible for such sport leadership positions (Schull, 2014). Madsen (2010) further stated: "the combination of the masculine nature of athletics and the masculine assumptions of leadership make athletic careers extremely difficult for women to successfully negotiate" (p. 3). Furthermore, if and when former female athletes display authoritarian leadership behaviors developed and nurtured in athletic contexts, they could get caught up in the double leadership bind, where they are scrutinized for acting in masculine ways that do not conform to their gender, and dismissed and overlooked as leaders when they comply with gender-appropriate leadership expectations. We have seen countless women leaders, both in sport and out of sport contexts, fall victim to the double bind mentality.

Social-oriented leadership

Social-oriented behaviors represented a second important dimension of peer leadership in sport contexts, and for 14–18-year-old female soccer players, this included the ability to demonstrate care and concern for teammates and to develop relationships and discussions with coaches (Price & Weiss, 2011, 2013). Peer leaders were also well liked among their team (Price & Weiss, 2011), and likability is a decidedly social element of leadership. Young women in college sport also valued social leadership among their peers; however, one notable difference is that likability was not necessarily a contributing factor of leadership for female college students. That is, peer leaders did not have to be liked to be effective leaders and female college athletes indicated that respect was more important to leadership than likability (Holmes et al., 2010). This difference could be a reflection of age and experience of the participants, as well as differences in sport and competition levels (i.e., youth sports compared to college sport).

Other important social leadership behaviors identified by female college athletes included the ability to demonstrate good interpersonal skills, to foster individual relationships, and to be trustworthy and caring (Holmes et al., 2008, 2010). In terms of relational leadership, one female athlete said: "I try to keep a relationship with every [teammate], too. I try to find something special about everybody that I can connect with, and it's not even about [team/sport]" (Schull, 2014). In addition to developing relationships with teammates, for some young women in college sport the ability to promote team cohesion and harmony outside of the athletic arena, to provide individual support, and to manage conflicts between teammates were all important aspects of social leadership (Schull, 2014). For example, another female athlete stated: "Being able to bring the team together … being able to keep the team cohesiveness together through the good times and the bad times, and I would definitely say a leader is somebody that any of the other players can go to for problems with [our team/sport] or school" (Schull, 2014).

Accounts of social-oriented peer leadership are in line with Eagly's (2007) and Fletcher's (2004) descriptions of collaborative and relational leadership practices. Such relational leadership practices are not only gaining traction and value in contemporary organizations, but are also socially constructed as feminine. For example, fostering interpersonal relationships and providing support and displaying empathy toward others are distinctly relational and feature more egalitarian, or equal and open leadership practices in contrast to the autocratic and hierarchical styles associated with traditionally masculine leadership. The increased focus on social and relational leadership has led to discussions around a potential female advantage in leadership (Eagly, 2007), which would seemingly serve many female athletes transitioning to work after their athletic careers conclude very well. However, women leaders should also be aware of gendered expectations associated with providing emotional support and labor—that is, women leaders are more often expected to provide emotional labor to their followers, and albeit important, emotional support is not valued as highly as other forms of leadership when displayed by women leaders (Eagly, 2007; Fletcher, 2004). The gendered expectations tied to social and relational leadership make up the second part of the 'double bind' facing women leaders. More specifically, the social and relational leadership contributions of women, while gender appropriate, are not rewarded to the same extent as the leadership contributions of men. Men in leadership roles do not face such binds—in fact, when they express more feminine and relational leadership and empathize with their followers, rather than face scrutiny for acting counter to gender appropriate expectations, they are praised for their interpersonal skills, making the very same leadership practices expressed by women expendable.

It is also relevant to note that Holmes and colleagues (2010) reported gender differences among female and male college athletes related to social peer leadership. More specifically, they found that female athletes often placed more emphasis on providing encouragement and demonstrating sensitivity, compared to male athletes who emphasized performance, experience, and trust. More recently, Schull's (2014) study found that female athletes in college sport discussed social leadership *less* frequently, compared to task-oriented leadership. That is, female athletes valued the task-oriented behaviors such as accountability, role modeling, communication and motivation to a greater extent than social leadership skills; however, this examination did not include comparisons to male athletes.

Communication

A third dimension of peer leadership is communication. Communication was often positioned within other leadership dimensions. For example, the ability to provide feedback and motivation through communication with teammates is also directly related to team task behaviors and social communication. However, positioning communication as a stand-alone category or dimension highlights the nuances of communication skills that contributed to peer leadership perceptions (Holmes et al., 2010; Schull, 2014). Communication leadership broadly included being verbal, motivating, and encouraging to teammates (Holmes et al., 2008, 2010; Schull, 2014). Communication leadership also played out in the expectations that some players would serve as liaisons between players and coach by interpreting coaches' instructions and representing teammates views with coaches.

For some young women (i.e., NCAA Division I female athletes), communication leadership included the ability to hold teammates accountable to certain team standards or expectations. Accountability was accomplished by a team leader's ability to 'call out' teammates, which was described by female college athletes as the ability to 'speak up' and to confront or reprimand teammates when they did not meet or comply with certain team standards (e.g., rules, performance expectations). For example, one participant highlighted that: "If you do something wrong, expect your teammates to call you out on it. Or if you're not playing hard, expect your teammates to call you out on it ... holding each other accountable is huge" (Schull, 2014).

Female athletes' descriptions of accountability communication featured autocratic and authoritarian leadership styles, including the ability to be assertive with one's peers. Fletcher (2004) describes authoritarian and autocratic leadership styles in terms of exercising 'power over' others, which is also linked to masculine leadership ideals. Authoritarian and 'power over' leadership behaviors are considered outdated and have lost some relevance in contemporary organizational settings where workers prefer collaborative and egalitarian leadership practices (Eagly, 2007). Sport, however, is not one of those setting as it has been argued that outdated and autocratic practices persist in sport leadership and coaching positions (Drago et al., 2005; Hanold, 2011; Knoppers & Anthonissen,

2005). Female college athletes also did not perceive the autocratic leadership behaviors associated with holding teammates accountable to be outdated. Rather, they saw it for the most part as instrumental in terms of team functioning and performance and a vital aspect of peer leadership within athletic teams (Schull, 2014).

While female leaders in various settings are often expected to express more sensitivity, empathy, and generally be more focused on relational aspects rather than team tasks (Eagly, 2007; Fletcher, 2004), the notion that young female athletes both value accountability among their peers and are expected to hold teammates accountable departs from gender-specific leadership styles that espouse egalitarian and collaborative leadership styles. The expectation for 'calling out' teammates and associated autocratic leadership practices thus challenges gendered leadership ideals and assists in demonstrating the complexity of gender (Ashcraft, 2009). In other words, not all young women in sport adhere to gendered expectations, nor do they prefer their female peers to display simply emotional support and relational leadership practices based upon their gender. However, young women in sport should be aware of how such leadership behaviors may be perceived by others and the challenges associated with those perceptions.

Likewise, it is important to note that for some young women, being assertive with teammates by 'calling them out' made them a little uncomfortable, and they described it as something they had to do based often upon their position as a captain or on their years of experience on the team (Schull, 2014). One female athlete noted: "That was the first time I ever made an [autocratic] statement knowing I wasn't going to be someone's friend and having to be okay with it … I don't like playing that role, but at the same time we [captains] have to" (Schull, 2014).

External behaviors

Peer leadership for young women in sport included external behaviors, which highlights the popular notion that peer leadership can emerge both in and out of sport contexts. External behaviors also feature a blend of both task and social leadership. For example, external behaviors consisted of representing and promoting the team at external functions and fundraising efforts (Loughead & Hardy, 2005; Loughead et al., 2006), as well as representing the team in the classroom by performing well academically and generally serving as a role model out of the sport contexts (Holmes et al., 2008, 2010; Schull, 2014). Other external peer leadership behaviors included administering individual support and the ability to understand the needs of the team and its members off the field or court (Loughead & Hardy, 2005). External leadership behaviors were specific to the college sport context where athletes are more visible within a campus and local community and thus expected to conduct themselves in a professional manner outside of their sport as they can come under great scrutiny.

External leadership behaviors can take the form of heroic individualism where behaviors and expectations for leadership center on individual leaders and what they do outside of the athletic arena. There is also agency at play given that certain individual players are expected to represent the team at external functions and their behaviors are perceived as acting on behalf of the team. For some athletes, external leadership overlaps with social leadership given that leaders are expected to provide individual support to other members of the team outside of sport contexts. External behaviors demonstrate the notion that leaders in sport should be able to balance a variety of leadership styles.

Hierarchical and positional leadership

Peer leadership, by its very definition, includes both formal and informal leadership roles (Loughead et al., 2006). Young women in sport also believe that leadership can be performed and displayed by a number of individuals in various roles. For example, a common belief among athletes—both female and male—is that you do not have to hold a formal position, such as a team captain to exercise leadership (Loughead & Hardy, 2005; Schull, 2014).

However, it is important to note that while many young women (and men) in sport subscribe to the belief that anyone can fulfill a leadership role regardless of formal position within team, formal leaders such as team captains and players with more experience were often more likely to display leadership and to be seen as leaders within their respective teams (Holmes et al., 2008; Loughead et al., 2006; Schull, 2014). Formal leaders include team captains, and the selection to formal leadership roles was influenced by player status including year of eligibility and previous sport experience. Athletes who fulfilled central roles on their team and athletes who possessed exemplary sport skills were also more likely to be perceived as leaders and exhibit leadership skills, such as the behaviors highlighted above (i.e., task, social, communication, external). Therefore, while it may be popular for athletes to espouse the notion that anyone can exercise leadership, it appears to be more hierarchical, top-down and positional in sport teams (Schull, 2014).

While the hierarchical- and positional-based nature of peer leadership is common in sport contexts, it provides a subtle departure from contemporary organizational leadership that promotes collaborative more 'bottom-up' styles of leadership where truly anyone can display leadership (Fletcher, 2004). Understanding leadership as hierarchical and positional may potentially impact young women as they transition to life after sport and enter the workforce. Gaining leadership experience and emerging as an informal leader in task-oriented groups are vital to individual leadership development. In the context of team sport, Schull (2014) found that emergent informal leadership was stifled—especially for younger female athletes. How this transfers to other work settings for former female athletes could present them with some leadership challenges. If young women believe they have to be in formal leadership positions or gain multiple years' work experience with organizations or firms before exercising leadership, this could place them at a distinct disadvantage compared to their peers.

It is also important to note that coaches play a role in prescribing leadership beliefs and expectations—particularly the hierarchical or positional leadership roles—by setting leadership expectations for captains and third and fourth year players who possess more sport experience. For example, one female athlete stated: "[Coaches] expect the captains to speak up. I practice when there's not enough energy ... it's kind of our job to hold each other accountable and call people out" (Schull, 2014). The positional and hierarchical nature of peer leadership is certainly a feature of the sport context with the importance of team captains and where athletes are often referred to by their years of experience with a team (e.g., rookie/novice, veteran). Sport practitioners and coaches should be aware of the hierarchical leadership perceptions and focus on leadership development for all participants—not just captains and players who fulfill central roles on the team. Emergent and informal leadership are vital to the growth of leaders and will serve young women well as they enter the work force.

Conclusions

Sport participation is often believed to contribute to the development of leadership skills, and it is widely assumed and accepted that leadership skills developed through sport participation can serve former athletes well in their selected careers. Schull (2014) found that female athletes construct peer leadership in the context of sport by drawing primarily on masculine styles, traits, and practices. Female athletes also value aspects of social leadership among their peers, but described leadership in more task-oriented terms. Much of the research reviewed in this chapter also featured implicit gendered leadership ideologies with a strong focus on task-oriented leadership. One possible explanation for the gendered leadership constructions could be due to the predominance of men sport leaders and coaches and the likelihood that they perhaps more often express and normalize masculine leadership practices. It is also quite likely that the sport context with its strong focus on task/team performance and outcomes contributes to the more masculine leadership constructions.

Considering the more recent shift in organizational leadership approaches that embrace collaborative and relational practices, masculinized leadership behaviors found in sport contexts could prove problematic for young women entering the workforce. For example, the different leadership styles could pose a 'double bind' for young women working in a variety of professions, including sport. The double bind exists when women are expected to adhere to gender-appropriate leadership practices such as being empathetic and collaborative, and in so doing they are valued less as leaders. At the same time, if women display agentic, assertive, and authoritarian leadership behaviors expected in certain contexts such as sport, they are frequently penalized because they are breaching gender expectations by leading ways that are socially constructed a masculine. Young women who aspire to leadership roles in a variety of organizational and sport settings should be aware of the challenges associated with the double bind and develop strategies to successfully negotiate the leadership challenges facing them. It could also be argued that because young women in sport draw on both masculine and feminine leadership styles, they are already gaining experience in negotiating some of these challenges.

An important implication for sport leadership practitioners, especially coaches, is that they play a vital role in not only establishing peer leadership expectations, but also modeling sport leadership behaviors. We know that group norms and culture are influenced by what leaders pay attention to, and focusing only on autocratic, individualist, and hierarchical leadership, while certainly valuable within a sport context, may have some limitations for leadership development more broadly. Leadership development programs for female athletes and other young women in sport should therefore continue to focus on a wide range of skills that can be transferred to a variety of other organizational leadership settings.

There are also important implications for young women who aspire to obtain a sport leadership career. As highlighted throughout this book, sport leadership careers remain quantitatively dominated by men at all levels of sport, and "the lack of female role models in coaching and athletic leadership sends a disturbing message to female athletes about their own likely professional opportunities" (Rhode & Walker, 2008, p. 14). Likewise, it is vital to explore how gendered leadership assumptions and dominant masculine ideals associated with sport leadership influence young women in sport. More specifically, researchers should explore how young women internalize masculine sport leadership ideals and how such internalization may impact or inhibit their intentions to pursue sport leadership careers. Female athletes represent a large pool of potential sport leaders and coaches, and it is possible that some candidates may be lost because the way they see their own leadership may not mirror their perceptions of sport leadership.

References

Acosta, R. V., & Carpenter, L. J. (2014). Women in intercollegiate sport: A longitudinal, national study thirty-five year update (1977–2012). Retrieved from www.acostacarpenter.org

Ashcraft, K. L. (2009). Gender and diversity: Other ways to make a difference. In M. Alvesson, T. Bridgman, & H. Willmott (eds.) *The Oxford Handbook of Critical Management Studies* (pp. 305–327). London: Oxford University Press.

Britton, D. M., & Logan, L. (2008). Gendered organizations: Progress and prospects. *Sociology Compass, 2*(1), 107–121.

Brown, S., & Light, R. L. (2012). Women's sport leadership styles as the result of interaction between feminine and masculine approaches. *Asia-Pacific Journal of Health, Sport, and Physical Education, 3*(3), 185–198.

Burton, L. J. (2015). Underrepresentation of women in sport leadership: A review of research. *Sport Management Review, 18*(2), 155–165.

Drago, R., Hennighausen, L., Rogers, J., Vescio, T., & Stauffer, K. D. (2005). *CAGE: The coaching and gender equity project.* Final report for NCAA, NACWAA and The Pennsylvania State University. Retrieved from http://lser.la.psu.edu/workfam/CAGE.htm

Eagly, A. H. (2007). Female leadership advantage and disadvantage: Resolving the contradictions. *Psychology of Women Quarterly, 31,* 1–12.

Eagly, A. H., & Johannesen-Schmidt, M. C. (2001). The leadership styles of women and men. *Journal of Social Issues, 57*(4), 781–797.

Elliot, C., & Stead, V. (2008). Learning from leading women's experience: Towards a sociological understanding, *Leadership, 4*(2), 159–180.

Ely, R. J., & Meyerson, D. E. (2000). Theories of gender in organizations: A new approach to organizational analysis and change. *Research in Organizational Behavior, 22,* 103–151.

Everhart, C. B., & Chelladurai, P. (1998). Gender differences in preferences for coaching as an occupation: The role of self-efficacy, valance, and perceived barriers. *Research Quarterly for Exercise and Sport, 69*(2), 188–200.

EY & espnW (2015). Where will you find your next leader? Retrieved from www.ey.com/gl/en/newsroom/news-releases/news-sport-is-a-critical-lever-in-advancing-women-at-all-levels-according-to-new-ey-espnw-report

Eys, M. A., Loughead, T. M., & Hardy, J. (2007). Athlete leadership dispersion and satisfaction in interactive sport teams. *Psychology of Sport and Exercise, 8*(3), 281–296.

Fasting, K., & Pfister, G. (2000). Female and male coaches in the eyes of female elite soccer players. *European Physical Education Review, 6*(1), 91–110.

Fletcher, J. K. (2004). The paradox of postheroic leadership: An essay on gender, power, and transformational change. *The Leadership Quarterly, 15,* 647–661.

Frey, M., Czech, D. R., Kent, R. G., & Johnson, M. (2006). An exploration of female athletes' experiences and perceptions of male and female coaches. *The Sport Journal, 9*(4). Retrieved from www.thesportjournal.org/article/exploration-female-athletes-experiences-and-perceptions-male-and-female-coaches

Glenn, S. D., & Horn, T. S. (1993). Psychological and personal predictors of leadership behavior in female soccer athletes. *Journal of Applied Sport Psychology, 5,* 17–34.

Hanold, M. T. (2011). Leadership, women in sport, and embracing empathy. *Advancing Women in Leadership, 31,* 160–165.

Holmes, R. H., McNeil, M., & Adorna, P. (2010). Student athletes' perceptions of formal and informal team leaders. *Journal of Sport Behavior, 33*(4), 442–465.

Holmes, R. H., McNeil, M., Adorna, P., & Procaccino, J. (2008). Collegiate student athletes' preferences and perceptions regarding peer leadership. *Journal of Sport Behavior, 31,* 338–351.

Hovden, J. (2000). "Heavyweight" men and younger women?: The gendering of selection processes in Norwegian sports organizations. *Nordic Journal of Feminist and Gender Research, 8*(1), 17–32.

Hovden, J. (2010). Female top leaders—prisoners of gender? The gendering of leadership discourses in Norwegian sports organizations. *International Journal of Sport Policy*, 2(2), 189–203.

Knoppers, A., & Anthonissen, A. (2005). Male athletic and managerial masculinities: Congruencies in discursive practices? *Journal of Gender Studies*, 14(2), 123–135.

Knoppers, A., & Anthonissen, A. (2008). Gendered managerial discourses in sport organizations: Multiplicity and complexity. *Sex Roles*, 58, 93–103.

Lapchick, R. (2012). The racial and gender report card. The Institute of Diversity and Ethics in Sport (TIDES), The University of Central Florida.

LaVoi, N.M. (2013). *The Decline of Women Coaches in Collegiate Athletics: A Report on Select NCAA Division-I FBS Institutions, 2012–13*. Minneapolis: The Tucker Center for Research on Girls & Women in Sport.

Lough, N., & Grappendorf, H. (2007). Senior woman administrators' perspectives on professional advancement. *International Journal of Sport Management*, 8(2), 193–209.

Loughead, T.M., & Hardy, J. (2005). An examination of coach and peer leader behaviors in sport. *Psychology of Sport and Exercise*, 6, 303–312.

Loughead, T.M., Hardy, J., & Eys, M.A. (2006). The nature of athlete leadership. *Journal of Sport Behavior*, 29(2), 142–158.

Madsen, R.M. (2010). Female student-athletes intentions to pursue careers in college athletics leadership: The impact of gender socialization. Doctoral dissertation. Retrieved from Digital Dissertations (UMI No. 3451398).

Messner, M.A. (2009). *It's All for the Kids: Gender, Families, and Youth Sports*. Berkley, CA: University of California Press.

National Federation of State High School Associations (NFHS) (2013). 2012–2013 high school athletics participation survey. Retrieved from www.nfhs.org/content.aspx?id=3282

Osborn, R.N., Hunt, J.G., & Jauch, L.R. (2002). Toward a contextual theory of leadership. *The Leadership Quarterly*, 13, 797–837.

Peachey, J.W., & Burton, L.J. (2011). Male or female athletic director? Exploring perceptions of leader effectiveness and a (potential) female leadership advantage with intercollegiate athletic directors. *Sex Roles*, 64(5–6), 416–425.

Price, M.S., & Weiss, M.R. (2011). Peer leadership in sport: Relationships among personal characteristics, leader behaviors, and team outcomes. *Journal of Applied Sport Psychology*, 23, 49–64.

Price, M.S., & Weiss, M.R. (2013). Relationship among coach leadership, peer leadership, and adolescent athletes' psychosocial and team outcomes: A test of transformational leadership theory. *Journal of Applied Sport Psychology*, 25, 265–279.

Rhode, D.L., & Walker, C.J. (2008). Gender equity in college athletics: Women coaches as a case study. *Stanford Journal of Civil Rights and Civil Liberties*, 4, 1–49.

Schull, V. (2014). Female college athletes' perceptions of leadership in college sport: A gendered approach. Retrieved from http://hdl.handle.net/11299/163286.

Schull, V. (2016). Female athletes' conceptions of leadership: Coaching and gender implications. In N.M. LaVoi (ed.) *Women in sports Coaching* (pp. 126–138). New York: Routledge.

Shaw, S. (2006). Scratching the back of "Mr. X": Analyzing gendered social processes in sport organizations. *Journal of Sport Management*, *20*, 510–534.

Shaw, S., & Hoeber, L. (2003). "A strong man is direct and a direct woman is a bitch": Gendered discourses and their influence on employment roles in sport organizations. *Journal of Sport Management*, *17*, 347–375.

Smith, M., & Wrynn, A. (2013). Women in the 2012 *Olympic and Paralympic Games: An Analysis of Participation and Leadership Opportunities*. Ann Arbor, MI: SHARP Center for Women and Girls. Retrieved from www.womenssportsfoundation. org/en/home/research/articles-and-reports/athletes/2012-olympic-report

Walters, J. (2016, March 30). You've got male: For the first time, only men are coaching women's Final Four teams. *Newsweek*. Retrieved from http://www.newsweek.com/youve-got-male-first-time-only-men-coaching-womens-final-four-teams-442213

Yukl, G. (2012). *Leadership in organizations* (8th ed.). Upper Saddle River, NJ: Pearson Prentice Hall.

Chapter 8

Future sport leaders: developing young women to lead

Sarah Leberman

Introduction

Leadership is something that takes time to develop (Nelson, 2010) and exercising leadership takes place in a myriad of ways on a daily basis in our homes, pre-schools and schools—but is most often associated with adults. If we compare this to developing elite athletes and the 10,000 hours of practice required to become an elite athlete or accomplished business person (Ericsson, Karmpe, & Tesch-Romer, 1993; Gladwell, 2008), at what age should we be fostering leadership opportunities? This chapter discusses leadership development models for young people and highlights programs specifically focussed on young women. Murphy and Johnson (2011), focusing specifically on leader development, advocate for a long-term approach starting at an early age and present a model of leader development across the lifespan. They posit that early developmental factors such as temperament and gender, parenting styles, and learning experiences, influence leader identity development, which in turn affects self-regulation, which is associated with future development experiences and leadership effectiveness. Leadership development needs to be intentional and to start at secondary school (Rehm, 2014). Rehm (2014) draws on four leadership development models which focus on young people to propose a practitioner-based model (see Table 8.1). The four models include Murphy and Johnson's (2011) life-span model, Komives, Longerbeam, Owen, Mainella, and Osteen's (2006) leadership identity model, Van Linden and Fertman's (1998) as well as Ricketts and Rudd's (2002) models which both focus on identifying stages and dimensions for leadership development. The resultant practitioner model identifies, self-efficacy, identity /personality and the best practices of leadership as the three areas of focus, all within the context of an experiential approach (Rehm, 2014). Anderson and Kim (2009) highlighted that effective youth leadership development should facilitate experiences that "allow them to explore their interests, discover their authentic selves, develop autonomy, and increase their decision-making power in a steadily advancing and nonthreatening environment" (p. 18). Many programs exist that focus on women who are identified as having leadership potential, with most of these being offered once women are either at university or in the workforce. There is a distinct lack of leadership training aimed at young women in high schools and in particular for those who do not 'fit' the dominant discourse of what a leader 'looks like.'

Table 8.1 Leadership development models for young people

Authors	Model name	Key characteristics
Van Linden & Fertman, 1998	Stage-orientated approach to adolescent leadership development	Identifies three stages of leadership development from awareness though interaction to mastery. Five dimensions of leadership development—leadership information, leadership attitude, communication, decision making, and stress management.
Ricketts & Rudd, 2002	Model for youth leadership curriculum	Identified five dimensions: leadership knowledge and information; leadership attitude, will and desire; decision making, reasoning, and critical thinking; oral and written communication skills; intra and interpersonal relations.
Komives, Longerbeam, Owen, Mainella, & Osteen, 2006	Leadership identity development model	Focuses on how leadership identity is developed. Identified six-stage developmental process in six different categories: awareness; exploration/ engagement; leader identified; leadership differentiated; generativity; integration/ synthesis.
Murphy & Johnson, 2011	Life-span model	Focuses on contextual-developmental stages, societal expectations and time in history. Considers early developmental factors which shape leader identity and self-regulation, which inform future development experiences and leadership effectiveness.

Leadership development for young women

Research suggests that boys and girls learn to lead in different ways (Hoyt & Johnson, 2011), reflecting to a large extent, society's expectations of how men and women should behave in leadership roles (Eagly, 2007), with women often being penalized for which ever approach they take—either too agentic or too communal (Koenig, Eagly, Mitchell, & Ristikari, 2011). With leadership often being associated with men, there is little focus on leadership development for girls, as the predominant messaging for girls focuses on how to behave and how to dress (Hoyt & Kennedy, 2008). Kelinsky and Anderson (2016) suggest that developing programs for young women need to actively take account of the gendered leadership environment within which participants are operating, and argue that in order to meet the expectations of effective leadership a transformational approach informed by inspirational motivation may be most powerful. The program they describe was framed within a feminist and appreciative pedagogy and applied three stages of learning leadership development: awareness, interaction, and integration. They conclude that "encouraging participants to develop an authentic leadership style that is more androgynous ... And a more transformational style of leadership, can serve as a catalyst for empowering young females to find their authentic voice and ability to lead in various situations" (p. 167). This is particularly important in the sport context, which is still dominated by male hegemony and ongoing challenges for women aspiring to leadership, associated with gender stereotyping and bias as discussed in Chapter 4 of this volume (see, for example, Anderson, 2009; Cundiff & Vesico, 2016; Fink, 2016).

Making gender visible in leadership development initiatives

Research focusing on leadership development for young women has grown slowly over the last five years, with most of this growth having been focused on university-level students, as opposed to young women in secondary schools (McNae, 2010; Rorem & Bajaj, 2012). Messages that young women hear in secondary school are often internalized and this is particularly so in the context of leadership. Young women who are not deemed 'leadership material' miss out on many leadership development opportunities provided by schools. Often these opportunities are only afforded to those young women who fit the box of a positional leader such as captain of a team, leader of the orchestra, or head of the student council. More often than not these young women are confident and outgoing. However, we must consider what happens to the quieter, shyer, and less confident young women, as they may be passed over for leadership development opportunities. Susan Cain in her excellent book *Quiet: The*

Power of Introverts in a World That Can't Stop Talking highlights the strengths that introverts can bring to leadership. Women like Rosa Parks and Eleanor Roosevelt "who achieved what they did not in spite of but *because* of their introversion" (Cain, 2012, p. 6, emphasis in original). She also draws on research that suggests being shy and being introverted are not necessarily connected. "Shyness is the fear of social disapproval or humiliation, while introversion is a preference for environments that are not over stimulating" (Cain, 2012, p. 12).

An example of a leadership development program aimed at young women who would not traditionally consider themselves as leaders is a six-week summer programme run in New York (Hoyt & Kennedy, 2008). Their findings suggest that after the programme the young women had a deeper understanding of leadership within a feminist context and had assisted them in developing a leadership identity that was reflective of who they are. Rorem and Bajaj (2012) suggest that there is a link between youth leadership development and civic engagement, but that it is an underresearched area. They highlight four key learnings—"leadership is the application of ability and agency to exercise authority, which is used to positively influence others"; "adults should model positive leadership through facilitation, apprenticeship and joint work"; "leadership strategies are either transformational or transactional"; and "women appear to be particularly effective as transformational leaders" (pp. 1–2). They cite two case studies aimed at young women in high school—Sadie Nash Leadership project in New York City and the Young Women's Leadership Program in central California.

Many leadership programs for young people are based on adult perceptions of what is needed and their frames of reference. Mita (2008) has called for more cooperative initiatives where young people and adults work together to create learning opportunities. Based on this, McNae (2010) co-developed a leadership development program for young women at a high school in New Zealand. Also in New Zealand is the Young Women in Leadership (YoWiL) program developed by Sarah Leberman, which facilitates vision and action in young women not in leadership positions, to collaboratively bring about change within their communities. This experiential program is aimed at 15–16-year-old female high school students who are not in leadership positions and are therefore rarely, if ever, exposed to leadership training opportunities or notions about exercising leadership. YoWiL was developed after reading Susan Cain's book *Quiet*, and recognizing that the message young women receive at an early age influences how they view their leadership potential in the future. The program is founded on the belief that as long as these young women can identify their values and their passions, they are all able to exercise leadership in different ways, irrespective of whether they have been 'identified' as leadership potential by their parents, teachers and/or peers.

In addition the program seeks to redress the confidence gap identified as a contributing factor as to why women remain underrepresented in leadership roles. The outcomes enable participants to:

- identify their values and passions and how this connects to the development of a leadership identity.
- learn about the many different ways and contexts within which leadership is exercised and that it is not based on position.
- develop leadership skills and experience in the delivery of a project.

Each participant:

- attends a day-long leadership training workshop focusing on leadership; identifying values and passions; ethical leadership; teambuilding and followership; project planning and development; an inspirational woman guest speaker.
- plans for and delivers a small-scale project with other students on the program from their school. Project examples include awareness raising, educational programs or campaigns, small-scale events, fundraising for charity.
- attends a second half day workshop eight weeks later, which includes a session on reflective practice, a presentation on their project and an inspirational woman guest speaker.

Nearly 500 young women have attended the program over the last three years, many traveling large distances to attend with the feedback from high schools being overwhelmingly positive. Feedback from participants includes: "This project has made a big impact towards my learning and my future career which is to serve people and being able to work together in a group"; "Working as a team to conduct the project; interacting with new people; explaining our project; and completion of project"; "Meeting new people and seeing what other people had done for their projects. It was awesome to see such cool things happening in the community—it was inspiring."

The role of playing sport in leadership development

Murphy and Johnson's (2011) model of leader development is contextual by being cognizant of developmental stages, societal expectations, and time in history. Pertinent to this chapter is that one of the early learning experiences highlighted as important for leader development in their model is sport, in addition to education and practice. If one accepts that initiative and team work are important for leadership development, then research findings by Larson, Hansen, and Moneta (2006) in the youth sport context would support this. In addition, Chelladurai (2011) highlighted how many skills developed through participating in sport are transferable to exercising leadership. Leadership development through physical activity and sport has been widely promoted in the youth sport literature (Gould & Voelker, 2012; Martinek & Hellison, 2009; Voelker, 2016). Programs with structured leadership opportunities for girls have shown to increase self-esteem, foster positive health behavior and physical activity (Barr-Anderson, Laska, Veblen-Mortenson, Farbakhsh, Dudovitz, & Story, 2012; Taylor, 2014). Voelker (2016) suggests that three areas are of particular importance in fostering girls leadership development. These are "(1) embracing leadership diversity and deconstructing gender stereotyping, (2) building networking and mentoring opportunities, and (3) encouraging girls to use their voice and exercise leadership skills" (Voelker, 2016, pp. 10–11).

Research by EY and espnW (2015) has also highlighted the value of sport to girls and women across their lives. They suggest that sport participation assists girls to grow up healthy and confident. Kay and Shipman (2014) emphasize the importance of girls playing sport to build confidence, which women often lack despite their educational and career achievements. They argue that the experience of both winning and losing teaches girls how to deal with setbacks and keep going, which is then helpful later on in life. One of their key concerns is the large number of girls who drop out of sport in their teenage years in developed countries. In many developing countries girls do not have access to sport and therefore their opportunities to develop confidence are even more challenging. Similarly, lessons learned from sport assist young women leaders to rise through their careers, and research by Stevenson (2010) indicates women who have been athletes in high school also earn more when they enter the workforce. She suggests that sport develops attributes such as teamwork, communication skills, assertiveness, discipline, and competiveness, all of which are valued in the workplace. In addition, the EY research suggests that sporting background has helped C-suite leaders succeed. However, other research would suggest that simply being an athlete and participating in sport does not necessarily translate into leadership as an adult (Extejt & Smith, 2009), and that it is therefore necessary to provide specific opportunities to exercise leadership (Gould & Voelker, 2012).

The Building Leadership in Young Women Through Sport Project (BYWLTS) was a three year (2013–2015) program implemented by Women Win and funded by the UK government's Department for International Development (DFID) with the objective of increasing leadership in adolescent girls and young women (AGYW) in formal and informal decision-making processes through sport and a life skills approach (Women Win, 2015). The programme evaluation recommends that it is essential to understand that women cannot, and will not, become leaders overnight and that leadership development needs to start with girls, especially during their adolescence when young people often start looking for ways to engage in the public sphere.

Two programs using sport and physical activity to develop young women as leaders are currently being piloted in New Zealand. The first is 'Shift: Shift your body, Shift your mind' and targeted at young women aged between 12 and 20 to become more physically active, with the concomitant outcomes of increased self-confidence, stress management techniques, self-esteem, strength and coordination, social connections and sense of achievement. The program develops Shift Leaders, through a weekly leadership program. Less active young women co-design a 10-week physical activity and well-being program in their high school. A fund has also been created that young women can apply to in order to facilitate access to sport and physical activity opportunities—'Give back, shift forward' (http://wellington.govt. nz/recreation/support-and-advice/shift-physical-activity-and-wellbeing). The second initiative, 'HERA; Everyday Goddess,' aims to develop confidence and self-belief in 13–18-year-old girls who are inactive through participation in sport and recreation. As with the 'Shift' initiative, the girls have co-developed and co-lead the implementation of the program.

Leadership development for girls through sport

Rauscher and Cooky (2016) provide a very timely critical analysis of girl-centered sport and physical activity programs in the USA based on a positive youth development approach. There is evidence to suggest that these programs benefit girls on many psycho-social dimensions (Tucker Centre, 2007). However, Rauscher and Cooky suggest that these programs do not prepare young women for the wider social environment within which they are situated, which is still largely gendered, and where privilege and inequalities (racial, ethnic, sexual, ability, religious) are experienced by many women on a daily basis. In essence the programmes are not preparing young women for the 'real' world they will encounter. They instead advocate for programs based on a transformative approach to positive youth development, which go beyond participation in sport and physical activity, by engaging the young women in projects focusing on social change within their communities. This approach focuses on connecting agency with structure and may go some way to redressing the gap identified in the conceptual framework for this book (Figure 1.1). Following are some programs worldwide that exemplify this approach.

Wijnen and Wildschut (2015) use a postcolonial feminist lens to analyse a Digital Storytelling (DST) workshop led by an international women's rights organization, Women Win (WW), who use sport as a tool to equip girls to exercise their rights and realize their leadership potential. The approach of Women Win's Digital Storytelling workshop (held in Amsterdam and involved young women from Cambodia, India, Kenya, Zambia, Ethiopia, and Rwanda) and framework of feminist transformational leadership reflects the idea that leadership is anchored within individuals and practiced by the self. DST is a program in which young women create and develop their digital story on if and how sport has influenced and empowered their lives. The authors investigate how these stories and identities are being constructed and how the process of representation develops. Wijnen and Wildschut (2015) strongly believe that young women's voices need to be included in adapting and improving the cross-cultural leadership development process, and programs need to be designed in collaboration with young women. Furthermore, they argue that young women can have the opportunity to exercise agency through storytelling if the true possibility of authenticity within and through stories can be supported and increased.

Research in Sweden by Meckbach and Larsson (2012) and Larsson and Meckbach (2013) focused on the experiences of young coaches. Sport in Sweden relies on sport associations and clubs built on democratic principles and fundamental values. Many young people indicated that they would like to become leaders if only they were asked and this was particularly the case for girls (The Swedish Sports Confederation, 2005). Significantly more young men than young women completed their leadership training (The Swedish Sports Confederation, 2005). In 2007 the Swedish government decided to invest EUR 200,000 for four years into children's and young people's sporting activities as part of the sporting initiative known as *Idrottslyftet* (Lift for Sport). This initiative included the recruitment and development of young coaches, a formal role in sport that requires leadership. Coach training was emphasized as an important factor in encouraging young people to seek leadership positions (Westerdahl, 2007). In addition, club support was regarded as particularly important for the effective development of young leaders (Redelius, Auberger, & Bürger Bäckström, 2004; Gerrevall, Carlsson, & Nilsson, 2006).

Meckbach and Larsson's (2012) findings are based on written material on the Young Coach initiative and focus group interviews with program participants. The analysis shows that the expectations placed on the young leaders are divided along gender lines; male leaders are expected to act in one way, and female leaders to some extent, in another. A gender coding of different activities was also identified. In the joint courses for young men and women, the focus was on knowledge of children and young people, whilst in the women-only courses, the focus was more on the participants who appeared to need a boost to their self-confidence, were nervous about speaking in front of a group, and were interested in diet, health, and equality. The results indicated that the male norm and the division into masculine and feminine-coded sports activities that have characterized, and are characterizing, the sport movement still exist and serve as an underlying classification principle for how coach training programs are designed.

Larsson and Meckbach (2013) explored young coaches' experiences and notions of influence in the Swedish sport associations, focusing on their articulation of what it was like to have been chosen to be coach, their resulting influence, and holding power. The data in this study consisted of focus group and semi-structured interviews with 37 young coaches, 20 of whom were women, who participated in leadership training for young coaches in sport clubs. They concluded that the opportunities for being considered for a leader assignment and having access to the sports field are not available to everyone. Only those young people with the habitus and the capital matching what is expected are provided the opportunity to coach. Having a background as an active sportsperson emerges as a given prerequisite, being Swedish, male and older also privilege access to both coaching and board positions. Larsson and Meckbach (2013) conclude that if sport associations genuinely want young people to influence sport organizations and have real access to power then 'the rules of the game' need to change.

The Scottish 'Girls on the Move' program is focused on specifically developing young women's (16–25) leadership capabilities and in particular self-esteem through attending and then facilitating leadership development programs based on dance. Completing the program led to being awarded a dance leadership qualification. The program had two main objectives, "(1) promoting opportunity and resilience by mobilising young women to provide for their local communities and (2) preventing delinquency and failure through engaging young women in purposeful activity" (Taylor, 2014, p. 66). The findings suggest that only the girls who went on to facilitate the program showed improvements in self-esteem (Taylor, 2014).

Globally, sport programs, including those mentioned above, have been reported to effectively raise self-esteem, confidence, and self-empowerment, transform and challenge gender norms, improve social relations, and provide opportunities for leadership development and advance communication skills (Levermore & Beacon, 2009). However, postcolonial scholars argue that programs designed to empower women through sport are often paradoxical, since sport is situated in a world of male privilege and power and a Euro-American dominance vis-à-vis the Global South is often tied to Sport Development Programmes (SDPs) (Adair, 2013). Notwithstanding this situation, most programs are centered on developing young girls' agency, rather than addressing the broader structural issues which are preventing women in general securing sport leadership roles. This in itself is not problematic as many of these programs need to evidence short-term outcomes to funders, and as highlighted in Figure 1.1, structural change is a long term endeavour. The key is being able to prepare these young women for the world they will encounter as they move through the sporting environment, as highlighted by Rauscher and Cooky (2016), whilst at the same time lobbying public and private sport organizations for structural change.

Recent graduate experience and suggestions for young women

Young women at university are another group who are critical to changing the future of sport organizations. Are they prepared adequately for the world of sport, and based on their experiences of working in sport, do they have advice for young women considering a career in sport? Similar to the observations by Rauscher and Cooky (2016) most of the discussion around the development of skills such as leadership for employability purposes has taken place in a socio-cultural vacuum. This does not address, for example, issues of gender which are particularly pertinent to this book, given the underrepresentation of women in leadership positions within the sport sector worldwide (Burton, 2015). Moreau and Leathwood (2006) conclude that "skills and qualities are not neutral" (p. 319), in that employers read these differently depending on the applicant. Social class, gender, and race are often perceived as irrelevant by graduates, until they enter the workforce. In research on accounting for instance, Gracia (2009) found that female students were not prepared for the gendered aspects of the accounting profession, meaning that they were left to work out for themselves *in situ* how to behave and what to do. It is therefore critically important to prepare female students whilst in tertiary education with the tools to navigate the realities of the workforce post-graduation, rather than naively assume it is an even playing field.

Leberman and Shaw (2015) sought to identify the key attributes or skills women needed to be successful in sport management based on research with female sport management graduates. The findings suggested that being able to build relationships was most important (98.1%), followed by having good communication skills (96.2%), interpersonal skills (90.6%), and being able to plan/organize (90.6%), and by having passion and drive (88.7%). One quarter of the respondents felt that being a woman had hindered their career. In their qualitative responses, they stated that the sport industry was run like an 'old boys club' and was male dominated. As one woman mentioned:

> The current sport environment holds male opinion over female opinion and boys give boys jobs (boys clubs) so I have found it useful to make friends with the right males and influence decisions via them – the way of the world right now is that a man in sport gets listened to more than a woman as illustrated by the fact there are more men on boards than women. But I know there are a lot of very good people working to change that. I will keep working at things alongside those people and keep trying to shift the balance.

Her last statement indicated that she was keen to change the structures in sport, rather than only focus on her individual agency. Another woman observed that being a woman in sport "hinders pay packets and salary. I think you are also less likely to get promoted. There is still a lot of the old boys' club attitude around."

The participants also highlighted the challenges of raising a family and working in the environment, not being taken seriously and how emotionally draining working in the sport industry can be:

> The workplace is still a male dominated arena. Most leadership is often based on long hours and hard work. Raising a family is still seen as the career interrupter and bosses give opportunities to others who don't have family commitments, e.g. travel.

The participants were asked what advice they would give to current female students based on their experience of the industry. Comments included being realistic about your expectations, finding something that you're really interested in, network, get experience, that the degree on its own is useless, being honest and not being complacent. Their response was to be very strategic about how they interacted with their environment and they knew that in order to survive, they had to build relationships and to navigate their way through the politics. There was, however, no mention of structural change within the organizations, which suggests these participants were more willing to adjust how they behaved to fit in, rather than change the situation they were in—a focus on agency, rather than structure.

The sport sector, like many traditionally male-dominated industries, requires female graduates to be equipped with the skills and knowledge to be successful, so that this "can mitigate against them interpreting a lack of success as a personal failure and to make collectivist interpretations and challenges seem possible" (Moreau & Leathwood, 2006, p. 320). As discussed in Chapter 4 in this volume, gender stereotyping and bias is still prevalent in the sport industry, and in many cases the message is that it is the women's problem rather than the fact that fundamental changes to the structures governing sport are required.

Conclusion

It is evident that there are numerous programs worldwide focusing on developing young women as leaders either through sport, or by using sport and physical activity as a catalyst to develop competencies associated with leadership. The main challenge is that many of these programs and tertiary education courses appear not to incorporate elements in the program design that expose the young women to the realities of the world they will encounter post-high school and tertiary education (Leberman & Shaw, 2015; Rauscher & Cooky, 2016). Longitudinal research is required to establish whether these programs have a long-term effect on not only young women's agency, but also making structural changes which in an ideal world would void the need for these programs.

References

Adair, D. (2013). *Sport: Race, Ethnicity and Identity: Building Global understanding*. Abingdon: Routledge.

Anderson, E. D. (2009). The maintenance of masculinity among the stakeholders of sport. *Sport Management Review, 12*(1), 3–14.

Anderson, J. C., & Kim, E. (2009). Youth leadership development: Perceptions and preferences of urban students enrolled in a comprehensive agriculture program. *Journal of Agricultural Education, 50*(1), 8–20.

Barr-Anderson, D. J., Laska, M. N., Veblen-Mortenson, S., Farbakhsh, K., Dudovitz, B., & Story, M. (2012). A school-based, peer leadership physical activity intervention for 6th graders: Feasibility and results of a pilot study. *Journal of Physical Activity and Health, 9*, 492–499.

Burton, L. J. (2015). Underrepresentation of women in sport leadership: A review of research. *Sport Management Review, 18*(2), 155–165.

Cain, S. (2012). *Quiet: The Power of Introverts in a World That Can't Stop Talking*. New York: Broadway Books.

Chelladurai, P. (2011). Participation in sport and leadership development. In S.E. Murphy & R. J. Reichard (eds.) *Early Development and Leadership: Building the Next Generation of Leaders* (pp .95–113). New York: Psychology Press/ Routledge.

Cundiff, J. L., & Vescio, T. K. (2016). Gender stereotypes influence how people explain gender disparities in the workplace. *Sex Roles, 75*(3–4), 126–138.

Eagly, A. H. (2007). Female leadership advantage and disadvantage: Resolving the contradictions. *Psychology of Women Quarterly, 31*, 1–12.

Ericsson, K. A., Krampe, R. T., & Tesch-Römer, C. (1993). The role of deliberate practice in the acquisition of expert performance. *Psychological Review, 100*(3), 363–406.

Evans, S. D. (2007). Youth sense of community: Voice and power in Community Contexts. *Journal of Community Psychology, 35*(6), 693–709.

Extejt, M. M., & Smith, J. E. (2009). Leadership development through sports team participation. *Journal of Leadership Education, 8*(2), 224–236.

EY & espnW (2015). Where will you find your next leader? Retrieved from www. ey.com/gl/en/newsroom/news-releases/news-sport-is-a-critical-lever-in-advancing-women-at-all-levels-according-to-new-ey-espnw-report

Fink, J. S. (2016). Hiding in plain sight: The embedded nature of sexism in sport. *Journal of Sport Management, 30*(1), 1–7.

Gerrevall, P., Carlsson, S., and Nilsson, Y. (2006). *Lärande och erfarenheters värde: en Studie avledare inom barn- och ungdomsidrott* [*The Value of Learning and Experiences: A Study of Leaders within Children's and Young People's Sport*], R&D Report 2006:1. Stockholm: The Swedish Sports Confederation.

Gladwell, M. (2008). *Outliers: The Story of Success*. New York: Little Brown & Co.

Gould, D., & Voelker, D. K. (2012). Enhancing youth leadership through sport and physical education. *Journal of Physical Education, Recreation & Dance, 83*(8), 38–41.

Gracia, L. (2009). Employability and higher education: Contextualising female students' workplace experiences to enhance understanding of employability development. *Journal of Education and Work, 22*(4), 301–318.

Hoyt, C., & Johnson, S. (2011). Gender and leadership development: The case of female leaders. In S. E. Murphy & R. J. Reichard (eds.) *Early Development and leadership: Building the Next Generation of Leaders* (pp. 205–228). New York: Routlege.

Hoyt, M. A., & Kennedy, C. L. (2008). Leadership and adolescent girls: A qualitative study of leadership development. *American Journal of Community Psychology, 42*, 203–219.

Johnson, S. K., Murphy, S. E., Zewdie, S., & Reichard, R. J. (2008). The strong, sensitive type: Evidence for gender-specific leadership prototypes. *Organizational Behavior and Human Decision Processes, 106*, 39–60.

Kay, K., & Shipman, C. (2014). The confidence gap. *The Atlantic*. Retrieved from www.theatlantic.com/features/archive/2014/04/the-confidence-gap/359815/

Kelinsky, L. R., & Anderson, J. C. (2016). Women's leadership development training for [program]. *Journal of Leadership Education, 15*(1), 161–170.

Koenig, A. M., Eagly, A. H., Mitchell, A. A., & Ristikari, T. (2011). Are leader stereotypes masculine? A meta-analysis of three research paradigms. *Psychological Bulletin, 137*(4), 616–642.

Komives, S. R., Longerbeam, S. D., Owen, J. E., Mainella, F. C., & Osteen, L. (2006). A leadership identity development model: Applications from a grounded theory. *Journal of College Student Development, 47*, 401–420.

Larson, L., & Meckbach, J. (2013). To be or not to be invited youth sport: Young people's influence in voluntary sport. *Sport Science Review, XXII* (3–4), 187–204.

Larson, R. W., Hansen, D. M., & Moneta, G. (2006). Differing profiles of developmental experiences across types of organized youth activities. *Developmental Psychology, 42*(5), 849–863.

Leberman, S., & Shaw, S. (2015). "Let's be honest most people in the sporting industry are still males": The importance of socio-cultural context for female graduates. *Journal of Vocational Education & Training, 67*(3), 349–366.

Levermore, R., & Beacom, A. (eds.) (2009). *Sport and International Development*. Hampshire: Palgrave Macmillan.

Martinek, T., & Hellison, D. (2009). *Youth Leadership in Sport and Physical Education*. New York: Palgrave Macmillan.

McNae, R. (2010). Young women and the co-construction of leadership. *Journal of Educational Administration, 48*(6), 677–688.

Meckbach, J., & Larson, L. (2012). Education: One way to recruit and retain young coaches. *Journal of Youth Sports, 6*(2), 25–31.

Mitra, D. L. (2008). Balancing power in communities of practice: An examination of increasing student voice through school-based youth-adult partnerships. *Journal of Educational Change, 9*(3), 221–242.

Moreau, M.-P., & Leathwood, C. (2006). Graduates' employment and the discourse of employability: A critical analysis. *Journal of Education and Work, 19*(4), 305–324.

Murphy, S. E., & Johnson, S. K. (2011). The benefits of a long-lens approach to leader development: Understanding the seeds of leadership. *The Leadership Quarterly, 22*, 459–470.

Nelson, A. E. (2010). Stepping in early to grow great leaders. *LIA, 29*(6), 20–24.

Rauscher, L., & Cooky, C. (2016). Ready for anything the world gives her?: A critical look at sports-based positive youth development for girls. *Sex Roles, 74*, 288–298.

Redelius, K., Auberger, G., and Bürger Bäckström, C. (2004). *Ung ledare sökes: En Studie av Riksidrottsförbundets satsning på unga ledare* [*Young Leaders Required: A Study of the Swedish Sports Confederation's Young Leader Initiative*]. Stockholm: Swedish Sports Education/The Swedish Sports Confederation.

Rehm, C. J. (2014). An evidence-based practitioner's model for adolescent leadership development. *Journal of Leadership Education*, Summer, 83–97.

Ricketts, J. C., & Rudd, R. D. (2002). A comprehensive leadership education model to train, teach, and develop leadership in youth. *Journal of Career and Technical Education, 19*(1). Retrieved from http://scholar.lib.vt.edu/ejournals/JCTE/v19n1/ricketts.html

Rorem, A., & Bajaj, M. (2012). Cultivating young women's leadership for a kinder, braver world. Kinder & Braver World Project: Research Series. Berkman Center for Internet and Society at Harvard University. Retreived from http://cyber.law.harvard.edu/node/8094

Shaw, S., & Leberman, S. (2015). Using the kaleidoscope career model to analyse female CEOs' experiences in sport organizations. *Gender in Management: An International Journal, 30* (6), 500–515.

Stevenson, B. (2010). Beyond the classroom: Using Title IX to measure the return to high school sports. NBER Working Paper 15728, National Bureau of Economic Research.

Taylor, J. A. (2014). The impact of the "girls on the move" leadership programme on young female leaders' self esteem. *Leisure Studies, 33*(1), 62–74.

The Swedish Sports Confederation. (2005). *Idrotten vill: Idrottsrörelsens verksamhetsidé och riktiinjer* [*Sport Wants To: The Sports Movement's Mission Statement and Guidelines*]. Stockholm: The Swedish Sports Confederation.

Tucker Centre for Research on Girls & Women in Sport. (2007). *The 2007 Tucker Center Research Report, Developing Physically Active Girls: An Evidence-based Multidisciplinary Approach*. Minneapolis, MN: Author.

Van Linden, J. A., & Fertman, C. I. (1998). *Youth Leadership: A Guide to Understanding Leadership Development in Adolescents*. San Francisco: Jossey-Bass.

Voelker, Dana K. (2016) Promoting the leadership development of girls through physical education and sport. *Journal of Physical Education, Recreation & Dance, 87*(3), 9–15.

Westerdahl, L. (2007). *Attitydundersökning bland ungdomar kring ledaruppdrag i internationella organisationer* [*A Survey of Young People's Attitudes Concerning Leadership Positions in International Organizations*]. Stockholm: SIFO Research International/The Swedish Sports Confederation.

Wijnen, E., & Wildschut, M. (2015). Narrating goals: A case study on the contribution of digital storytelling to cross-cultural leadership development. *Sport in Society, 18*(8), 938–951.

Women Win (2015). Building young women's leadership through sport 2013–2015: programme evaluation. Retrieved from https://womenwin.org/files/BYWLTS%20Programme%20Evaluation_1.pdf

Networking, mentoring, sponsoring: strategies to support women in sport leadership

Janelle E. Wells and Meg G. Hancock

Introduction

To ascend the career ladder, one cannot do it alone. Individuals, especially women sport leaders, need networking, mentoring, and sponsoring strategies to achieve career success. While general research on these topics is plentiful, specific research in the sport context is scant. The majority of networking, mentoring, and sponsorship literature pertains to general business management, and where possible the literature specific to sport will be highlighted, but much in this context remains unknown. Although this may be troubling, it is fruitful for prospective research. Given the static, and at times declining, presence of women sport leaders, this chapter discusses opportunities and strategies for women sport leaders in the male-dominated field of sport.

This chapter is organized into sections based on three topics: networking, mentoring, and sponsoring. All three of the concepts are grounded in theory, but the mentoring and sponsoring sections take an applied focus. The structure of the sections begin with a discussion on the importance of the topic and then transition into a discussion on the type, benefits, and advantages of networking, mentoring, and sponsoring. Throughout each section examples of gender differences will be weaved into the text. The sections will conclude with a discussion on strategies to increase women leaders in sport organizations.

Networking: defining relationship patterns

A significant predictor of career success is an individual's network and the size of the network (Seibert, Kraimer, & Liden, 2001). A network is a pattern of relationships among individuals (Seibert et al., 2001). For the remainder of the chapter, a network will be discussed as the action of networking.

Networking is referred to as the building and nurturing of professional and personal relationships to create a system of support, information, and contact crucial for career and personal success (Whiting & De Janasz, 2004). Networking allows increased exposure to people within the organization, which may enhance access to information, resources, and the understanding of organizational practices (Lankau & Scandura, 2002). In sport especially, the need for networking is vital given the competitive tight-knit nature of the industry. It is not unusual for hundreds, if not thousands, of applicants to apply for one position. To stand out in a pile of one hundred resumes, knowing someone within the organization is key to having your application considered.

In general, specific elements of networking relate differentially to men and women. Social role theory has been used as a framework to examine potential gender differences in networking behaviors. Since agentic qualities align more with the male role, and communal qualities align more with a female role, networking researchers suggest men tend to be more instrumental (e.g., task and goal oriented), while women tend to be more relational (Macintosh & Krush, 2014). Van Emmerik (2006) indicates that men specialize in obtaining "hard social capital," based on task-related benefits, compared to women acquiring emotional support or "soft social capital." There is also evidence suggesting women value networking differently than men. For example, women have attributed career success to external influences, such as networking, while men have attributed career success to internal factors, such as ambition (Ackah & Heaton, 2004).

So what is social capital and what does it have to do with networking? Social capital includes the skills, organizational knowledge, and relationships acquired through professional networks (Sagas & Cunningham, 2004). An individual's social capital increases when access to resources come from higher-level organizational members, such as those with authority, power, and influence (Seibert et al., 2001). While having connections with supervisors is important, social capital theorists also suggest having a vast network with peers and direct reports (James, 2000), because access to information and resources encourages career advancement (Seibert et al., 2001).

In the context of sport, participation in networks is integral for advancement within sport organizations, particularly, for women (Bower, 2009; Hancock & Hums, 2016; Hums & Sutton, 1999; Shaw, 2006). For example, a recent study on collegiate women athletic administrators showed that of the 20 women interviewed, all attributed their current positions as an assistant or associate athletic director and career advancement to their professional networks (Hancock & Hums, 2016). Specifically, networks provide opportunities to develop new and continuing relationships with peers, mentors, and potential employers in intercollegiate athletics and sport more generally.

Network types

Formal and informal networks

Distinguishing between formal and informal networks is relevant for this chapter because engagement in either form of network may have differing implications (McGuire, 2002). Informal social networks at work are organically formed, and have been known to encourage job embeddedness and to provide more access to job leads (Mitchell, Holtom, Lee, Sablynski, & Erez, 2001). On the contrary, formal networks are official, publicly recognized organizational networks that have identifiable membership and explicit structure. Furthermore, formal networks are more accessible for change policies to advance careers. For example, if a member was excluded from a formal network, he or she could refer to a policy to argue they have been treated unfairly. In contrast, a member excluded from an informal network has little recourse because organizations lack responsibility over informal work ties (McGuire, 2002).

Homogenous and heterogeneous networks

Although individuals prefer to function in homogeneous groups (e.g., individuals of similar demographic groups and/or organizational positions) (Levine & Moreland, 1990), having diverse ties enhances individuals' access to valuable information (Lin, 2001). Homogenous networks have led to increased social support and exchange of information, which has benefited individual career outcomes (James, 2000). Yet, homogenous networks have also created conformity and exclusion (Blackshaw & Long, 2005). This has occurred in the affluent homogenous network of collegiate athletic directors, where the majority are white men (Lapchick, 2015) and underrepresented individuals have been less likely exposed to these networks (Bettie, 2003). Speaking more generally, especially amongst sport leaders, this lack of acceptance into homogeneous networks may promote insular behavior and norms that engender institutionalization without bridging relationships and diversifying representation.

Diversity amongst resource users, which can be found in a heterogeneous network, potentially influence the use and creation of one's social networks. Ibarra (1995) discovered underrepresented individuals in the workplace have greater heterogeneous support networks compared to their majority counterparts. Underrepresented individuals are a part of more heterogeneous networks because they must reach beyond the boundaries of the organization or occupation to reach similar demographic individuals (Ibarra, 1995). As such, heterogeneous networks have provided individuals with new and unique resources, while also increasing their access to better resources (Lin, 2001). While heterogeneous networks promote diverse thought and resources, they also have limitations. For example, in common-pooled resource systems, which exist in sport, demographic differences have created strong divides between individuals (McPherson, Smith-Lovin, & Cook, 2001). Divides can be caused by the interactions experienced by members, the quality of information received, and attitudes formed in heterogeneous networks (Ibarra, 1995; McPherson et al., 2001).

Networking outcomes

Networking has positive effects on both individual careers and organizational success. Over the years, researchers have revealed networking facilitates the formation of common norms and rules (Pretty, 2003), provides greater social support (Chiaburn & Harrison, 2008), enhances an individual's reputation (Steward, Walker, Hutt, & Kumar, 2010), creates clearer role expectations (Podolny & Baron, 1997), improves task performance, increases access to career and emotional coping resources (Van Emmerik, 2006), and advances careers (Metz & Tharenou, 2001).

Even though women engage more in networking behaviors, men had greater success gaining promotions through their effective use of networks (Cannings & Montmarquette, 1991) and benefited more from the satisfaction of networking (Macinstosh & Krush, 2014). One form of networking, external networking, has benefited women more than men. Clarke (2011) discovered women benefited more because of greater opportunities to connect with peers, mentors, or role models of the same sex.

Despite the clear benefits of networking, having a networking conversation may not be comfortable or attractive for some, but it is necessary because individuals are hungry for real relationships and conversations (McKeown, 2015). While networking can be timely, often intentional and selective, authentic and sincere networking may help overcome an individual's hesitation to network.

Networking in the sport industry

Across the world, sport organizations have recognized the vital role of networking. Due to social networking sites such as Twitter, Facebook, and LinkedIn, connecting and networking have never been easier than before. As such, the virtual networks allow individuals and organizations a platform to access and create targeted connections. Virtually, Ernst & Young Global Limited (EY) created a platform, specifically for women, to take advantage of networking opportunities to reach the executive suite. EY notes women athletes are "by nature, high achievers, influential leaders and team players who have tremendous value for businesses, governments and NGOs around the world. The transition from sport to post-athletic success, however, can be daunting. That's why we created the Women Athletes Business Network" (WABN, 2016, p. 1). Additionally, the Australian Sport Performance Network (ASPN) provides an online forum to collaborate with all allied health care providers and sport science disciplines throughout the country (ASPN, 2016). In the United Kingdom, the Sport Business Network created a movement through businesses, clubs, charities, and governing bodies to change lives through the power of business and sport (SBN, 2016). In the United States, sport organizations such as the National Association of Collegiate

Women Athletic Administrators (NACWAA) and the Alliance of Women Coaches have supported the advancement of women through networking activities. NACWAA consistently champions "our members' achievements and encourages advancement through leadership education, networking and career guidance" (2016a, p. 1) through multiple workshops and conventions held throughout each year. Additionally, one of the reasons the Alliance of Women Coaches exists is because they believe "that a national network and community of women coaches not only serves the individual but will make it possible for other women to follow in their footsteps" (AWC, 2016, p. 1). These few examples are only a snapshot of sport organizations dedicated to creating networking opportunities specific to and for women.

Since networking is prevalent across and throughout all sport careers (Rice, 2015), it is important for sport leaders, particularly women, to note that networking provides greater access to expertise, which can lead to higher status and career success (Forret & Doughterty, 2001). Furthermore, researchers have shown that not only is respect, support, and advice shaped by the structure of an organization, but it is even more strongly molded by the demography of individuals' job level and titles (Ibarra, 1992, 1995). Given that the majority of sport leaders are men, especially at the most commercialized, lucrative, and powerful levels (Acosta & Carpenter, 2014; Adriaanse & Crosswhite, 2008; Burton, 2015, Lapchick, 2015), this is of particular interest to note. Since women, at times, have been excluded from networks, especially those that are above the glass ceiling, an invisible barrier to career advancement (Lyness & Thompson, 2000), it is imperative women make connections to higher-level organizational members to increase their access to information, influence, and resources (Seibert et al., 2001).

Mentorship and outcomes

Mentoring is a popular buzzword in conversations regarding professional success and career advancement. Fortune 500 companies like Google and Deloitte have well-established programs designed to inspire and cultivate mentoring relationships within their respective organizations. Not surprisingly, both companies are also on Fortune's list of '100 Best Companies to Work For' (Fortune, 2016). Sport organizations like the NACWAA and the National Association of Collegiate Directors of Athletics (NACDA) have also recently started mentoring programs for various constituencies across college and university athletic programs. NACWAA offers a 'Mentor Program' that "matches accomplished veteran administrators with talented up-and-comers committed to advancing and excelling in college athletics" (NACWAA, 2016b, para. 1). More specifically, the year-long program is divided into three phases – introduction (a face-to-face meeting at the national convention), coaching (a series of phone conversations with themed guidelines for each call), and closing (in-person meeting). The NACWAA program has desired outcomes for the up-and-comer, as well as the mentor. NACDA offers a 'Senior Administrators Mentoring Institute' designed to "assist and prepare those individuals that are Senior Level Administrators in athletics administration who are one step away from becoming an athletics director" (NACDA, 2016, para. 1). Programming for the Institute includes leadership and management strategies, student-athlete welfare, and organizational culture. In addition, NACDA also supports and promotes mentoring programs for the National Association of Academic Advisors for Athletics (N4A) and the National Association for Athletics Compliance (NAAC).

Internationally, the US Department of State also created the Global Sports Mentoring Program (GSMP), a one-month mentorship program that connects emerging female leaders from around the world with women executives at leading US organizations in the sport industry (US Department of State, 2016). The goal of the GSMP is to empower emerging leaders to "serve their local communities by increasing access and opportunities for participation in sport" (US Department of State, para. 1). Other examples of mentoring programs outside the United States also exist. Sport New Zealand (2016) offers a year-long mentorship program for women serving on governance boards of sport organizations. The program is designed to offer guidance and advice on promoting evidence-based best practices. Women Ahead is a mentorship in the United Kingdom comprising "global experts that specialize in designing, implementing, and evaluating world-class mentoring partnerships between and within worlds of sport and business" (Women Ahead, 2016, para. 1). More specifically, Women Ahead's '30% Club' is a mentoring program that pairs male and female leaders with women in different sport and business organizations to build learning, development, and professional networks. Similar to Women Ahead, the Australian Woman and Recreation Association established an e-mentoring program to "assist women in middle management in sport to make the next step" (AWRA, 2016). The online program includes activities for mentors and their mentees, information and discussion groups relevant to women in sport management, and web-based workshops on various professional development topics (e.g., networking, establishing career goals, defining skills and experience).

The term 'mentor' and the action of 'mentoring,' as well as the role of the mentee are broad and come with many perceived expectations (Haggard, Dougherty, Turban, & Wilbanks, 2011). When not clearly defined, the mentor/mentee relationship may become marred with confusion and frustration. The purpose of this section is to define the role of a mentor, types of mentorship, the benefits of having a mentor, and strategies for cultivating a mutually beneficial mentor/mentee relationship.

A mentor provides specific "guidance focused on professional issues, such as talking about goal setting, pursuing education, and seeking the right experiences to be successful in a position" (Baumgartner & Schneider, 2010, p. 568). With this in mind, mentors often serve a mentee primarily in one of two functions—career or psychological (Kram, 1983; Kram & Isabella, 1985). Career functions prepare the protégé for career advancement. The mentor may provide the mentee career advice, access to networks, professional coaching, challenging work, and professional protection. The purpose of the career function is to help the mentee learn about an organization and/or industry and develop competencies for career growth and advancement. Psychological functions include a mentor's role in: building a mentee's sense of professional self, acting as a sounding board, developing problem-solving strategies, and giving respect and support. Mentors who perform psychological functions may also develop friendships with their protégés, while still serving as a role model. Additionally, mentors benefit from a relationship with a mentee in that a mentor also gains experience in providing support, feedback, and guidance, which can help the organization by developing talent (Kram & Isabella, 1985).

Types of mentoring relationships

Informal and formal mentoring

Mentoring relationships may be cultivated formally or informally. Informal mentoring relationships "develop on the basis of mutual identification and the fulfillment of career needs" (Ragins & Cotton, 1999, p. 530). Often informal mentoring occurs at the early stages of a mentee's career and involves a mentor who identifies as a mid-level manager. Mentors in informal relationships may select mentees they perceive to be less experienced versions of themselves in an effort to pass down knowledge and wisdom to future generations. Conversely, the mentee, selects a mentor they view as a role model and someone who can provide guidance to help achieve long-term career goals (Ragins & Cotton, 1999). For both the mentor and the mentee, mentorship is grounded in the perceived competence and the strength of an interpersonal relationship. In short, an informal mentoring relationship is one in which mentors seek mentees they perceive to be capable of successful career growth; mentees seek mentors who possess a desired skill set, offer advice that protects the mentee's best interests, and reflect the professional values of the mentee (Boddy, Agllias, & Gray, 2012). Given the close interpersonal nature of informal mentorships, the relationship may last several years. As such, informal mentoring is likely to fulfill psychosocial, as well as career functions (Boddy et al., 2012; Ragins & Cotton, 1999).

In recent years, research on mentoring relationships has shifted to an examination of formal mentoring. To contend with and keep up with an increasingly global environment, organizations are implementing formal mentoring programs to "develop and sustain a knowledgeable and connected talent pool" (Chun, Litzky, Sosik, Bechtold, & Godshalk, 2010, p. 422). A formal mentor/mentee relationship is sanctioned by an organization in which mentors and mentees are matched in an effort to share organizational knowledge, build strong cultures, enhance political skill, and build professional connections (Chun et al., 2010). Mentors and mentees are often paired on the perceived competency of the mentor and for the purpose of meeting organizational needs (Blake-Beard, O'Neill, McGowan, 2007).

Based on the matching process, the mentor and mentee never meet or converse until the match is made. Previous role modeling and interpersonal relationship cultivation is absent; thus, psychosocial functions may occur less (Ragins & Cotton, 1999) or in later stages of the formal mentoring relationship as the mentor and mentee develop rapport. As such, formal mentoring relationships tend to focus on career functions like skill development and access to networks, rather than developing self-confidence or friendships with the mentee. Furthermore, the lack of rapport may significantly inhibit the mentoring relationship, thus negating organizational and professional goals of a formal mentoring program. With this in mind, Chun and colleagues (2010) explored the role of Emotional Intelligence (EI) and trust in formal mentoring relationships. A mentor's EI was positively related to their ability to effectively mentor as well as build trust with the mentee. More importantly, when mentees had a positive experience with their mentor, mentees expressed a greater desire and willingness to mentor others. This is particularly important given that most formal mentorships are time based and generally last 6 to 12 months (Ragins & Cotton, 1999). It should be noted that while formal mentorship may be time-based, the relationship may continue beyond the original parameters of the mentorship program if the mentor and mentee develop a strong friendship and rapport. Although formal mentoring programs offer benefits, the creation and implementation come with challenges. When selection choices are unavailable to mentors and mentees unrealistic expectations may exist, reciprocity between the two parties lacks, and the two may have reduced opportunities for identifying with one another (Blake-Beard, 2001).

Internal and external mentors

In addition to formal and informal relationships, a mentor can exist inside (i.e., internal) or outside (i.e., external) of an organization (Baugh & Fagenson-Eland, 2005). Internal mentors are more physically accessible than external mentors and can provide assignments and immediate feedback to enhance mentee self-confidence (Haggard et al., 2011). Moreover, mentors in the same organization are particularly helpful when a mentee seeks advancement. Internal mentors often have more knowledge of organizational personnel, policies, and politics, which the mentee can then access to navigate the organization (Murrell, Blake-Beard, Porter, &

Perkins-Williamson (2008). On the other hand, mentors external to the organization may offer a more objective perspective for mentees seeking advice or guidance on career-related issues (Arthur, Khapova, & Wilderom, 2005; Ragins, 1997). External mentors also extend the mentees professional network, which may be beneficial for career mobility (Arthur et al., 2005; Baugh & Fagenson-Eland, 2005; Haggard et al., 2011). It is important to consider the advantages and disadvantages of an internal versus external mentor, as well. Perhaps not surprisingly, mentees with internal mentors reported higher levels of career and psychosocial support than protégés with external mentors (Baugh & Fagenson-Eland, 2005). In a study on coaching, internal and external mentors were equally beneficial to a mentees learning and performance; however, internal coaching mentors had a stronger effect on learning and performance than external coaching mentors (Jones, Woods, & Guillaume, 2015). Despite this, mentees with external mentors may be more independent and have greater self-efficacy, because mentors are not immediately available for guidance (Baugh & Fagenson-Eland, 2005).

Whether a mentee has a formal or informal mentor who is either internal or external to an organization, identifying the purpose for the mentoring relationship is critical for both parties to derive the most benefit. The following section details the professional career benefits of having a mentor.

Who can be a mentor?

Traditionally, mentorship has been defined by age and rank; that is, an older, more senior person (i.e., the mentor) provides guidance to the younger, less experienced person, also known as a protégé. Traditional mentorship also suggests that the mentor is at a higher position in the organizational hierarchy than the mentee. Therefore, the traditional mentor may be more likely to supply the mentee a broader range of mentoring function, more exposure/visibility in the organization, and provide more access to organizational resources (Haggard et al., 2011). Interestingly, traditional mentorship may have limited applicability to women and people of color (Ragins, 1997) especially in the sport industry, which tends to be dominated by white men (IOC, 2016; Lapchick, 2015). As our understanding of mentorship has evolved, so too has the definition. Certainly, mentors may be older or more senior in the organization, but mentors can also be colleagues who are one 'step-ahead' in a career path (Ensher, Thomas, & Murphy, 2001). Moreover, a peer mentor can be just as beneficial and may be more accessible than other mentoring relationships (Kram & Isabella, 1985). Peer mentors provide important professional and social support for protégés (Bauer, Bodner, Erdogan, Truxilla, & Tucker, 2007). Likewise the professional reciprocity experience by both the mentee and the mentor is likely to be greater than in a traditional mentorship (Haggard et al., 2011). Still peer mentors often have less organizational power by virtue of their position in the hierarchy and are likely to have less access to organization resources. Regardless of relationship (e.g., traditional, step-ahead, peer), support, guidance, and counseling are hallmarks of mentorship that have the potential to "enhance career development and psychosocial development of both individuals" (Kram, 1983, p. 613).

Mentoring outcomes

Given the developmental nature of the mentor/mentee relationship, mentoring affords the mentee many opportunities for career development, growth, and advancement. When engaged in a mentoring relationship, mentees demonstrate higher rates of promotion (LaPierre & Zimmerman, 2012), higher salaries (Ramaswami, Dreher, Bretz, & Wiethoff, 2010), greater levels of job and career satisfaction and higher rates of organizational commitment (Allen, Eby, Poteet, Lentz, & Lima, 2005). For most mentees, these benefits are related to personal perceptions of career success and advancement (Singh, Ragins, & Tharenou, 2009). For the mentor, the opportunity to increase employee satisfaction and organizational commitment may result in less turnover (Baranik, Roling, & Eby, 2010); thus, the mentor and the organization not only retain talent, but also reduce costs associated with recruiting and hiring practices (Baranik et al., 2010).

In male-dominated industries like sport, mentorship is particularly important to women, as women are more likely to experience barriers to advancement (Bower & Hums, 2013; Shaw, 2006). Moreover, engaging in a mentoring relationship is an effective way for women not only to advance, but also to reach top management and leadership levels (Dworkin, Maurer, & Schipani, 2012). Through mentorship, women understand themselves, styles of operating, and the ways they might need to change to gain more opportunities for career success (Ibarra, Carter, & Silva, 2010). The success women mentees experience is also due, in part, to the career opportunities afforded by virtue of the guidance, support, and protection of the mentor (Metz & Tharenou, 2001).

Despite the clear advantages and benefits of mentorship, many women have difficulty engaging in a mentoring relationship. In the sport industry, this has been attributed to the low proportion of women in top-management levels. This perspective, however, assumes that women seeking mentorship must seek another woman. The following section details the role of gender when selecting a mentor.

Gender in mentorship

Male mentors have been found to be more likely to provide career functions of mentoring, while women mentors were more likely to provide more psychological functions of mentoring (Cullen & Luna, 1993). Not surprisingly, mentees had similar expectations of their mentors. For example, mentees expected female mentors to exhibit outreach and support, while male mentors were perceived to be more content-focused and less comfortable with certain discussions like those pertaining to work–life balance (Levine, Mechaber, Reddy, Cayea, & Harrison, 2013).

Women with a senior-male mentor in a male-dominated industry had the highest level of career progress satisfaction (Ramaswami et al., 2010). Conversely, some benefits may occur from having a female–female mentee–mentor such as understanding the unique challenges facing women in the workplace. Despite the benefits, females are less likely to have a female mentor, "probably due to too few women in sufficiently advanced positions to provide mentoring to junior colleagues" (Dworkin et al., 2012, p. 366).

In sum, men and women in management and leadership positions are likely to possess the ability to provide both career and psychological functions of mentoring. Overall, it is most important to consider *what* an individual will need as a mentee and *who* might fulfill those needs as a mentor.

Sponsoring: having influence and a voice

Many may confuse sponsoring with mentoring. Although a mentor may be a sponsor, a sponsor goes beyond the traditional career and psychosocial support provided by a mentor. A sponsor is an individual in a decision-making position who advocates, protects, and fights for a mentee's career advancement (Ibarra et al., 2010). Furthermore, a sponsor uses his or her platform to publicly support the advancement of an individual who has untapped talent or potential (Foust-Cummings, Dinolfo, & Kohler, 2011; Hewlett, Peraino, Sherbin, & Sumberg, 2011).

The position and power of a sponsor is critical because conversations regarding opportunities for advancement occur at the leadership table, where a sponsor can advocate for unrecognized talent. Sponsors can effectively catapult a hopeful talent from unknown status to rising-star. Given there are few women sport leaders, a talented female may go unrecognized or discussed, remaining untapped without a sponsor. Researchers have shown women begin their career behind and remain behind men, even with men supporting their advancement (Ibarra et al., 2010). However, when a women's advocate has high organizational status, women are just as likely as men to be promoted (Ibarra et al., 2010). Thus, more women need to have sponsors *and* more women need to be at the leadership table.

Sponsor versus mentor: what is the difference?

While mentors may act as sponsors, the roles and positions differ from one another. Kathy Hopinkah Hannah, a managing partner at KPMG LLP US, notes the distinction between mentors and sponsors as "a mentor will listen to you and speak with you, but a sponsor will talk about you" (Catalyst, 2011, p. 1). Additionally, Harris (2014) suggests mentoring relationship are passive and low risk for the mentors, while sponsoring is a high-risk venture, especially sponsoring a talented rising woman, because senior male leaders "don't see obvious rewards for themselves. And there's no reference manual on how to go to bat for a rising female star" (p. 1). As previously noted, a sponsor has significant decision-making power, usually holds a higher-status organizational position, acts as an advocate, gives brutal constructive feedback, and puts his or her reputation on the line (Harris, 2014). Distinct from a traditional mentor, a sponsor provides sophisticated coaching and advice to stretch a role, position, or assignment to assist a mentee. In contrast, a mentor does not put his or her prestige on the line for a mentee, usually provides positive constructive feedback, may not have position or power and the relationship may be behind the scene serving in the role as a counselor. For example, in US intercollegiate athletics, an Assistant Athletic Director can serve as a mentor to an Athletic Director but, by virtue of the position, he or she is unlikely to be a sponsor for the Athletic Director.

As previously noted in this chapter, mentors can be male or female and both have advantages and disadvantages. However, when men and women are sponsored by men, the sponsors often have greater representation and more opportunities to publicly endorse their mentees. This is because, in most industries including sport, organizational decision-making structures are male dominated. Thus, individuals with male sponsors are more likely to receive exposure to greater resources and affluent networks. It is clear from the underrepresentation of women as league commissioners, heads of national and international governing bodies, intercollegiate and interscholastic athletic directors, head coaches, and youth coaches that mentoring, though necessary, has not been sufficient to help women leaders reach the pinnacle positions in sport.

Sponsorship importance

Sponsors put their reputation on the line to open doors of opportunities and raise the visibility of mentees, enhancing their recognition and credibility. In addition, increased salaries and job satisfaction have been the results of a sponsor (Hewlett, Marshall, & Sherbin, 2011). Sponsors do not advance unqualified individuals; rather, they identify 'high potential' individuals who may go unrecognized by the leadership team, many of whom are men (Dinolfo, Silva, & Carter, 2012). By nominating a mentee for a promotion or an opportunity supportive of a promotion, a sponsor provides instrumental career support (Friday, Friday, & Green, 2004).

Sponsorship is particularly important for women. Hewlett and colleagues (2011) found men, compared to women, were 46% more likely to have a sponsor. Without a sponsor, women are far more likely to be unsatisfied with their career progression (Rezvani, 2014), are less likely to be appointed to top positions, and even more importantly, are less likely to apply for such positions (Travis, Doty, & Helitzer, 2013). A sponsor may help challenge a women to volunteer for an appropriate stretch assignment, rather than waiting to be asked. Ibarra and colleagues (2010) noted women operate under a meritocracy system believing that their hard work will advance their career, but it takes more, ideally it takes a sponsor. Without sponsorship, women are less likely to be appointed to top positions or 'hot jobs' (Silva, Carter, & Beninger, 2012), and we know jobs in sport are 'hot.'

As a sponsor, there is personal and professional satisfaction gained from the relationship (Foust et al., 2011; Hewlett et al., 2011). Being able to identify and develop a mentee into a leader gives many sponsors a deep sense of satisfaction. Building a legacy of developing talent for the future is also highly valued by sponsors (Travis et al., 2013). As such, the growing network of high-achieving loyal employees creates an in-depth understanding of the organization, or more broadly the industry (Harris, 2014). Being or becoming a sponsor can be instrumental to creating a culture of sponsorship where identifying and developing talent becomes a recognized and appreciated skill set. In particular, male sponsors of emerging female talent also reap an abundance of potential rewards. For example, they become key agents of change and learn to work effectively in increasingly diverse settings (Harris, 2014).

Once an individual has solidified a sponsor they should be sure to create and maintain reasonable relationship expectations, regularly inform the sponsor about accomplishments, freely discuss career opportunity hesitations, and thank them for their support. They should also ensure that they sponsor women once they are in a position to do so.

Summary

Think of networks, mentorships, and sponsoring as a pyramid (Figure 9.1).

Foundationally, it begins with a broad network, possibly inclusive of professional colleagues who may or may not have diverse career interests,

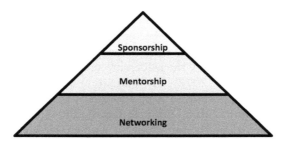

Figure 9.1 A conceptual pyramid of networking, mentorship, and sponsorship

skills, values, and success. From that network, mentoring relationships are derived. Mentors may provide career or psychosocial functions or both, and may extend over years or be sustained for only a brief period of time. Regardless of the function or duration of time, a mentor may become a sponsor if the sponsor is in a position of decision-making power and is willing to be an advocate. Ultimately, cultivating relationships to create a network, and garnering mentors and sponsors are key factors to career success and advancement.

References

Ackah, C., & Heaton, N. (2004). The reality of "new" careers for men and for women. *Journal of European Industrial Training*, 28(2), 141–158.

Acosta, R. V., & Carpenter, L. J. (2014). Women in intercollegiate sport: A longitudinal, national study, thirty-seven year update – 1977–2014. Unpublished manuscript. Retrieved from www.acostacarpenter.org

Adriaanse, J. A., & Crosswhite, J. J. (2008). David or Mia? The influence of gender on adolescent girls' choice of sport role models. *Women's Studies International Forum*, 31, 383–389.

Allen, T. D., Eby, L. T., Poteet, M. L., Lentz, E., & Lima, L. (2004). Career benefits associated with mentoring for protégés: A meta-analysis. *Journal of Applied Psychology*, 89(1), 127–136.

Arthur, M. B., Khapova, S. N., & Wilderom, C. P. M. (2005). Career success in a boundaryless career world. *Journal of Organizational Behavior*, 26, 177–202.

ASPN. (2016). What is ASPN? Retrieved from www.aspn.com.au/about/

AWC. (2016). Alliance of Women Coaches. (2016). What is the alliance? Retrieved from http://gocoaches.org/about/overview/

AWRA. (2016). AWRA e-mentoring program. Retrieved from www.australianwomensport.com.au/content.aspx?file=47474|34175f

Baranik, L., Roling, E. A., & Eby, L. T. (2010). Why does mentoring work? The role of perceived organizational support. *Journal of Vocational Behavior*, 76(3), 366–373.

Bauer, T. N., Bodner, T., Erdogan, B., Truxillo, D. M., & Tucker, J. S. (2007). Newcomer adjustment during organizational socialization: A meta-analysis review of antecedents, outcomes, and methods. *Journal of Applied Psychology*, 92, 707–721.

Baugh, S. G., & Fagenson-Eland, E. A. (2005). Boundaryless mentoring: An exploratory study of the functions provided by internal versus external organizational mentors. *Journal of Applied Social Psychology*, 35(5), 939–955.

Baumgartner, M. S., & Schneider, D. E. (2010). Perceptions of women in management: A thematic analysis of razing the glass ceiling. *Journal of Career Development*, 37(2), 559–576.

Bettie, J. (2003). *Women without Class: Girls, Race, and Identity*. Berkeley, CA: University of California Press.

Blackshaw, T., & Long, J. (2005). A critical examination of the advantages of investigating community and leisure from a social network perspective. *Leisure Studies*, 17, 233–248.

Blake-Beard, S.D. (2001). Taking a hard look at formal mentoring programs. *Journal of Management Development*, *20*, 331–345.

Blake-Beard, S.D., O'Neill, R.M., & McGowan, E.M. (2007). Blind dates? The importance of matching in successful formal mentoring relationships. In B.R. Ragins & K.E. Kram (eds.) *The Handbook of Mentoring at Work: Theory, Research, and Practice* (pp. 617–632). Thousand Oaks, CA: Sage.

Boddy, J., Agllias, K., & Gray, M. (2012). Mentoring in social work: Key findings from a women's community-based mentoring program. *Journal of Social Work Practice*, *26*(3), 385–505.

Bower, G.G. (2009). Effective mentoring relationships with women in sport: Results of a meta-ethnography. *Advancing Women in Leadership*, *29*(3), 1–21.

Bower, G.G., & Hums, M.A. (2013). The impact of title IX on career opportunities in intercollegiate athletic administration. *Journal of Intercollegiate Sport*, *6*(2), 213–230.

Burton, L.J. (2015). Underrepresentation of women in sport leadership: A review of research. *Sport Management Review*, *18*, 155–165.

Cannings, K., & Montmarquette, C. (1991). Managerial momentum: A simultaneous model of the career progress of male and female managers. *Industrial and Labor Relations Review*, *44*, 212–228.

Catalyst. (2011). Fostering sponsorship success among high performers and leaders. Retrieved from https://linniecarter.com/files/2012/02/Fostering-Sponsorship-Success-Among-High-Performers-Leaders.pdf

Chiaburu, D.S., & Harrison, D.A. (2008). Do coworkers make the place? Conceptual synthesis and meta-analysis of lateral social influences in organizations. *Journal of Applied Psychology*, *93*, 1082–1103.

Clarke, M. (2011). Advancing women's careers through leadership development programs. *Employee Relations*, *33*, 498–515.

Chun, J.U., Litzky, B.E., Sosik, J.J., Bechtold, D.C., & Godshalk, V.M. (2010). Emotional intelligence and trust in formal mentoring programs. *Group & Organization Management*, *35*(4), 421–455.

Cullen, D.L., & Luna, G. (1993). Women mentoring in academe: Addressing the gender gap in higher education. *Gender and Education*, *5*(2), 125–137.

Dinolfo, S., Silva, C., & Carter, N.M. (2012). *High Potentials in the Pipeline: Leaders Pay it Forward*. New York: Catalyst.

Dworkin, T.M., Maurer, V., & Schipani, C.A. (2012). Career mentoring for women: New horizons/expanded methods. *Business Horizons*, *55*, 363–372.

Ensher, E., Thomas, C., & Murphy, S. (2001). Comparison of traditional, step-ahead, and peer mentoring on protégés' support, satisfaction, and perceptions of career success: A social change perspective. *Journal of Business and Psychology*, *15*, 419–438.

Forret, M.L., & Dougherty, T.W. (2001). Correlates of networking behavior for managerial and professional employees. *Group and Organization Management*, *26*, 283–311.

Fortune. (2016). 100 best companies to work for. *Fortune*. Retrieved from http://learn.greatplacetowork.com/rs/520-AOO-982/images/GPTW_100Best_List_2016.pdf

Foust-Cummings, H., Dinolfo, S., & Kohler, J. (2011). *Sponsoring Women to Success*. New York: Catalyst.

Friday, E., Friday, S. S., & Green, A. L. (2004). A reconceptualization of mentoring and sponsoring. *Management Decision, 42*, 628–644.

Haggard, D. L., Dougherty, T. W., Turban, D. B., & Wilbanks, J. E. (2011). Who is a mentor? A review of evolving definitions and implications for research. *Journal of Management, 37* (1), 280–304.

Hancock, M. G., & Hums, M. A. (2016). "A leaky pipeline?" Perceptions of barriers and supports of female senior-level administrators in NCAA Division I athletic departments. *Sport Management Review, 19*(2), 198–210.

Harris, J. (2014). She breaks into the inner sanctum of top management, with his sponsorship. Retrieved from www.linkedin.com/pulse/20140325211506–275490660-she-breaks-into-the-inner-sanctum-of-top-management-with-his-sponsorship

Hewlett, S. A, Marshall, M., & Sherbin, L. (2011). The relationship you need to get right: How to be an effective sponsor—and a good protégé—throughout your career. *Harvard Business Review, 89*, 131–134.

Hewlett, S. A., Peraino, K., Sherbin, L., & Sumberg, K. (2011). *The Sponsor Effect: Breaking through the Last Glass Ceiling.* Boston, MA: Harvard Business School Press.

Hums, M. A., & Sutton, W. A. (1999). Women working in the management of professional baseball: Getting to first base? *Journal of Career Development, 26*(2), 147–158.

Ibarra, H. (1992). Homophily and differential returns: Sex differences in network structure and access in an advertising firm. *Administrative Science Quarterly, 37*, 422–447.

Ibarra, H. (1995). Race, opportunity, and diversity of social circles in managerial networks. *The Academy of Management Journal, 38*, 673–703.

Ibarra, H. (2010). Women are over-mentored (but under-sponsored). Retrieved from https://hbr.org/ideacast/2010/08/women-are-over-mentored-but-un.html

Ibarra, H., Carter, N. C., & Silva, C. (2010). Why men still get more promotions than women? *Harvard Business Review, 9*, 80–85.

IOC. (2016). Fact Sheet: Women in the Olympic Movement. Retrieved from https://stillmed.olympic.org/Documents/Reference_documents_Factsheets/Women_in_Olympic_Movement.pdf

James, E. H. (2000). Race-related differences in promotions and support: Underlying effects of human and social capital. *Organization Science, 11*(5), 493–508.

Jones, R. J., Woods, S. A., & Guillaume, Y. R. F. (2015). The effectiveness of workplace coaching: A meta-analysis of learning and performance outcomes from coaching. *Journal of Occupational and Organizational Psychology, 89*(2), 249–277.

Kram, K. E. (1983). Phases of the mentoring relationship. *Academy of Management Journal, 26*, 608–625.

Kram, K. E. (1985). *Mentoring at Work: Developmental Relationships in Organizational Life.* Glenview, IL: Scott Foresman.

Kram, K. E., & Isabella, L. A. (1985). Mentoring alternatives: The role of peer relationships in career development. *Academy of Management Journal, 28*(1), 110–132.

Lankau, M. J., & Scandura, T. A. (2002). An investigation of personal learning in mentoring relationships: Content, antecedents, and consequences. *Academy of Management Journal, 45*(4), 779–790.

Lapchick, R. E. (2015). The 2015 racial and gender report card: College sport. Retrieved from www.tidesport.org/college-sport.html

LaPierre, T. A., & Zimmerman, M. K. (2012). Career advancement and gender equity in healthcare management. *Gender in Management: An International Journal*, 27(2), 100–118.

Levine, J. M., & Moreland, R. L. (1990). Progress in small group research. *Annual Review of Psychology*, 41, 585–634.

Levine, R. B., Mechaber, H. F., Reddy, S. T., Cayea, D., & Harrison, R. A. (2013). "A good career choice for women": Female medical students' mentoring experiences: A multi-institutional qualitative study. *Academic Medicine*, 88, 527–534.

Lin, N. (2001) *Social Capital: A Theory of Structure and Action*. New York: Cambridge University Press.

Lyness, K. S., & Thompson, D. E. (2000). Climbing the corporate ladder: Do female and male executives follow the same route? *Journal of Applied Psychology*, 85, 86–101.

Macintosh, G., & Krush, M. (2014). Examining the link between salesperson networking behaviors, job satisfaction, and organizational commitment: Does gender matter? *Journal of Business Research*, 67, 2628–2635.

McGuire, G. M. (2002). Gender, race, and the shadow structure: A study of informal networks and inequality in a work organization. *Gender & Society*, 16, 303–322.

McKeown, G. (2015). 99% of networking is a waste of time. Retrieved from https://hbr.org/2015/01/99-of-networking-is-a-waste-of-time

McPherson, M., Smith-Lovin, L., & Cook, J. M. (2001). Birds of a feather: Homophily in social networks. *Annual Review of Sociology*, 27, 415–444.

Metz, I., & Tharenou, P. (2001). Women's career advancement: The relative contribution of human and social capital. *Group & Organization Management*, 26(3), 312–342.

Mitchell, T. R., Holtom, B. C., Lee, T. W., Sablynski, C. J., & Erez, M. (2001). Why people stay: Using job embeddedness to predict voluntary turnover. *Academy of Management Journal*, 44, 1102–1122.

Murrell, A. J., Blake-Beard, S., Porter Jr., D. M., & Perkins-Williamson, A. (2008). Interorganizational formal mentoring: Breaking the concrete ceiling sometimes requires outside support. *Human Resource Management*, 47, 275–294.

NACDA. (2016). Senior administrators mentoring institute. Retrieved from www.nacda.com/nacda/nacda-mentoring-institute.html

NACWAA. (2016a). We champion women leaders. Retrieved from www.nacwaa.org/

NACWAA. (2016b). Mentor program. Retrieved from www.nacwaa.org/connect/mentoring-networking/mentor-program

Podolny, J. M., & Baron, J. N. (1997). Resources and relationships: Social networks and mobility in the workplace. *American Sociological Review*, 62, 673–693.

Pretty, J. (2003). Social capital and the collective management of resources. *Science*, 302, 1912–1914.

Ragins, B. R. (1997). Diversified mentoring relationships in organizations: A power perspective. *Academy of Management Review*, 22, 482–521.

Ragins, B. R., & Cotton, J. L. (1999). Mentor functions and outcomes: A comparison of men and women in form and informal mentoring relationships. *Journal of Applied Psychology*, 84, 529–550.

Ramaswami, A., Dreher, G. F., Bretz, R., & Wiethoff, C. (2010). Gender, mentoring, and career success: The importance of organizational context. *Personnel Psychology*, *63*, 385–405.

Rezvani, S. (2014). *The career-changing value of a sponsor.* Retrieved from www.selenarezvani.com/blog/142/The-Career-Changing-Value-of-a-Sponsor/

Rice, T. (2015). Sport professional stress the importance of networking. Retrieved from http://sportsfitnessnetwork.com/2015/05/sport-professionals-stress-the-importance-of-networking/

Sagas, M., & Cunningham, G. B. (2004). Does having "the right stuff" matter? Gender differences in the determinants of career success among intercollegiate athletic administrators. *Sex Roles*, *50*(5), 411–421.

SBN. (2016). Welcome to the SBN. Retrieved from http://sportbusinessnetwork.com/

Seibert, S. E., Kraimer, M. L., & Liden, R. C. (2001). A social capital theory of career success. *Academy of Management Journal*, *44*(2), 219–237.

Shaw, S. (2006). Scratching the back of "Mr. X": Analyzing gendered social processes in sport organizations. *Journal of Sport Management*, *20*, 510–534.

Silva, C., Carter, N. M., & Beninger, A. (2012). *Good Intentions, Imperfect Execution? Women Get Fewer of the "Hot Jobs" Needed to Advance.* New York: Catalyst.

Singh, R., Ragins, B. R., & Tharenou, P. (2009). What matters most? The relative role of mentoring and career capital in career success. *Journal of Vocational Behavior*, *75*(1), 56–67.

Sport New Zealand. (2016). Search for a resource. Retrieved from www.sportnz.org.nz/managing-sport/search-for-a-resource/news/2016-recipients-women-in-sport-governance-scholarships-and-mentor-programme

Steward, M., Walker, B., Hutt, M., & Kumar, A. (2010). The coordination strategies of high-performing salespeople: Internal working relationships that drive success. *Journal of the Academy of Marketing Science*, *38*(5), 550–566.

Travis, E. L., Doty, L., & Helitzer, D. L. (2013). Sponsorship: A path to the academic medicine C-suite for women faculty? *Academic Medicine*, *88*(10), 1414–1417.

US Department of State. (2016). Global sports mentoring program: The initiative. Retrieved from https://globalsportsmentoring.org/global-sports-mentoring-program/

Van Emmerik, I. J. H. (2006). Gender differences in creation of different types of social capital: A multilevel study. *Social Networks*, *28*(1), 24–37.

WABN. (2016). EY women athletes business network. Retrieved from www.ey.com/BR/pt/About-us/Our-sponsorships-and-programs/Women-Athletes-Global-Leadership-Network-About

Whiting, V. R., & de Janasz, S. C. (2004). Mentoring in the 21st century: Using the Internet to build skills and networks. *Journal of Management Education*, *28*(3), 275–293.

Women Ahead. (2016). Women ahead: Mentoring. Retrieved from www.women-ahead.org/mentoring-v2

Chapter 10

New leadership: rethinking successful leadership of sport organizations

Laura J. Burton and Sarah Leberman

Introduction

A shift in understanding of what the measures of successful leadership are is required in order for leadership in sport organizations to be more inclusive and open to differing views and objectives, as well as diverse individuals. However, without a clear understanding of how success is conceptualized in sport organizations, we cannot embark on more inclusive ways to exercise leadership. In this concluding chapter, we explore how success is most often defined in sport organizations and suggest other ways of conceptualizing success that may assist in the quest for gender equity in sport leadership. We challenge thinking on how existing structures operating in sport organizations can be adapted to better support all individuals and argue that fundamental change to structures is required in order to bring about meaningful change to leadership in sport organizations. Further, we continue to urge those in positions of power to be held responsible and accountable for providing more inclusive structures in order for more individuals to exercise leadership in sport. We suggest that one way to achieve this is for sport organizations to consider both adopting the quadruple top and bottom line as a strategic guiding force and focusing on the United Nations Sustainable Development Goals, in particular Goal 5: Gender Equality and Goal 8: Decent Work and Economic Growth.

Leadership success within the dominant paradigm: 'winning at all costs'

Winning at all costs: reinforces a model that privileges men

We argue that the 'winning at all costs' model, as a measure of organizational success in sport, serves to reinforce hegemonic masculinity and male privilege in sport leadership. With an emphasis on winning over all else, leaders can perpetuate systems and structures that are inclusive only for a certain few. As an example, the emphasis on US football as the primary source of revenue generation in the US intercollegiate system at the highest level of play (i.e., Division I Football Bowl Subdivision) negatively impacts women in sport leadership, as women are often excluded from athletic administrative positions that support football and are thus denied opportunities to work with the sport deemed most important to the success of the organization. The highest level of leadership, athletic director, is often perceived as out of reach for women, as women are denied access to football administration and therefore are denied access to learning how to lead and manage the most complex and revenue-intensive areas of the organization (Grappendorf & Lough, 2006). Similarly, women were absent in the leadership of Rugby Union in New Zealand until late 2016 when Dr Farah Palmer as Chair of the Māori Rugby Board was appointed to the board of the NZRU, and apart from Raelene Castle, CEO of the Canterbury-Bankstown Bulldogs Rugby League club, are also absent from Rugby League in Australia—two sports closely associated with the national identities of these countries.

The priority to win encourages coaches and administrators to spend the majority of their time working, whether that is time in the office, travel with teams, or recruiting new athletes. The expectations to prioritize work over all other aspects of life has a negative impact on the work–life interface, as time spent either in the office or out 'on the road' has a negative impact on family and personal needs (Dixon & Bruening, 2005, 2007). With this emphasis, only those who have partners who are able to take on the majority of domestic and family responsibilities, or those who are not in relationships, are able or perhaps willing to make such significant personal/family trade-offs to meet work requirements. This model most often benefits men with stay-at-home partners, who can serve as primary caretakers of their personal and family needs. Increasingly, women with stay-at-home partners are also able to be successful within this paradigm. However, such a system devalues the importance of active participation in family life and importantly holistic enrichment in one's own life.

It is important to note that we should not assume that all men want to make these trade-offs to prioritize work over personal and family needs. In recent research conducted by Gallup (2016), a larger percentage of men (78%) who aspire to senior leadership roles (e.g., CEO) than women (72%) would be discouraged from seeking that position if it required working more than 60 hours per week. Therefore, organizational structures that prioritize excessive work hours and demand that work is privileged above family and personal needs must be changed to enable and value different ways of working, which benefit both women and men. Anecdotally it has been speculated that motherhood makes women less interested in seeking senior leadership positions. However, research by Lean In and McKinsey Company (2015) suggests that motherhood can make women more ambitious, and they feel well placed to be successful in high-profile leadership roles. Women are also less likely than men to leave organizations, particularly at the senior level (Lean In and McKinsey & Company, 2015).

Second-generation bias is also evidenced in the 'winning at all costs' model of success. Second-generation bias is described as "powerful but subtle and often invisible barriers for women that arise from cultural assumptions, organizational structures, practices, and patterns of interaction that inadvertently benefit men while putting women at a disadvantage" (Ibarra, Ely, & Kolb, 2013, p. 64). Organizational practices within sport leadership also support gendered career paths and gendered work. Leaders in sport organizations who aspire to gain higher status positions are often expected to move to new positions that provide greater challenges and opportunities to demonstrate success (e.g., win championships, generate profits). These new positions are likely to require movement to a new part of a country or internationally. Such moves often assume there is a 'trailing spouse' and family that is willing and able to move. As noted by Ibarra et al. (2013) in their work describing second-generation bias, men typically are able (and expected) to move to enhance their careers and their families (partner, children) are expected and will follow. This same dynamic does not always apply to women, and women are more likely to pass up opportunities for career advancement if such advancement requires moving their families (Ibarra et al., 2013). Further, Leberman and Hurst (2017) describe this as a linear career approach, "where a person aspires to organizational advancement characterized by upwards mobility, greater responsibility, and increased pay, all of which are more consistent with the way the careers of men tend to develop" (p. 255).

The 'winning at all costs' model may also deter some women from seeking advancement to positional leadership in sport organizations. The ways in which men and women value career success in general may favor men in this model. Though financial rewards and promotion are important factors in career success for both men and women, research to date from different parts of the world suggests that women also focus on the concept of life success (Bostock, 2014; Heslin, 2005; Ituma, Simpson, Ovadje, Cornelius, & Mordi, 2011). This includes maximizing congruence between their work and personal lives, having quality work and personal relationships, as well as personal happiness and contentment (Leberman & Hurst, 2017). Gallup (2016) research suggests, however, that what men and women are seeking from the workplace is not as different as expected or conventionally assumed, and that changes to the workplace will benefit all employees. They suggest that "it is not enough to hire the right 'numbers' to improve diversity. An organization's culture should be mission rich; support and expect high performance; and appreciate, develop and recognize people for their unique talents and strengths" (p. 74).

'Winning at all costs': contributing to ethical impropriety

If we take a more reflective view of leadership in sport organizations, we can critically evaluate how leadership is rewarded and who and what is privileged in these dominant paradigms of leadership. This type of critical analysis allows us to examine why we continue to see failings of leadership, including ethical scandals that have a negative impact on all those involved in sport. Under the current paradigm of sport leadership, we contend that success in sport organizations is most often defined by objective measures including win–loss statistics and generating revenue in profit-driven, high-performance sport organizations. Success evaluated only through the lens of 'winning at all costs' can create environments that focus leadership and leadership outcomes on objective measures only, and can lead to and/or contribute to unethical practices in sport organizations. With a focus on winning, often winning at all costs, leadership may take on more destructive forms (e.g., pseudotransformational leadership, personalized charismatics, toxic leaders) that result in structures, systems, rewards and organizational norms which value winning (and profit generation) above any other organizational goals.

Several scholars have critiqued the publically espoused organizational goals of the national governing body for US intercollegiate sport—the NCAA. One of the core values of the organization reads, "The collegiate model of athletics in which students participate as an avocation, balancing their academic, social and athletics experiences" (NCAA, 2016, n.p.). However, in sports which generate the most revenue for the university (i.e., football and men's basketball), the majority of the players on those teams (i.e., black men) graduate at significantly lower rates than the male student population (Southall, Eckard, Nagel, & Randall, 2015). Similarly, inappropriate behavior by male athletes with respect to women is often minimized when these athletes are associated with high-profile sports and teams, such as Football in the US, Soccer in the UK, Rugby Union in New Zealand and Rugby League in Australia. If winning is the only or most significant measure of organizational success, societal, broader organizational, and individual needs at all levels of sport organizations can get distorted or worse, lost. This focus on winning is not merely emphasized at the highest level (i.e., international/professional competition), but permeates all levels of sport including amateur and youth sport.

We witness this in the challenges and issues facing individuals leading US-based youth sport organizations, from the increased incidents of injuries in youth soccer (football) and declining participation in US football as a result of concerns regarding concussions. In many countries the win at all costs mentality drives youth sport coaches away, athletes (and unfortunately parents/guardians) to disregard resultant injuries, burnout, and other negative health and psychological development-related problems in the quest for championships (see, e.g., Bergeron et al., 2015; Strachan & Davies, 2015; Walters, Schluter, Oldham, Thomson, & Payne, 2012).

In the US intercollegiate model, a focus on winning and revenue generation in a non-for-profit model has resulted in an emphasis on resource allocation to football at the expense of other men's and all-women's sports (Grasgreen, 2014). At the international/professional levels of sport, the win at all costs model of success has led to massive corruption (e.g., FIFA), state-sponsored doping of athletes (e.g., Russia's ban from 2016 Summer Olympics for track and field events), and denial and then delayed response to addressing head trauma incurred by athletes (e.g., NFL).

Alternative leadership success paradigms beyond winning

As discussed throughout this book, women contribute to sport on a daily basis in a myriad of ways, but more often than not their leadership is not seen, let alone recognized. Their contributions are often 'disappeared' (Fletcher, 1999). When this leadership cannot be counted it is considered less important than the positional leadership which is publically visible. When women are in positions of leadership they are visible, can be counted and given the context within which they operate, are measured as being successful along the same criteria as their male counter parts in sport—winning. Women in sport want to win just as much as men, however, the 'winning at all costs' paradigm, similar to the economic profitability motive of big business, comes at a real cost. So what happens if sport teams do not win—the coach may be sacked, funding reduced or withdrawn, and CEOs may lose their jobs. This singular focus on winning detracts from the other contributions that sport makes to individuals and society—are these less important than winning? How are they valued and if your team does not win, does this equate to poor leadership? Conversely, can the assumption be made that organizations that do win represent 'good' leadership? The challenge we have is to identify those other measures of success which are often neglected within sport, and arguably are much more important to long-term sustainability than a 'winning at all costs' approach.

Success beyond winning: what would an alternative model look like?

If using the 'winning at all costs' model to demonstrate success in sport organizations is detrimental to sport in general, and to women in leadership in particular, we should consider alternate models to measure success in sport (e.g., success beyond winning). Of course we acknowledge that sport is based on the concept of competition, and to remove winning from sport is not realistic, desirable or necessary. What we are calling attention to and believe needs to be reconciled through leadership in sport, is the singular emphasis on winning or the 'winning at all cost' model. Sport, provides much more to individuals and collectively to society, when it is considered outside of the 'winning at all cost' model, as noted in work provided by the United Nations.

Before proposing a new model of 'success beyond winning', we want to acknowledge the critically important work that takes place in the context of sport for development and peace models (SDP). Broadly defined, SDP models use "sport to exert a positive influence on public health, the socialization of children, youths and adults, the social inclusion of the disadvantaged, the economic development of regions and states, and on fostering intercultural exchange and conflict resolution" (Lyras & Peachey, 2011, p. 311). We recognize that the focus of SDP programs have and will continue to measure 'success beyond winning' and that SDP programs are providing benefits to individuals and groups internationally that cannot be captured by measuring success in the context of winning/losing and/or profit/losses. In the model to follow, we are not proposing that sport leadership follow a SDP model, but we do recognize that SDP can provide opportunities for those leading other types of sport organizations to rethink success beyond winning.

To help guide us in shifting the focus to a new model, one that holds to a 'success beyond winning' model, we look to the work being done through the United Nations. In 2000, the UN provided a long-term vision and plan for a better world entitled the 'Millennium Development Goals' that included the following goals (poverty eradication, universal primary education, gender equality, child mortality reduction, improving maternal health, combating HIV/AIDS and other diseases, environment sustainability, and global partnership for development). As an extension of the work introduced in 2015 are the 17 Sustainable Development Goals (SDGs) (Table 10.1). The purpose of the SDGs "is to have a globally agreed holistic approach to the three major pillars of sustainable development: economic development ...; social inclusion meaning gender equality, human rights and the reduction of inequalities; and environment sustainability" (Sachs, 2015, pp. 56–57). Sport plays a prominent role in meeting these goals:

> Sport is also an important enabler of sustainable development. We recognize the growing contribution of sport to the realization of development and peace in its promotion of tolerance and respect and the contributions it makes to the empowerment of women and of young people, individuals and communities as well as to health, education and social inclusion objectives.
>
> (UN, 2015)

The opportunity to shift the focus of success to a model as outlined by the UN provides greater opportunity for women to exercise leadership, both positional and non-positional. In fact, one of the 17 SDGs is to achieve gender equality and empower all women and girls. Sport is ideally suited for this objective:

> Gender equality and changes in norms and attitudes towards it can be promoted in sport contexts, where sport-based initiatives and

Table 10.1 UN sustainable development goals

#	Goal	Description
1	No Poverty	End poverty in all its forms everywhere
2	Zero Hunger	End hunger, achieve food security and improved nutrition and promote sustainable agriculture
3	Good Health and Well Being	Ensure healthy lives and promote well-being for all at all ages
4	Quality Education	Ensure inclusive and quality education for all and promote lifelong learning
5	Gender Equality	Achieve gender equality and empower all women and girls
6	Clean Water and Sanitation	Ensure access to water and sanitation for all
7	Affordable Clean Energy	Ensure access to affordable, reliable, sustainable and modern energy for all
8	Decent Work and Economic Growth	Promote inclusive and sustainable economic growth, employment and decent work for all
9	Industry, Innovation and Infrastructure	Build resilient infrastructure, promote sustainable industrialization and foster innovation
10	Reduce Inequality	Reduce inequality within and among countries
11	Sustainable Communities and Cities	Make cities inclusive, safe, resilient and sustainable
12	Responsible Growth and Consumption	Ensure sustainable consumption and production patterns
13	Climate Action	Take urgent action to combat climate change and its impacts
14	Life Below Water	Conserve and sustainably use the oceans, seas and marine resources
15	Life On Land	Sustainably manage forests, combat desertification, halt and reverse land degradation, halt biodiversity loss
16	Peace, Justice and Strong Institutions	Promote just, peaceful and inclusive societies
17	Partnerships for the Goals	Revitalize the global partnership for sustainable development

Note: Retrieved from www.un.org/sustainabledevelopment/sustainable-development-goals/

programmes have the potential to equip women and girls with knowledge and skills that allow them to progress in society.

(UN, 2015, n.p.)

If sport organizations adopted the UN model of sustainable development and shifted emphasis to success beyond winning, then the economic rationale and organizational practices would need to follow. Within business there are parallel objectives to sustainable development as demonstrated in corporate social responsibility initiatives (CSR). The rationale for CSR has been well made in the business literature, suggesting that there is a need to move away from a purely economic model of business focused exclusively on profits to one that includes social, cultural, and environmental sustainability—referred to as the quadruple bottom line (Werbach, 2009). Much of the CSR research refers to the triple bottom line which conflates social with cultural issues (see, e.g., Marques-Mendes & Santos, 2016; Mostovicz, Kakabadse, & Kakabadse, 2009), but together with Laszlo and Laszlo (2011) we would argue that these dimensions are quite different, with the inclusion of cultural issues going some way to acknowledging intersectionality, so often ignored in both research and practice, yet crucial in moving toward gender equity in organizations. In addition to the quadruple bottom line, Laszlo and Laszlo (2011) advocate for the quadruple top line, which focuses on the organization's value add of their service and/or product to their sector, rather than only considering the return on investment (the bottom line) of the service and/or product.

Driven by the strategic leadership of the organization, in most cases the board, structural change can be achieved to secure sustainable and ethical outcomes over the long term (Laszlo & Laszlo, 2011; Mostovicz et al., 2009). By adopting an integrated holistic approach which focuses on social, cultural, financial, and environmental sustainability, fundamental changes in overall organizational structures are likely to occur. Recent research in Australia and New Zealand indicates that organizations are aware of the SDGs (Australian Centre for Corporate Social Responsibility, 2016). The most important goals identified were Gender Equality, Good Health and Wellbeing, Decent Work and Economic Growth, Industry Innovation and Infrastructure, and Climate Action. The key challenge for organizations was to match desired priorities with concrete action plans. When examining gender and CSR in this context, research has shown that corporate boards that have women serving as directors are more likely to engage in CSR activities (Harjoto, Laksmana, & Lee, 2015; Jain & Jamali, 2016). As organizations acknowledge the benefits to CSR engagement, findings in this area have highlighted the importance of women in leadership positions to help maximize these benefits (Kaspereit, Lopatta & Matolcsy, 2016). Most of the CSR research in sport has focused on professional sport and the reasons for engaging in CSR (see, e.g., Babiak & Wolfe, 2009; Hamil &

Morrow, 2011). An exception is the work by Palmer and Master's (2010) with Māori women in sport leadership. They indicate that many Māori businesses seek to focus on the quadruple bottom line, but that achieving this is a challenging process.

Returning to the conceptual model introduced in the introduction, we posit that structural change could be achieved more expediently by sport organizations adopting a quadruple top- and bottom-line approach, with a particular focus on the UN Sustainable Development Goals of Gender Equality and Decent Work and Economic Growth. This would necessitate a paradigm shift away from the focus of 'winning at all costs' to one where the multiple benefits of sport to individuals and society are recognized (see Figure 10.1).

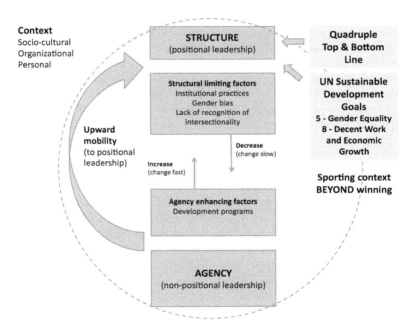

Figure 10.1 Structure-Agency quadruple top and bottom line conceptual model to redress the underrepresentation of women in sport leadership © Sarah Leberman and Laura J. Burton

Men and women in power: need for those voices to make change

As was described in the final section of Chapter 3, one of the ways that institutional change occurs is through advocacy by those in positions of power. Within sport organizations, men hold the majority of leadership positions at all levels of sport throughout the world (Lapchick, 2016). When men in sport leadership advocate for and provide opportunities for women in sport leadership, especially in areas where there have been few women historically (e.g., senior leadership in men's professional sport, international sport governing bodies), it makes a meaningful difference to all women. Importantly, women who have obtained positions of power and leadership in sport organizations must not only provide opportunities to women within their organizations, but also advocate more broadly for changes to the structures within which they operate. Women in leadership positions in sport organizations must be aware of and resist the narrative that there is only one seat at the table for women and that one 'token' woman is able to speak for all women in the organization. Research would suggest that to make a meaningful difference in organizations there needs to be at least three women on a board (see, e.g., Adriaanse & Schofield, 2014; Torchia, Calabro, & Huse, 2011). As discussed in Chapter 6, quotas are one means of ensuring more women are on boards. However, what is unclear is whether mandating this legislatively is having a positive impact on organizations. Recent research by Korn Ferry (2016) highlights Catalyst (2015) data which indicates that in Norway women currently make up 35.5% of board members on stock index companies, where mandatory quotas of 40% women on boards was introduced in 2008. Finland and France also have mandatory quotas and currently have female representation of 29.9% and 29.7% respectively. However, this approach has not worked in Italy, which set a 33% target and is currently sitting at 6%.

It is useful to remind readers that the benefits of diversity are well researched as highlighted in the introduction. This is reinforced by a recent Korn Ferry (2016) report that highlights five key organizational benefits from having women represented at the highest level of organizations from the board down. They are:

- Better corporate performance—it makes a positive difference to the financial bottom line.
- A more innovative working culture—this is of critical importance in the fast-paced world of sport.
- Help in closing the growing skills gap—drawing on the expertise of women broadens the talent pool.
- Better connections for organizations to their customers—participation in sport by girls and women in growing, as is consumption of sport at all levels. Women control about 70% of consumer spending so having their voice represented in decision making can only be good for organizations.
- Improvements in brand image—and providing women as role models in leadership positions.

Gallup (2016) identifies 10 areas in which organizations can focus on to "attract, engage and retain a female workforce" (p. 75), whilst recognizing that addressing these areas will benefit the organizations in terms of diversity more generally, applying to both women and men.

1   Review performance management systems to enable employees to play to their strengths and engage in meaningful work.
2   Hire, develop, and reward great people managers who enable others to maximize their potential, achieve performance outcomes, engage their teams, and actively pursue a diversity hiring agenda.
3   Create trust and transparency to make flexibility work by advocating flex policies and using them. "True flexible working arrangements do not give workers permission to slack—they give employees freedom to succeed" (p. 78).
4   Communicate and activate organizational values and mission. "Women are more apt to see work and life as one holistic entity ... They care about values, and they care about purpose and cause" (p. 78).
5   Develop a culture of coaching.
6   Rehire, re-engineer, and retain—an organization that is loyal and makes work 'work' for its employees, at different stages of their lives is valued.
7   Pay attention to strengths over stereotypes.
8   Build a culture of well-being.
9   Encourage people to get to know one another. Women in particular value friendships at work and indicate they are missing out on opportunities to build meaningful relationships.
10 Make your organization child friendly. For mothers the greatest influence of whether to stay at work or not is their children.

The other very important strategy is to focus on accountability and not only collecting data, but also sharing of results (Lean In and McKinsey & Company, 2016).

When women are included in leadership positions, unfortunately, they can face undue burdens based on lower legitimacy perceptions. When compared to powerful men, powerful women are less likely to be perceived as legitimate authorities (Vial, Napier, & Brescoll, 2016). Perceptions of legitimacy can be further reduced for women in high-status positions that are gender incongruent (e.g., sport organizations) if they make a mistake in the role of leader (Brescoll, Dawson, & Uhlmann, 2010). An additional challenge for women in leadership is that their legitimacy can be compromised when their leader behaviors highlight power differentials between them and subordinates (Vial et al., 2016). When we consider that sport organizations in general, and leadership positions in particular, continue to be dominated by men, these challenges to women's legitimacy in leadership positions can be significant because being a leader in a sport organization continues to be seen as gender incongruent for women (Heilman, Wallen, Fuchs, & Tamkins, 2004). Men in leadership positions who support developing women as leaders must work with women and other individuals in the organization to mitigate questions of legitimacy for women in leadership.

Research is increasingly suggesting that changing the way organizations are structured and how they are led is important to both women and men (Lean In and McKinsey & Company, 2016). The main reason both women and men (42%) do not want to be a top executive is their perceived inability to manage their work–life interface, followed by the level of politics involved (39%; 40%) and not being interested in the type of work (35%; 37%). Thirty-two percent of women, compared with 21% of men indicated that they did not want the pressure. Interestingly, more men (21%) than women (15%) indicated that senior roles were not consistent with who they were and 13% of both women and men were not confident they would be successful (Lean In and McKinsey & Company, 2016). What this means is that if sport organizations fundamentally change their structures to focus on both the quadruple top- and bottom-line, not only will this ensure more women and diversity at the strategic level, but also it will benefit everyone in the organization.

Conclusion

For the last 40 years we have seen numerous attempts to increase the number of women in sport leadership positions across the world, both legislative and voluntary, but overall progress has been glacial. It is now time to make significant structural changes which address the three key issues we have identified as reasons that continue to contribute to the lack of women in these senior positions—institutional practices; gender bias; the lack of recognition of intersectionality—and change the paradigm from one which focuses on 'winning at all costs,' to one that recognizes and celebrates the value of sport beyond winning (see Figure 10.1). We urge you to consider how adopting this approach within your organization can start today. We cannot wait another 40 years for gender equity in sport leadership. As scholars and advocates we must challenge the dominant paradigm of 'winning at all costs,' and demonstrate that all people can and do benefit from a 'success beyond winning' model in sport, and that the future of sport leadership must reflect the knowledge, passion and commitment of all individuals involved in sport.

References

Adriaanse, J. A., & Schofield, T. (2014). The impact of gender quotas on gender equality in sport governance. *Journal of Sport Management*, 28(5), 485–497.

Australian Centre for Corporate Social Responsibility. (2016). Pathways to the Sustainable Development Goals: Annual review of the state of CSR in Australia and New Zealand 2016. Retrieved from http://accsr.com.au/wp-content/uploads/dlm_uploads/2016/06/ACCSR-State-of-CSR-Report-2016.pdf

Babiak, K., & Wolfe, R. (2009). Determinants of corporate social responsibility in professional sport: Internal and external factors. *Journal of Sport Management*, 23(4), 717–742.

Bergeron, M. F., Mountjoy, M., Armstrong, N., Chia, M., Côté, J., Emery, C. A., ... & Malina, R. M. (2015). International Olympic Committee consensus statement on youth athletic development. *British Journal of Sports Medicine*, 49(13), 843–851.

Bostock, J. (2014). *The Meaning of Success: Insights from Women at Cambridge*. Cambridge, UK: Cambridge University Press.

Brescoll, V. L., Dawson, E., & Uhlmann, E. L. (2010). Hard won and easily lost the fragile status of leaders in gender-stereotype-incongruent occupations. *Psychological Science*, 21(11), 1640–1642.

Catalyst (2015). 2014 Catalyst census: Women board directors. Retrieved from www.catalyst.org/

Dixon, M. A., & Bruening, J. E. (2005). Perspectives on work-family conflict in sport: An integrated approach. *Sport Management Review*, 8(3), 227–253.

Dixon, M. A., & Bruening, J. E. (2007). Work-family conflict in coaching I: A top-down perspective. *Journal of Sport Management*, 21(3), 377.

Fletcher, J. K. (1999). *Disappearing Acts: Gender, Power and Relational Practice at Work*. Cambridge, MA: MIT Press.

Gallup (2016). Women in America: Work and life well-lived. Retrieved from www.gallup.com/topic/category_leadership.aspx

Grappendorf, H., & Lough, N. (2006). An endangered species: Characteristics and perspectives from female NCAA Division I athletic directors of both separate and merged athletic departments. *The Sport Management and Related Topics Journal*, 2, 6–20.

Grasgreen, A. (2014). Weighing value in sports. January 6. Retrieved from www.insidehighered.com/news/2014/01/06/temple-cuts-highlight-cost-big-time-football

Hamil, S., & Morrow, S. (2011). Corporate social responsibility in the scottish premier league: Context and motivation. *European Sport Management Quarterly*, 11(2), 143–170.

Harjoto, M., Laksmana, I., & Lee, R. (2015). Board diversity and corporate social responsibility. *Journal of Business Ethics*, 132, 641–660

Heilman, M. E., Wallen, A. S., Fuchs, D., & Tamkins, M. M. (2004). Penalties for success: Reactions to women who succeed at male gender-typed tasks. *Journal of Applied Psychology*, 89(3), 416.

Heslin, P. A. (2005). Conceptualizing and evaluating career success. *Journal of Organizational Behavior*, 26(2), 113–136.

Ibarra, H., Ely, R., & Kolb, D. (2013). Women rising: The unseen barriers. *Harvard Business Review*, 91(9), 60–66.

Ituma, A., Simpson, R., Ovadje, F., Cornelius, N., & Mordi, C. (2011). Four "domains" of career success: How managers in Nigeria evaluate career outcomes. *The International Journal of Human Resource Management*, 22(17), 3638–3660.

Jain, T., & Jamali, D. (2016). Looking inside the black box: The effect of corporate governance on corporate social responsibility. *Corporate Governance: An International Review*, 24, 253–273.

Kaspereit, T., Lopatta, K., & Matolcsy, Z. (2016). Board gender diversity and dimensions of corporate social responsibility. *Journal of Management and Sustainability*, 6(2), 50.

Korn Ferry. (2016). The real gap: Fixing the gender pay divide. Retrieved from www.kornferry.com/institute/reports-and-insights/

Lapchick, R. (2016). Gender report Card: 2016 International Sports Report Card on Women in Leadership Roles. The Institute for Diversity and Ethics in Sport, University of Central Florida, USA. Retrieved from www.tidesport.org/women-s-leadership-in-international-sports.html

Laszlo, A., & Laszlo, K.C. (2011). Systemic sustainability in OD practice: Bottom line and top line reasoning. *OD Practitioner*, 43(4), 10–16.

Lean In and McKinsey & Company (2015). Women in the workplace 2015. Retrieved fromwww.mckinsey.com/global-themes/women-matter

Lean In and McKinsey & Company (2016). Women in the workplace 2016. Retrieved fromwww.mckinsey.com/global-themes/women-matter

Leberman, S.I., & Hurst, J. (2017). The connection between success, choice and leadership for women (pp. 254–267). In S.R. Madsen (ed.) *Handbook of Research on Gender and Leadership*. Cheltenham: Edward Elgar.

Lyras, A., & Peachey, J.W. (2011). Integrating sport-for-development theory and praxis. *Sport Management Review*, 14(4), 311–326.

Marques-Mendes, A., & Santos, M.J. (2016). Strategic CSR: An integrative model for analysis. *Social Responsibility Journal*, 12(2), 363–381.

Mostovicz, I., Kakabadse, N., & Kakabadse, A. (2009). CSR: The role of leadership in driving ethical outcomes. *Corporate Governance: The International Journal of Business in Society*, 9(4), 448–460.

NCAA (2016). NCAA core values. Retrieved from www.ncaa.org/about/ncaa-core-values

Palmer, F.R., & Masters, T.M. (2010). Māori feminism and sport leadership: Exploring Māori women's experiences. *Sport Management Review*, 13, 331–344.

Sachs, J.D. (2015). Achieving sustainable development goals. *Journal of International Business Ethics*, 8(2), 53–62.

Southall, R.M., Eckard, E.W., Nagel, M.S., & Randall, M.H. (2015). Athletic success and NCAA profit-athletes' adjusted graduation gaps. *Sociology of Sport Journal*, 32(4), 395–414.

Strachan, L., & Davies, K. (2015). Click! Using photo elicitation to explore youth experiences and positive youth development in sport. *Qualitative Research in Sport, Exercise and Health*, 7(2), 170–191.

Torchia, M., Calabro, A., & Huse, M. (2011). Women directors on corporate boards: From tokenism to critical mass. *Journal of Business Ethics*, 102 (2), 299–317.

United Nations (2015). Sport and the Sustainable Development Goals. Retrieved from www.un.org/wcm/content/site/sport/home/sport/sportandsdgs

Vial, A.C., Napier, J.L., & Brescoll, V.L. (2016). A bed of thorns: Female leaders and the self-reinforcing cycle of illegitimacy. *The Leadership Quarterly*, 27, 400–414.

Walters, S.R., Schluter, P.J., Oldham, A.R.H., Thomson, R.W., & Payne, D. (2012). The sideline behaviour of coaches at children's team sports games. *Psychology of Sport and Exercise*, 13(2), 208–215.

Werbach, A. (2009). *Strategy for Sustainability: A Business Manifesto*. Boston, MA: Harvard Business Press.

Moving the conversation forward: future research directions

In the process of writing this book, a number of areas for future research have been identified to help us better understand the topic of women in sport leadership. The list provided below is by no means exhaustive; rather, it provides a starting point for scholars. Based on the existing research we suggest that, in general, future research is required to better understand how leadership is conceptualized within sport organizations in particular through more in-depth qualitative and potentially ethnographic studies. Similarly, adopting a broader range of alternative methodologies would provide deeper insights into the issues at play, together with a consideration of wider theoretical models of leadership. Currently most of the published research is dominated by research conducted within the US intercollegiate sport system, yet there is a need for a broader understanding of issues beyond the United States, particularly from countries outside of North America, Europe, and Oceania. We have limited understanding of women in sport leadership in Asia, Africa, and South America.

The following is a list of areas we have identified as worthy of further research, listed in no particular order:

- Leadership as practice and need for this to be studied in sport.
- What are sustainable outcomes in sport?
- Longitudinal research is needed to evaluate the conceptual model presented in Figures 1.1 and 10.1—do the programs designed to increase agency have influence and change the structure? If these programs do affect change, what is the process.
- There is a need to understand the impact of quotas more widely. Questions to explore include: Have quotas impacted on the day-to-day lived experience of girls and women in sport in terms of interest, funding, media coverage and coaching? Why has it worked in some countries better than others and what are the key factors to making quotas work?
- Longitudinal research on the impact of mentoring and sponsoring in sport. Much of the research is from the business context.
- Do women in leadership positions bring other women through and do they change the culture? There is a need for in-depth qualitative studies

of sports organizations where this may occur and also where women make up the majority, if not all of the leadership team.

- Understanding who applies for leadership roles, who constitutes the selection panel, who is selected for interview and who is appointed—this is still a black box and limits our ability to target interventions at the appropriate point in the process.
- To what extent is mobility required to take on leadership roles in sport? Do the experiences in the sport domain mirror those in business, which suggest the structure benefits men with willing partners who are prepared to move.
- In-depth case studies of sport organizations leading the way and which showcase the benefits of diversity and model something different than wining at all cost.
- In all research take an intersectionality approach as the experiences of women are not homogenous and need to reflect the diversity of women engaged in sport.
- Research required at all levels of sport from youth sport through to the international level, from not-for-profit through to corporate business.
- Longitudinal research on the impact of sport leadership programs for young women—are they important and more importantly do they make a difference? Are they accessible to all or only a privileged few?
- What are other conceptualizations of leadership in sport that represent the myriad of ways that women exercise leadership often hidden from the public domain and therefore not able to be counted? How do we make this leadership visible and show that there is not only one form of leadership that is valued?
- Aside from examining the experiences of women coaches in the US sports system, we are not aware of research to date that has explored self-limiting behaviors of women in sport leadership positions.
- Future research should examine how to encourage cultural changes within sport organizations, how to develop and empower male allies, and explore other techniques for the de-institutionalization of barriers to women in sport leadership.
- The glass cliff has not been examined empirically in the field of sport management, but may provide an interesting avenue to explore women's experiences in sport leadership.

Index

·

For Product Safety Concerns and Information please contact our EU
representative GPSR@taylorandfrancis.com
Taylor & Francis Verlag GmbH, Kaufingerstraße 24, 80331 München, Germany

www.ingramcontent.com/pod-product-compliance
Ingram Content Group UK Ltd.
Pitfield, Milton Keynes, MK11 3LW, UK
UKHW021611240425
457818UK00018B/491